DATE DUE

THE
REFERENCE
SHELF

TELEVISION AND AMERICAN CULTURE

edited by CARL LOWE

THE REFERENCE SHELF
Volume 53 Number 2

THE H. W. WILSON COMPANY

New York   1981

THE REFERENCE SHELF

The books in this series contain reprints of articles, excerpts from books, and addresses on current issues and social trends in the United States and other countries. There are six separately bound numbers in each volume, all of which are generally published in the same calendar year. One number is a collection of recent speeches, each of the others is devoted to a single subject and gives background information and discussion from various points of view, concluding with a comprehensive bibliography. Books in the series may be purchased individually or on subscription.

Library of Congress Cataloging in Publication Data
Main entry under title:

Television and American culture.

(The Reference shelf ; v. 53, no. 2)
Bibliography: p.
Summary: A compilation of articles about television and its effects on politics, religion, education, and other aspects of American culture.
1. Television broadcasting—Social aspects—United States—Addresses, essays, lectures.   2. Television and children—United States—Addresses, essays, lectures.   3. Television in politics—United States—Addresses, essays, lectures.   4. Television broadcasting of news—United States—Addresses, essays, lectures.
[1. Television broadcasting—Social aspects]   I. Lowe, Carl.   II. Series:
Reference shelf ; v. 53, no. 2.
PN1992.T378   791.45′0973   81–7557
ISBN 0-8242-0649-5   AACR2

PRINTED IN THE UNITED STATES OF AMERICA

CONTENTS

3

PREFACE

Television, in modern America, is all pervasive. When CBS broadcast the segment of the TV series "Dallas" that revealed JR's assassin, in the fall of 1980, more than 80 million people watched—almost as many people as voted in the last presidential election. But what is television? From a conceptual point of view its identity and function are controversial. As this selection of articles suggests, it is different things to different people. Television is one technology amidst a host of others brought to us in the second half of the 20th century. All of them have had a profound, interrelated influence on America's lifestyles and ways of thinking.

From one point of view, television is strictly a marketing medium, a creature whose soul is owned by advertisers. Critics with this perspective claim that TV programming's only purpose is to fill in the gaps between commercials and somehow keep the audience from changing channels. This school of thought argues that the search for meaning or quality in TV programming is a fool's errand since quality is irrelevant to the people who control the medium. The commercial is the medium. Paying attention to the programming is like looking at the donut's hole—you are missing the real substance of the object.

Not even public TV, with its mix of mainly cultural and informational programming, is immune to these charges. An advertising executive, quoted by Peter Andrews in *Saturday Review*, states "If I want to brush up a corporate image, I'll buy time on PBS; and don't think PBS isn't under the gun to produce numbers, too." The "numbers" referred to are the Nielsen numbers, the all-powerful survey that reports the total audience of each program. The larger the audience, the more attractive it is to sponsors. And almost all TV shows need sponsors to stay on the air. Without them they die.

An opposing perspective on television reverses this picture. This point of view sees TV as an important means of communication that makes a modern, widespread, and complicated society like the United States workable. Ideas and information can be spread via television instantly to virtually the whole country. For the price of a television set, citizens have access to "free" entertainment and information to an extent unprecedented in human history. The commercials that interrupt this programming are merely the small price we pay for this modern wonder. The programming is not really chosen by the networks or the sponsors. The shows that appear on TV are actually chosen by the viewers. If they don't choose to watch them, these shows go off the air and are replaced by others more to the public's liking.

As Leonard Goldenson, the Chairman of the Board and Chief Executive Officer of the American Broadcasting Companies states in a speech to the National Press Club (quoted in Section V) "free television . . . has been available to all for many years. It is the most important source of news, information and entertainment in our society." Goldenson sees the growing power of cable and pay TV as threats to the public's right to view TV without charge.

But critics of the traditional TV system reply that the term "free television" is a misnomer. They believe that the advertising dollars that support the system actually come out of the consumer's pocket in the form of surcharges for goods and services. Corporations that advertise simply add the cost of advertising into the prices they charge and pass on to the public.

It is primarily within the context of these two perspectives that the arguments over television's effect on America emerge and our compilation reflects this. Those who view the marketing aspect of TV as a penetrating negative influence in society tend to see television as one of the ultimate alienating forces. Television's defenders see the medium as a great unifier that informs and entertains.

Section I gives an overview of television, giving some sense of the medium's history and exploring its general societal and economic role. Section II discusses politics and religion on TV, touching on how both politicians and evangelists attempt to use the small screen (not always successfully) to promote themselves and their beliefs. Section III examines TV news, its changing role in the medium, how it has changed viewers' perspective on world events, and its relationship (if any) to reality. Section IV takes a look at television's effect on children and education, an important area since youngsters are probably TV's most frequent users. The subject of Section V is TV's current programming and advertising trends—as the medium grows older, its techniques for gauging viewer preferences become more sophisticated and the shows seem to grow more ridiculous. Section VI focuses on the future of television. The spread of home video tape recorders, cable systems, and satellite transmissions may weaken the power traditionally held by the networks and their affiliate stations.

The compiler wishes to thank the authors and publishers who have courteously granted permission for the reprinting of their materials.

CARL LOWE

April 1981

I. HISTORY

EDITOR'S INTRODUCTION

"We have been living with television in uneasy alliance for thirty years now. Only recently, however, have we begun to come to terms, critically, with this curious, evidently influential, sometimes frightening medium/art/industry/social force." Thus begins James Monaco as he reviews the history of television in *Sight and Sound*, the first article in this section. Television has grown large at the same time as our modern American technological society. Television is a constant flow of images, sound, and ideas flowing through the center of computerized, electronic America.

Shortly after World War II, television, as we know it today, began to evolve. From its early beginnings as a stumbling imitation of other media (mainly radio and stage), it became a slick, almost irresistible force overshadowing other modern forms of communication. Today it dominates the entertainment and information fields. But inherent in its domination is the question of whether it controls society or society controls it. Has America made TV into a picture of itself? Or has TV molded America in its own image?

A. R. Saldich, a research associate at the University of California at Berkeley, in a speech at Stanford University, discusses how television has taken over the governing process. Because of the medium's power, the political process has changed to accommodate its idiosyncrasies. As she states: "Whenever important public policy is decided for the nation the TV factor is always weighed: how will it play on the home screens?"

Crime shows on television are rampant. An article from *Psychology Today* discusses studies showing that "heavy viewers (defined as those watching TV more than four hours a day) [were] much more likely than light viewers to associate crime with psychological abnormality and to discount unemployment as a possible cause." According to this article police shows on TV tend to convince viewers that the distorted images portrayed on the tube really do reflect the shape of actual events.

Peter Andrews, contributing editor to *Saturday Review,* argues that television executives work to keep TV dull so that the "entertainment" doesn't distract the audience from the commercials. "The people who run the networks do not perceive of television as primarily a conduit for information, enlightenment, or amusement. To them it is first a marketing medium."

THE TV PLEXUS[1]

We have been living with television in uneasy alliance for thirty years now. Only recently, however, have we begun to come to terms, critically, with this curious, evidently influential, sometimes frightening medium/art/industry/social force. Throughout the 50s and 60s, American television criticism was relatively low-grade, and essentially Manichean. In the popular mythos, TV was a shining force for Good. It brought bountiful quantities of information and entertainment to millions of people, and it did so, through the wondrous system of commercial advertising, apparently cheaply. It united us in a national (if not global) village to celebrate and mourn, and it forged a social network that was more than metaphorical. Intellectual critics, on the other hand, have generally tended towards the opposite view. For most serious commentators, TV is ultimately Bad. It's a 'vast wasteland', it rots the brain, it stifles cultivated conversation and social interaction, it teaches children the efficacy of violence and it's the prime cause of illiteracy.

The strength and constancy of this running critique of the

[1] Reprint of magazine article "The TV Plexus," by James Monaco, *Sight and Sound.* 48:19–22. Winter '78/79. Reprinted by permission of *Sight and Sound* and the author.

medium is unique. In the 50s and much of the 60s, the censure of television could be attributed at least in part to elite intellectual attitudes towards popular culture. TV is clearly the most popular medium in the sense that it reaches more people, quicker, more often. So, while film for example was being grudgingly accepted in academic circles as an art, and PhDs were gingerly venturing into the foreign world of pop with iconoclastic encomiums to Bob Dylan and the Beatles, the boob tube remained a safe target for intellectual ire.

Yet in the late 70s, when we no longer make so many invidious distinctions between popular culture and elite culture—we've learned to treat them as parts of the same continuum—censure of television is escalating geometrically. Most recently, Jerry Mander's jeremiad *Four Arguments for the Elimination of Television* (William Morrow and Co., 1978) has suggested that reform is futile; there's nothing else to do but cancel the entire medium outright. As an act of collective will, this would be unprecedented. It's very likely impossible, thcugh Mander makes a surprisingly strong case for his position. (The title of the book is only partly hyperbolic.)

Like most of the new critics of TV, Mander focuses on the form of the medium and its effect on us rather than its content. This shift, in itself, marks a significant advance in the level of sophistication of television criticism. So long as analysis of the medium was devoted to programme materials, it was logically difficult if not impossible to develop an understanding of the true social and political context of television. If the programme is the problem, change the programme. This channel-switching approach was at best reformist. The growing interest in television-as-form, however, permits a radical interpretation, centred on the psychoactive nature of the medium. The title of Marie Winn's influential book *The Plug-In Drug* (Viking Press, 1977) is more than metaphorical. Most of the new criticism of television has about it the vague flavour of semiotics, which is certainly not surprising. Our attention has shifted from the signified to the signifier in the television sign, and that now enables us to begin to understand TV in context.

I'd like to suggest, however, that a second quantum jump is necessary. If the content of television is plotted on a horizontal axis, and the form on a vertical axis, then this third level in the development of TV criticism could be described as a calculus combining the two. Form and content don't exist separately in the medium, nor should they in our critical model of it. We need to investigate the *écriture* of television, as Roland Barthes might say: in other words, 'the relationship between creation and society, the language [of television] transformed by its social finality, form considered as a human intention and thus linked to the great crises of History.'

This pattern of the development of criticism isn't unique to television, of course. It has occurred in literary, film and art criticism—TV criticism is just a little behind chronologically. First we want to understand the significance of the message ('the moral of this story is . . .'); then we develop an interest in style and form ('the medium is the message'); finally we want to understand the human and social dimensions ('language transformed by its social finality'). We want to understand the *function* of television, in the broadest sense of that word, not only as a political instrument, or economic activity, or psychological force, but also as a transcendent model.

The first step here, it seems to me, is to stop thinking of television as one factor among many that go to make up the social equation. Talking about television *and* politics, television *and* children, television *and* advertising (to take three of the most common examples), forces an essentially misleading dichotomy. As the dominant medium of social expression, television is pervasive in a profound way that we seldom recognise fully. (Jerry Mander is on to this, although he doesn't state it explicitly. It's the reason the medium, in his view, is not salvageable.) Because most of us get most of our information about the society most of the time from television, it becomes the primary social fact of our lives. It doesn't simply mirror the society; in a way it *is* the society because it is such a powerful record of it.

This is true, in general, of all media (television is simply first among the various forms of information gathering, transmission and recording that we now use), and Raymond Williams—to my mind, the most important TV theorist now at work—has expressed this new view of the relationship between reality and the media and the rationale for it most succinctly. In *Communications,* he wrote: 'Many people seem to assume as a matter of course that there is, first, reality, and then, second, communication about it. We degrade art and learning by supposing that they are always second-hand activities: that there is life, and then afterwards there are these accounts of it. Our commonest political error is the assumption that power—the capacity to govern other men—is the reality of the whole social process, and so the only context of politics. Our commonest economic error is the assumption that production and trade are our only economic activities, and that they require no other human justification or scrutiny. We need to say what many of us know in experience: that the life of man, and the business of society, cannot be confined to these ends: that the struggle to learn, to describe, to understand, to educate, is a central and necessary part of our humanity. This struggle is not begun, at second hand, after reality has occurred. It is, in itself, a major way in which reality is continually formed and changed. What we call society is not only a network of political and economic arrangements, but also a process of learning and communication.' Williams is writing here more about the uses to which the media are put, but what he says holds true, I think, for the whole complex of uses and media.

Clearly, this reinterpretation of the function of audiovisual and print means of communication is in line with the great 20th century movement to picture the world not *in* language, but *as* language. It is just the next logical step to recognise that the channels of the expression of language are co-equal with 'political and economic arrangements'. Assuming we accept this new triad of the forces of reality, it might be useful to give the third thing a name. On the model of 'economy' (production, distribution and consumption of commodities) and 'ecology' (natural relationships between beings and their environments), let's call it 'ecomedia'. The jargon we use isn't important; what is important is that we start to recognise the equality between the powerful means of communication which we use and our economic and ecological (including political) models.

One advantage of the neologism 'ecomedia' is that it tends towards a singular usage ('media' is often singular in common usage now, anyway) and therefore forces the very real connections among the (plural) media. In reality, television is no longer an entity separate from newspapers, magazines, books, radio, recordings or movies—if it ever was. They are all united in a complex web of interrelationships, both economic and practical. The media *'is'* a sprawling, but unified, whole.

If ecomedia is of equal stature and range with, for example, economics, then we should expect some of the basic concepts of other types of human relationships to operate in the media, the necessary changes being made. Indeed they do. Take the concept of economic value, for example. The producer of a commodity adds value to the raw material he uses by transforming it into usable material: bauxite becomes aluminium sheet. This is a very simple idea. Television acts economically mainly by transporting images and sounds. In purely economic terms, the value added is that these 'commodities' are brought closer. (They are also packaged in seemingly more usable forms.) But what gives the images and sounds value in the first place? Entertainment and news have intrinsic value for most of us, but this basic quantity is multiplied considerably by the cultural values which television markets. Advertising creates artificial needs not only for consumer products but also for television itself as a social fact, and its programming.

So, immediately, we have two levels on which the concept of value works in television. Both are essentially economic. (Mander has discussed them.) But there is a third level, more exclusively ecomedial, as well. Like the stage and movies, only more effectively, television gives value to its sounds and images by *dramatising* them. Raymond Williams has pointed out the remarkable nature of this dramatic transformation in historical terms. 'In societies like Britain and the United States,' he notes in *Television Technology and Cultural Form*, 'more drama is watched in a week or a weekend, by the majority of viewers, than would have been watched in a year or in some cases a lifetime in any previous historical period.'

The effect of this vast inflation of the experience of drama can only be guessed at but, Williams concludes: 'It is clearly one of the unique characteristics of advanced industrial societies that drama as an experience is now an intrinsic part of everyday life, at a quantitative level which is so very much greater than any precedent as to seem a fundamental qualitative change.' Certainly the need for drama (or more generally for the artistic transformation of raw experience) is in part deeply rooted, psychologically. But it seems more than likely that the five or six hours of it now consumed on television alone by the average American household each day is the result of artificial inducement of need.

So we have the concept of value operating in several different ways in the structure of television. First as a simple economic fact: the transportation of the images and sounds has a real value for us and we are willing to pay for it. Second, in terms of the 'creative' economics of advertising, which induces a false need for the medium which can then be satisfied at a profit. Third, in purely ecomedial terms, value being equated with drama and the adding of value with dramatisation. Finally, in a combination of modes two and three, as the very existence of the medium together with its own self-promotion creates an inflated need for the experience of drama.

There are, of course, numerous ways in which 'ecomedial dramatic value' affects the way we perceive reality. Life imitates art these days not only in content (how could it not? with the vast amounts of dramatic commodities being produced in the media, the odds grow better all the time that the plot has already been used) but also in form. The average American TV is turned on more than six hours per day. It's unlikely people are actually watching TV for that amount of time; nevertheless, when we exclude work time and sleep,

simple arithmetic suggests that we spend more time experiencing television than reality. Naturally, during those
relatively brief periods when we do enter out into the world
on our own, we should expect things to happen the way they
do on the tube.

We expect drama, it is what we are used to, and if we
don't get it we perceive a lack. Reality is often disappointing.
But luckily, actors in reality are learning more about their
craft, a fact which is evident over the full range of experience,
from the political demonstration (the French word, *manifes-
tation,* is more precise) staged to dramatise ideas, to the
human potential movement which helps us to become stars in
our own right, better able to cope with the exigencies of our
lifescripts.

None of this is really new. The dramatisation of everyday
life began very early on with the advent of films and mass
newspapers. Pirandello understood the dimensions of the new
social structure; Brecht experimented with de-dramatisation.
But, as Williams has noted, the quantitative change has, with
television, become a qualitative change as well. In the economic metaphor, television creates value out of drama. But
how precisely does it do so? To understand the structure of
TV, perhaps it's best to switch to the biological metaphor.

The media are neural systems of the body politic, since
they distribute information. Television is a plexus. Because
the medium is more highly centralised than most, and because value in its system is essentially a matter of dramatisation and therefore singularly determined, TV exhibits an 'artistic coherence' (or uniformity of style) that is remarkable.
TV distributes information, unlike other media, in discrete
but carefully formulated quanta. We can categorise these
quanta—news and entertainment, action and comedy, commercials, talk and sports—but the categories come after the
fact. Structurally, they are all experienced in the same way,
and the particular genius of television is that it has been able
to integrate such seemingly disparate categories into a homogeneous whole.

Raymond Williams has analysed the distribution of televi-

sion forms and come to the conclusion that 'planned flow is
. . . the defining characteristic of broadcasting, simultaneously
as a technology and as a cultural form.' On the simplest level,
that flow results in effortless transitions from shot to disparate
shot and scene to scene, best evidenced in any newscast.
(Williams' own example, from a 1973 San Francisco broadcast: 'Meanwhile, the Justice Department is considering legal
action and it is very tense and touchy at this moment in
Wounded Knee. *Still of French Château.* And in picturesque
France Georges Pompidou is still President of the Republic
. . .') On the succeeding levels, television flow gives us the art
of programming a prime time sequence, with lead-ins and
lead-outs, hummocks and hills; and the dominance of serials
and series, time-slots and schedules, which stretch the flow
beyond the borders of a particular day or week.

The flow obviously depends on breaking down information into manageable particles. This is the definition of homo-
genisation. The result is that we tend not to notice when categories are mixed. The voice that tells us about the vaginal
deodorant spray has the same quality and form as the announcement that Georges Pompidou is still president. Moreover, the categories, as they become homogenised, tend to inform each other.

Ron Rosenbaum has brilliantly described one salient example of this feedback relationship between categories in his
recent article 'The Four Horsemen of the Nightly News'
[*MORE: The Media Magazine,* Mr. '78]. The nightly network
newscasts, he notes, are saturated with commercials for laxa-
tives, denture creams, stomach remedies, arthritis and head-
ache formulas, and sleeping pills—'dramas of bodily disinte-
gration, of systemic failures, of the depredations and
indignities of age, of the pain, suffering, and minutiae of mortality.'

The simple reason for this is that more than a third of all
people over 55—the prime market for these products—watch
the nightly network news. Demographically, these shows
provide the most efficient exposure for such advertisers. The
complex reason, in Rosenbaum's view, is that such commer-

cials provide a 'reality check': behind the news, 'behind all these ephemeral dramas of institutions, the spectre of mortality stalks through the Pepto-Bismol and Dentu-Grip commercials, the skull beneath the skin of official news.' Older people watch the news programmes, not because they are more interested in news than younger people, but because they are more attuned to this underlying dramatic conflict, and the news itself provides them with 'the spectre of mortality', a drama in which they are more than a little interested.

Rosenbaum chose one week in early September 1977 for close analysis. The newscasts that week included commercials for Dentu-Creme, Ex-Lax, Arthritis Pain Formula, Primatene Asthma Remedy, Preparation H, Sominex, Nytol, Metamucil, Tums, Orafix Special, Rolaids, Geritol, Polident, Anacin, Pepto-Bismol, Fasteeth Denture Aid, among others. Meanwhile, the news stories covered that week included: Panama Canal Treaty signed, Senate passage in doubt; Bert Lance money-moving practices lead to resignation calls; progress toward Middle East peace conference blocked as talks stall; internal probe by Congress into Koreagate; strikes and work stoppages; Liddy paroled; Energy bill in trouble. The two lists are strikingly parallel. Almost all the commercials present images of blocked, constricted passageways, and so do the news stories. The body politic perfectly reflects the body commercial, at least in the nightly network news.

Rosenbaum also makes an interesting case for denture creams as emblems of 'the traditional reformist solutions of a liberal democracy.' He points out that the classic denture drama mirrors Watergate morality: denture-wearer at a party . . . corn or apples offered . . . two choices . . . stonewall it, declaring he doesn't like corn or apples . . . go the modified, limited hang-out, accepting the food but not really eating it. He then asks: 'Can you fix things by pasting on socially engineered improvements? Can the inequities of monopoly capitalism be fixed merely by "adding teeth" to regulatory legislation, by putting a new "tax bite" on big corporations? Has America, in its global role, bitten off more than it can chew? Does the fact that Jimmy Carter's real teeth *look* like false teeth make us reconsider whether fraud is inherent in the porcelain or the person?'

The structure of television inherently produces this kind of interrelationship between categories. Constipated, arthritic, indigestible news stories attract a specific audience; that audience attracts a certain kind of advertiser; the commercials, to complete the circle, serve as models for the news stories, intensifying and sharpening the metaphor: a classic case of feedback. (The feedback itself fits the metaphor.)

There are numerous other ways in which the quanta of television interact and inform one another. It is a commonplace now that news and documentary materials are distorted to fit dramatic formulas, but the reverse is true as well: the rise of 'docudramas' reminds us that drama based on news is at a high premium. Commercials and sitcoms continually reflect each other, a situation that was parodied rather effectively in *Mary Hartman, Mary Hartman.* Over the years, all these categories have been refined through a process not unlike natural selection to such a degree that we are now confronted with a homogenised model—perhaps even a replacement—for the life of the home. TV life is family life. From the Ricardos to the Waltons, from the *Father Knows Best* Andersons to the Bunkers and the Bonos, from avuncular Walter Cronkite to adolescent Hollywood Squares, family life is the prime formal force in American television.

This is true not only in terms of subject matter, but also, and more importantly, in terms of the *écriture* of television. The 'tube', the 'box'—a piece of domestic furniture—is integrated into the flow of domestic life like no other medium before it. Instead of taking our information and entertainment whole, at specific times and in specific places, we now absorb it continually, in a thin, processed stream. The elaborate 'meals' of books, newspapers, magazines and movies— over which we exert some control—have been replaced by the 'intravenous' steady diet of television (together with radio). This is the ultimate level of television flow: it merges indistinguishably with private reality. And it is able to do so, not only because it is always with us, but also because television structure has evolved in such a way that its discrete quanta are small enough to be linearised and therefore more easily injected into the flow of experience. In this respect, the operating medical metaphor isn't constipation, but rather the runs. TV is diarrhetic and diuretic. Its continual, diluted flow dries us out. (Another reason the news shows are fixated on blockages may just be the difficulty their producers confront in forcing solid chunks of reality into this slurry—'Meanwhile, in picturesque France . . .')

One good example of the way this flow theory works in practice is the success of *TV Guide*, which is one of the two largest-circulation magazines in the world. (The other is the structurally similar *Reader's Digest.*) TV is successful because it makes limited demands. It needn't be worked at. It leaves viewers room for other activities. *TV Guide* is successful because its easily consumable quanta of information fit into this pattern. The schedules aren't of primary importance. They are available in newspapers and free 'shoppers' publications. The articles are attractive, but this material, too, is available elsewhere. But the *Guide* is meant as a companion to the television experience. Even its pocket size permits readers to keep one eye on the set. The recent success of non-books (experienced the way television is experienced) and mass-market paperback tie-ins with mini-series suggests it is only a matter of time before the *TV Guide/Reader's Digest* format is adapted to books designed to be read along with television rather than separately from it.

If television creates its own equivalent of value through dramatisation, then it creates its own meaning through a type of abstract personalisation. In general, people don't watch television shows, they watch television. This is part of the flow. More specifically, viewers are notably less interested in plot and information than they are in character and mood. The limited visual capabilities of TV don't lend themselves very well to the communication of detailed information. The discrete quanta structure militates against intricate plots. The domestic connection suggests a low-keyed approach to significance and a concentration on character/personality. In financial terms, this has proved a successful style in every area, from 'Happy Talk' news in which we are more interested in the reporters than in the events, to personality-laden game shows, to so-called situation comedies, in which the interest lies not at all with the situation but with the characters, the people.

We watch television to be with people—nice people, mildly interesting people, sometimes witty people. This is why newscasters are stars. This is why the talk show is the ultimate form of television. This is the reason for the success of nearly all entertainment shows from Jackie Gleason to Mary Tyler Moore, from *Father Knows Best* to *Kojak* and *Columbo*. The recent rise of static 'action' shows like *Charlie's Angels* is simply a refinement of the character approach into caricature. The aim of the Angels isn't to do anything, but to be. They pose, they walk, they talk, they wear clothes, they jiggle, they are. They have the same appeal as dolls—curious microcosmic reproductions that condense our experience of reality at the same time as they abstract it—and sometimes parody it. So the ultimate function of TV thus becomes surrogation. To a large extent, it replaces experience. It talks for us, it thinks for us, it has more character than we do, more drama, more style. It gently chides us for not being more like its people, and thus remains a powerful political tool and an unprecedented advertising medium: it is the keystone of consumer capitalism. Yes, it certainly is insidious.

But it doesn't have to be. Over the last thirty years television has developed an *écriture* best characterised by quantum flow. This is the way it has been able to integrate itself so effectively into the public life and our experience of it. That flow gives it the power it has to create its own equivalents of value and meaning in terms of drama and character. But TV isn't alone in this. To argue for its elimination is to argue by implication against all media, print and audiovisual. There's no doubt that television as a form has a measurable psychological effect which is most likely negative. It may even be physiological. But at least a part of this effect is inherent in the experience of any medium, even print.

Our aim shouldn't be to dismiss the medium out of hand.

It is not going to go away. If it were outlawed it would simply create a generation of underground secret watchers. We lost whatever ultimate social control we have over the medium with the advent of videotape cassette marketing. What we should be doing as critics of the medium is giving people a measure of power to confront it intellectually and emotionally. First, we have to make it clear that the media are so pervasive that it is incorrect to assume that 'there is, first, reality, and then, second, communication about it'. The two are intimately related on a basis of equality. Then we have to learn to deal with television's inherent power to dramatise and characterise. In short, we have to develop a dialectical adversary relationship with the medium.

Television did not cause consumer capitalism, it just made it easier to construct a society built on waste and economic exploitation. If we can conceive of a society that redefines economic value in more human and appreciable terms, then there seems to me to be no reason why we cannot restructure television (and by extension the other media) so that value is predicated upon information instead of drama and meaning is the result of intellection rather than character.

Even as a surrogate reality, television isn't essentially evil. Our view of it as such depends on our own evaluation of reality, which is personal. Intellectuals and academics don't like to admit it, but there are significant numbers of people for whom Johnny Carson's nightly panel provides enlightenment, useful information and even political wisdom. To think otherwise simply betrays a profound lack of understanding of the way most Americans live. Putting Alistair Cooke (or Ralph Nader) in Johnny Carson's chair doesn't change anything in reality; it just provides a different surrogate.

Clearly, television isn't going to change until its matrix, society, does. Ecomedia works in tight conjunction with economics and ecology. But until that happens, we can begin restructuring the medium so that it is easier for us to deal with it objectively. The flow has to be interrupted, and with it dramatisation and characterisation. How to do this is another question.

ELECTRONIC DEMOCRACY: HOW TV GOVERNS[2]

Last December when TV's coverage of the mideast crisis was at full flood an Iranian was quoted as saying: "We've got America right by the networks." What he meant was that our hearts and minds soon would follow. That idea just about sums up two centuries of journalism's growth in the United States: our once-penny sheets are now powerful institutions. Perhaps because it is accepted political practice in his country, the Iranian seems to have understood better than we that television does govern. That is the pivot around which I will develop three problems in electronic democracy: how TV governs, why the First Amendment should apply differently to television than to print, and the need for public accountability.

My content is commercial network news, specifically ABC, CBS and NBC. Although technological innovations, such as cable and satellite communication, now challenge their leadership it is instructive, nonetheless, to trace how television gradually moved beyond reporting events and influencing the government to functioning as government itself.

By network TV I mean national television. Hundreds of local stations throughout the country choose to affiliate with one of several conventional broadcast networks from which they get much of their programming, including the network's news feed of national and international events. Some stations are independent of networks. They pick and choose their programming from a wide variety of suppliers but most stations are affiliated with one of the big three.

In deference to the practice of defining one's scope and terms, I would like to say what I mean by "government" and by "sovereignty of the people".

"Government" is used here in two ways: the institutionalized government that we think of on the national, state and

[2] Reprint of address entitled "Electronic Democracy: How TV Governs," by Anne Rawley Saldich, research associate, Department of Political Science, University of California, Berkeley. *Vital Speeches of the Day.* 46:487–493. Je. 1, 1980. Used by permission.

local levels which, in all cases, is divided into three branches: executive, legislative and judicial. The other definition of "government" is all-encompassing. To use Thomas Jefferson's phrasing it means the people themselves acting in their political capacity.

The other term that can do with a bit of citation is "sovereignty of the people". I am told by a well-known political scientist who specializes in American government that this country has no sovereign. That may be modern but I have decided it is inaccurate. I believe Alexis de Tocqueville's interpretation of this phrase is still valid. In Part II of his *Democracy in America* he wrote that "above all the institutions, and beyond all the forms, there is a sovereign power, that of the people [because] they can abolish or change them as it will." This classic definition is the one that I use.

Let me begin, now, to crystallize the three points that I make. First, observation shows that television has openly usurped certain functions that are traditionally governmental. In addition, TV continually shapes our political values and most of our electoral process in ways that are far from open.

Second, freedom of the press belongs to the people, not to journalists. Therefore, it seems to me that the First Amendment should not protect TV in the same way that it protects print because the airwaves are public property, legally. Broadcasters would like us to think television news is an extension of print but it is not. It is different, intrinsically and profoundly.

My last point is that television has a potential for tyranny. We can guard against it only if TV's vast powers are checked and balanced through public accountability, just as all political power is checked and balanced wherever democracy is strong.

Well, in what way does TV govern? The ways are numerous and subtle but four are obvious. Network executives have taken over what political scientists call gatekeeping, setting the nation's political agenda, being a court of last resort, and a conduit for TV diplomacy. Television's bid for a fifth governmental function collapsed when the networks tried to control the start of TV's presidential campaign last fall.

Gatekeeping is just what it sounds like, control of access to power. In this context it means control of the airwaves. No one may appear on national TV without network permission. That includes presidents. Until recently presidential requests were quickly met, usually without question. However, after Nixon and Watergate gave us the journalist-as-hero, network executives began to flex their political muscle. They have denied access to President Carter on more than one occasion. An example will suffice. CBS turned down the president's proposal for a nationwide speech on energy in 1977. The White House wanted to broadcast "live" but CBS decided the subject did not warrant interruption of their programming. Since the big three march in lockstep, it surprised no one when ABC and NBC followed suit. So, for the first time since his inauguration, Carter formally requested broadcast time, citing national urgency as his reason. Face was saved on all sides: he got access and the networks demonstrated independence.

Consider the political implications, even the absurdity of this situation. Who gave network executives this gatekeeping function? Ours is an electronic democracy, by which I mean much of the information in our society is transmitted electronically, and democracy assumes an informed citizenry. Presidents must have access to the viewing public because they comprise a majority of the body politic. It is not unusual for eighty million people to watch a televised presidential address and millions more listen on radio. After all, the public owns the airwaves and the president is our duly elected representative. No one elected or appointed broadcasters to control presidential access to the nation's electorate or our access to the president.

Another governmental function that networks exercise every day is this: on their evening news they set the country's political agenda, which simply means they pick and choose what is important for us to know about public affairs. We have no nationwide, general newspaper in the United States except for electronic news on radio and television. Of the two, TV has the greater impact.

Historically it was a nation's leaders, whether religious or secular, who decided what the people would know about public affairs. I am not saying that that was a better system. There was a great deal of deception in the good old days just as there has been in our recent past and as there may be now. But that is how government did work and in a democratic society such as ours people could at least vote their leaders out of office if they thought they were wide of the mark. Today, however, broadcasters pick and choose what many people will know and when they will know it. Despite the fact that TV has a long, well-documented track record of not telling us what we need to know, in order to make intelligent political choices, broadcasters cannot be voted out of this governmental function. Furthermore, they think that we the people should have no say about news content. This attitude reflects a certain arrogance of power. Journalists have forgotten that freedom of the press belongs to the people. It does not belong to a particular profession. Furthermore, the airwaves are public property, legally. They are licensed to stations for three years and are relicensed on condition that the public's interest, convenience and necessity is ascertained by the station and met. Otherwise the Federal Communications Commission, an arm of Congress, may reassign the license to another station manager. The conclusion is obvious: the public has a right to influence news standards that govern content because they have a right to influence the use of their property.

Because democracy requires an informed citizenry news sources receive special privileges. Print is posted at lower rates than otherwise would apply and broadcasters are awarded monopolies when they are assigned space on the TV spectrum. But TV news is superficial, fragmented, and often irrelevant to the needs of its viewers. Its prime mover is not the public's interest but the public's pocketbook. TV's "half hour" news is twenty-two minutes long. The other eight are sold to advertisers for rates that swing widely between eighty to a hundred and fifty thousand dollars, or more, for every thirty seconds of publicity, depending on how many warm bodies a network delivers to advertisers. X number of viewers are sold for Y number of dollars, like so many bales of hay. Therefore, networks try to build up massive audiences by having something for everyone. The result is that we learn very little about a lot. This has serious consequences for democracy because most Americans use TV as one of their information sources about public affairs and a majority of that group use it as their sole source. That alone is impressive. But TV also enjoys the highest credibility rating of all media, not because the quality of the news is good but because it reaches a national audience and people tend to believe what they see. We often forget that cameras can lie, and there are myriad ways to distort reality on television, intentionally or inadvertently. The superficiality of TV news is a disservice to democracy because it is unsuitable as a source of information for participation in the political process. As long as broadcasters control the nation's daily political agenda the public should oblige them to produce quality news that is relevant.

Ironically, it is news coverage which gave network executives another governmental function. TV has become a court of last resort, a corridor to power, for many people who are normally shut out of our political process. When the have-nots decided to have more they took their case to the viewing public. Through massive demonstrations and occasional violence anti-war protestors, blacks, American Indians, women, the aged and infirm dramatized their problems to the nation as a whole and this forced authorities to respond. Street politics became a carefully honed fine art as each group taught others how to manipulate public opinion, via TV, with the same skill and insight as advertisers, government leaders and media managers.

The story of democracy in America parallels closely the development of communications. New technology facilitates the flow of information and allows the underprivileged to see how the other half lives. This has led to an electronic revolution of rising expectations. Although we live in the age of fu-

ture shock the same maxim is true today that was true in biblical times: knowledge is power. In this context, television's
contribution to democracy cannot be overestimated. Ordinary people have used TV to widen and deepen the meaning-
fulness of America as a land of opportunity for themselves.
They have learned that the political process is not limited to
an occasional turn at the ballot box. Four years separate one
presidential election from another, but TV's combined network news reaches 55 million people night after night during
those intervening 208 weeks. Now, that's what you call raw
political power.

With regard to television's role as diplomat, the bench-
mark year was 1977 when Walter Cronkite facilitated an Is-
raeli-Egyptian rapprochement. On a news program that was
carried overseas by satellite he helped to arrange an historic
visit between the leaders of two nations whose previous relationship had been one of war and bitterness. The most recent
sample of TV diplomacy is the Iranian crisis, but that is so familiar it needs no recounting.

Still, it is worth asking: what is the significance of TV diplomacy? In one sense the simple answer is: not much.
There's a long history of business serving as a conduit for diplomacy when normal channels of official communication
break down. While I wouldn't say that broadcasting is a business like any other (because it has more power than any governmental, economic or social institution) it is, nonetheless, a
multinational corporation with profit motives and business interests that are much the same as Mobil Oil, IBM or IT&T.
Like them, networks have governmental contacts in nations
where they station personnel, who are similarly subject to
temptations of privilege and corruption. So, in this regard,
journalists trod a well-worn path when they were chosen as a
conduit for information exchange by both governments.
(We've heard a great deal about the Iranians manipulating
television, but the White House spokesman for the Iranian
crisis was Hodding Carter III, whose professional credentials
include seventeen years as a reporter and editor. That is not a
coincidence.)

The yet undefined significance of TV diplomacy allows one's fantasies to roam. Perhaps modern warfare could be ritualized on TV as global theatre. Why not a war of words? Why not a holocaust of orchestrated street demonstrations and video frenzy? We could have a military draft system that would train an army of camera crews to fight on foreign soil, shooting film instead of missiles. Staging centers could be set up, under allied protection, where other military personnel study intensively for starring roles as tyrants or government negotiators. Instead of the classic infantry we could have a sort of televised Greek chorus, chanting in unison: The whole world's watching! Then, if a Canadian camera crew comes along to film, the chorus could salute or exploit that country's separatist tendencies by switching to French: le monde entier nous regarde!

Ridiculous? Sure. But not more so than many a ridiculous war that is now part of history.

The point is this: television received a lot of instant criticism for filling a function that is normally governmental, even though there is a long tradition of business becoming an information exchange when diplomatic channels break down. Perhaps it would be worthwhile to consider the positive possibilities of international TV as a forum, an electronic United Nations, through which nations could let off steam when the pressure builds up.

Is there a conspiracy among networks to take over the government? I doubt it. Most broadcasters have been slow to understand the nature of their vast political power, and few admit they threaten or have taken over certain facets of governing. Television acquired political power gradually, almost imperceptibly, without plotting and scheming, as a spillover effect from video technology. However, a recent move by the networks to take on another governmental function did seem to be calculated.

In the fall of last year television executives decided they would not sell half hour time segments to political candidates. They said it was too soon to start TV's presidential campaign. Again, the question arises: should broadcasters control the start of a governmental function of this magnitude? As it happens, they did not succeed because candidate Carter appealed to the FCC and the commission overruled the networks.

The issues surrounding this event are enormously complex. One can sympathize with broadcasters because the fairness rule and equal time provision require them to make air time available to all candidates once one has appeared on television. At first glance it does seem "unwarranted," as the networks put it "to interrupt their regularly scheduled programming" for the campaign. But if we look at that explanation from a different angle it doesn't make any sense. After all, TV programs are designed to be interrupted, by advertisements that are sold at a princely sum. The CBS news magazine, "60 Minutes" earns $200,000 per minute of advertising. And specials are really special when it comes to the bottom line. When the Steelers and Rams met in the Rose Bowl this year advertising sold for $476,000 a minute. With twenty-two commercial minutes during that game we're talking about really big money. Therefore, we could reinterpret the networks' position as follows: presidential campaigns do not warrant the interruption of our regularly scheduled profits. Now they may be right. Surely more people would watch the Rose Bowl than a political candidate. But the start of TV's presidential campaign, in an electronic democracy, is a decision about governing America and it is far too important to be left solely to broadcasters. While the excessive length of our campaigns is worthy of debate it is one in which the public should participate since it is the use of public property that is being discussed.

These are the obvious ways that TV governs. There is not time to elaborate on the subtle ways in which TV affects our political values and how it restructures the electoral process. All I can do is mention a few in passing.

Personalizing power is one that comes to mind. Whoever is before the camera's eye gains ground for that episode of Who Governs? During Watergate it was the Congress; in the era of street politics it was the protestors; often it is the presi-

dent; at the end of last year it seemed to be the Ayatollah.
There are a few notable exceptions where TV is impressively destructive (for instance, Ted Kennedy's televised condemnation of the Shah) but these prove the rule rather than weaken it.

Another example of subtle shaping is immediacy. Electronic news is hard and fast. Its negative impact on democracy is that it conditions viewers to want immediate answers. But democracy is a bumbling, stumbling, inefficient form of government. It was designed that way to guard against tyranny. Dictatorships seem to be efficient. When journalists ask questions of a dictator the answers can be given immediately and without qualification because few people need to be consulted. In fact, the answers might be given to journalists before they are asked along with a list of questions from which reporters are not to deviate. But in a democracy the best way to preserve freedom is to have an open exchange of ideas, a public debate on matters of consequence. Democracy therefore takes time, whereas television is intolerant of reasoned discourse. Its emphasis is visual and visceral, not rational.

Officials know this. They often think they will look foolish or uncooperative if they don't answer a question put by a TV journalist and so they almost always do. That quickly but imperceptibly reverses the leadership role, putting the journalist in charge. It also reinforces the viewers' impression that there are immediate answers to all issues, no matter how complex, and if officials don't supply them they are guilty of some misdoing.

This kind of thinking ties in with another hidden governmental power that TV exercises daily. Whenever important public policy is decided for the nation the TV factor is always weighed: how will it play on the home screens? This means that TV personnel participate in the government's decision-making process even when they are not there personally. It's a kind of Orwellian remote control, a sort of grey eminence that subtly shapes policy with an invisible hand.

As for restructuring the electoral process, television coverage has weakened parties and conventions and it has caused campaign costs to skyrocket. It is not simply that politicians buy expensive air time, if stations will sell it to them. It has to do with candidates entering as many primaries as possible, with the hope that they will get TV coverage and therefore win national recognition on the nightly news. Every primary costs money, lots of money. If there were a neck and neck race here in California among Brown, Carter and Kennedy, the state democratic headquarters tells me that each candidate might be expected to spend between two and three million dollars. In other states where there's not much of a fight (for example, Georgia would probably go to Carter) the contestants might spend as little as a few hundred thousand dollars or less. As . . . [has been] pointed out, the political significance of this is that candidates spend a large part of their time fundraising instead of dealing with issues. For those candidates who already hold office this getting and spending of money takes time away from their governmental responsibilities. For everyone who makes politics a career it is important to accommodate TV by maintaining a good rapport with its reporters and managers. Again, the Orwellian syndrome: even after an office is won there is always the next election to think about, and this gives television personnel additional leverage in day-to-day government. Although much more could be said on this subject it's time to move on to the First Amendment and why I think it should apply differently to television than to print.

Television's immense political power flows from a combination of several qualities that are not found elsewhere. Its powerful imagery gives viewers a you-are-there feeling, which tends to shut down one's critical, analytical faculties. This, in turn, gives the medium high credibility. People are inclined to believe what they see even if it contradicts their knowledge or experience. Because television news has the highest credibility of all media it also enjoys the kind of authority that every institution in America envies. Credibility is the keystone of all power relationships because belief is the engine of action.

Another unique quality that TV enjoys is its vast audience, which can be compared with radio. While the combined network news reaches 55 million viewers on week nights the space shots, President Kennedy's funeral, the Watergate hearings, and President Nixon's resignation, as well as many other TV specials, were seen by billions throughout the world.

And, television news is received more or less simultaneously, depending on time zones. This is unlike newspapers and magazines whose readers read at their convenience, rather than having their news consumption orchestrated nationally as TV's is. Still another characteristic of television is that it is a continuum and cannot be scanned. Just as the TV set dictates at what time people will get their nightly news so it also dictates that everything must be viewed if one is looking for a particular report.

While radio shares many of these characteristics it does not have the visuals, or the highest credibility, nor does it personalize power in the same way. The source of TV's impact is the mix of all these qualities. That is why all of the still photos in all of the print media did not create the same degree of furor that TV's coverage of the Iranian hostages did. To cite one source, *Newsweek* had dramatic color photos of two Iranians carrying garbage in a large American flag, they showed a black hostage against a wall poster that was covered with anti-American propaganda, other hostages were photographed in humiliating positions—on the floor with hands bound. This kind of picture was not confined to *Newsweek*. Why, then, was there such an outcry when similar images appeared on the home screen? It is because of the medium's unique combination of qualities which are also its source of potential for tyranny: immediacy, moving pictures, a vast audience, and more or less simultaneous reception. The impact has a terrific effect that strains a democratic process because viewers want instant solutions. But international diplomacy is a ritual that takes time.

Freedom of the press is a great tradition in America, and ours has been a model for many countries. Journalists are quick to defend themselves against tendencies to abridge that freedom and they are right to do so. However, the press controls most information sources in the U.S. but media managers seldom admit that they have unmatched political power for that very reason. Others may spend as much time, money and talent in advancing their interests but no institution has the media's power to investigate for publication, and do so with social approval. Even the FBI, CIA and the police need media cooperation in order to round off their investigations with publicity. Big business may influence policy at home and abroad, as do the multinational broadcasting networks, but they cannot tell their story to the American people unless the press will sell or give them space and time. Similarly, television executives almost never allow their network or station problems to be aired and in this way the public is cleverly manipulated.

Let's consider the case of free TV. Americans who visit Western Europe are often surprised to learn that an annual tax is paid on each television set. For color it is about $50 a year and for black and white it is about $35. Figures vary from country to country and are subject to change. Everything about this is fairly straightforward but American tourists are almost always shocked and they usually tell their European friends: Why in our country we have free TV. But that isn't true. We pay a hidden TV tax, because prices of all TV-advertised products are raised a few cents so that we may have the pleasure of viewing commercials. It's a simple little system. Broadcasters use our airwaves at no cost to themselves. Consumers (not just people who own television sets) pay for them to have this opportunity. Manufacturers use our airwaves at no cost, also, because they have passed the advertising bill on, and it is from that fortune in advertising revenue that broadcasters make their enormous profits, enough to pay Barbara Walters a million a year, and to budget eighty thousand dollars annually so that Charlie's angels will have their hair nicely combed when you watch that program. In short, what we have in America is an undeclared system of pay-TV, or, in political terms, of taxation without representation. Why don't most Americans realize this? Because broadcasters have carefully controlled that information. For the same reasons the networks don't like to have themselves discussed as multinational big business. But they are. Nor will their managers readily admit to having government power. But they do. And certainly journalists are unlikely to tell us that their role as guardians of the public interest is a self-appointed one. But it is. The First Amendment on which they base their claim also protects religion. Using the same logic that the press has used, there is no reason why legitimate religious leaders and their less respectable counterparts should not appoint themselves as the public's watch dog.

The First Amendment is a part of the Bill of Rights that was written for the people, not for the press. Its wording is clear and simple: "Congress shall make no law abridging the freedom of speech, or of the press . . ." Note, there is no mention of this nation's sovereign, the people. If the First Amendment is not taken out of context, if we keep in mind that the overall purpose of the Constitution is to separate and divide power so that it cannot become tyrannous, then simplicity gives way to complexity. Then, a strong argument can be made that television has staggering political power which should be checked and balanced. Naturally, this interpretation of the Constitution is not the broadcasters' favorite.

Tyranny is the arbitrary use of power in the absence of accountability. This describes television before 1968, which is when Paul Simpson founded this nation's first television news archive for public use. Speaking politically, what he did was to provide us with the means for checking TV's tyrannous potential by documenting how its power is used, and making it accountable to the public.

To set the tone for this last theme on accountability I would like to quote Freeman Dyson, an eminent physicist, from his new book, which is titled *Disturbing the Universe:* What he says is this: "Through science and technology, evil is organized bureaucratically so that no individual is responsible for what happens." Think of that in connection with television. A dozen years ago, when there were no TV archives, broadcasters were fond of saying their medium is merely a neutral conduit of information, that their reporters are objective, without bias, that TV is simply a window on the world. What they did not tell us is that what we see depends on where they put the window. Objectivity does not exist but it is a wonderful thing if we can convince others that it does because that frees us from responsibility.

Usually when we think about making TV accountable to the public the first thing that comes to mind is regulation through institutionalized government, such as the FCC. That is not what I advocate. The public accountability that I am thinking of would find expression in press councils, classroom instruction in electronic literacy so that we learn how to watch and listen to television with a new awareness; I would like television archives to expand and proliferate, and I would like to see citizens' groups influence standards for news content. That last one is bound to raise the ire of broadcasters for they have accustomed themselves to think that freedom of the press means freedom to do what they please, even though we the people pay them to use our property for their profit. It is a favorite axiom in business that "there ain't no free lunch". I think it is time to let the wealthy multinational networks pick up the tab for some part of this accountability process. Unlike most other businesses they have never had a year without profit since 1940. Wall Street analysts tell us that NBC had a bad year in 1978 when its pretax profits bottomed out at $122 million. In the language of transactional analysis that would come under the game called: "Ain't it awful?" We should all have such a bad year.

Teaching electronic literacy should be done in the schools and over the air. Everyone should learn about the absence of truth in advertising, when it occurs, and how to recognize it. We should know how TV shapes values and what the mechanics are for distorting reality. For instance, when blacks rioted in Watts, California during the sixties TV did not have the fast film that they now have, which allows crews to shoot in the dimmest of light. So, to accommodate the technology that was then available TV photographers, filming at night, sought out available light sources, most of which were fires set by arsonists. Without intending to they distorted reality because the televised version of Watts gave the impression of an entire city aflame, which was not the case, though it did provide good visuals. Electronic literacy would also teach us to find out the source of video materials. Much of the TV film that we saw during the early years of our war in Indochina came from the government in the form of "handouts" which were used by broadcasters without telling us that we were viewing propaganda instead of reports filmed by TV journalists. If Watergate gave us the journalist as hero those early years of fighting in Southeast Asia gave us the journalist-as-dupe. We should all learn how TV technicians can splice together bits and pieces of what a person says so that it bears no resemblance to the actual event. Some astute interviewees prevent this by insisting that they be taped to time, which means that if they grant a ten minute interview the broadcasters must agree to air all ten minutes of it. Or, they might refuse an interview altogether unless it is broadcast "live," thereby circumventing the lab where so much of reality ends up on the cutting room floor. We should also learn to see what is not on our TV screens. Broadcasters keep telling us that TV mirrors society. Really? Where are the American Indians? Where are the Mexican Americans? The Puerto Ricans? Where and when do we see on our home screens images of intelligent, capable, hardworking people with physical infirmities? Where are the analyses of media's influence on every facet of our lives?

In addition to press councils and electronic literacy much can be done on behalf of public accountability by encouraging interest groups to form media evaluation centers. This has already been done with success by Action for Children's Television, and by the United Church of Christ which is to television what Nader's Raiders are to car manufacturers. Many other organizations have also been effective media activists but TV managers don't like people to know what a lot of power we have. For example, in the spring of 1978 the Parent Teachers Association met in Chicago with nearly twenty executives whose products are advertised on children's programs. The PTA had a simple message: use your influence to get sex and violence off of children's programs or we will lead a nationwide boycott of your products, and we have the clout to get others, such as churches and medical institutions, to join us. Their threat was successful. This was a giant step for grass roots democracy. It was an extraordinary coming together of issues and events but network news gave it the silent treatment. They invoked that principle of journalistic folklore that says: if it wasn't reported it didn't happen.

The fourth expression of public accountability is television archives and all the others are really based on their existence, but most particularly on adequate access to their resources.

It was while doing research here at the Hoover Institution that I began to appreciate how important TV archives are to the vitality of electronic democracy. They are as important as the public library system was in the linear era when most information came through print. When I was doing that research I wanted to analyze how each network had reported the American Indians' takeover of Wounded Knee as a protest against injustice. I was able to do this efficiently, at minimal cost, because there is an excellent television news archive at Vanderbilt University in Nashville, Tennessee, which was started by a private citizen with his own funds in 1968. This is not the place to tell you the story of that remarkable institution and how CBS tried to put it out of business. What you want to know is that it exists, that it is service oriented, and that its materials are accessible because that TV archive has troubled itself to put out an index and abstract of its resources that is comparable in comprehensiveness and quality to the New York Times Index. Both the Hoover and the Green libraries have these, here at Stanford. To get videotapes from Vanderbilt you simply go through their indices, select news segments that you want to see, list your selections (which are really a reflection of your editorial judgment) and mail it off to Nashville. You will pay a modest user fee, a refundable deposit for the tapes, and you will sign a promise that you will not have public showings of the materials except under certain conditions. In Tennessee the archive technicians will splice together the selections that have been made and in short order you will receive a compiled video subject tape that can be studied with ease. Or, you can request an entire evening's broadcast, as well as certain documentaries and public affairs programs.

There are few video archives in America. The Vanderbilt Television News Archive is the only one that sends materials from its institution to the user, so that research can be done wherever a playback facility exists, whether in libraries, business offices or homes. This gives the researchers considerable flexibility because they do not have to conform to an institution's business hours. Here at Stanford playback machines are available in the Communications library, at the Hoover, in the Education department and probably in several other places of which I have no knowledge.

It is important to know that Vanderbilt's is the only archive that will compile a subject tape for you. The other major video archive is our National Archives in Washington, D.C. Unwisely, they have let CBS dictate the terms of government policy with respect to their collection and how it is used. CBS, whose whole empire turns on the ability to sell, simply sold the director of the National Archives a bill of goods that prevents the archives from compiling subject matter tapes or sending tapes directly to users. Materials are mailed only from one institution to another. If your library in northwestern Alaska does not have a playback machine, too bad. Try Seattle. In return for letting CBS dictate its policy, the National Archives gets CBS news free of charge and CBS has issued nationwide press releases to advertise its generous gift to the nation.

The political issues involved here are essentially these: CBS is making government policy which denies public access to public events that were broadcast over public property from which activity CBS accrued considerable revenue. Let me give you an example of what I mean by denying access. When I did my research on Wounded Knee it took me three hours to run through those segments of the networks' news coverage that I had asked the Vanderbilt Television News Archive to splice together. Had Vanderbilt signed one of CBS' agreements about the use of video tapes I would have had to request 9 weeks of evening news for each of the networks. That's a total of 135 video cassettes. Imagine retrieving all that from the shelves, packaging it up, mailing it out, being handled by me. Think of the expense in terms of retrieval time and postage. Think of how long I would tie up a playback machine in order to get to one 45 seconds or three minute news segment. Think of how awkward and cumbersome that makes the mechanics of doing research. This is what Dyson means when he says that evil is organized bureaucratically through science and technology.

At this point you are not surprised to learn that NBC and ABC have followed CBS' policies in lemming-like fashion. What the networks are doing is not unlike techniques that were used to keep blacks from voting in the south. This is the broadcasters' version of the poll tax and unreasonable literacy laws. It denies access while appearing to be in the public's interest.

Researchers and educators who understand the importance of television archives should take the lead in petitioning Congress to change our National Archives' policy so that big business (the networks) do not dictate access to public resources. And we should take the lead in working out a system whereby the networks help to support and multiply archives. They can well afford to do this from their profits, as part of their legal commitment to the public interest. There is not much point in knowing about all this unless someone takes action, and I think that burden falls on scholars who understand how documentation is related to accountability, and how accountability is related to freedom.

In closing, I want to say again that television has been a great asset to democracy. Sure, there are problems but there are problems everywhere: in education, religion, government, business and volunteer associations. Broadcasters have not cornered the market on imperfection. The medium is no longer in its infancy but it, and we, are on the learning curve.

While we must have the courage to study its political power and governing functions with care, we should do this with the intention of building on its strengths in such a way that future communications technology will continue to protect not only freedom of the press but the people for whom that press is free.

THE UNREALITY OF PRIME-TIME CRIME[3]

More pernicious vidiocy. Craig Haney, a psychologist at the University of California at Santa Cruz, and John Manzolati, a graduate student at Stanford, have analyzed more than 500 hours of prime-time television crime shows since 1974. They find that violent crime, particularly murder, occurs far more frequently on the tube than it does in real life. In contrast, white-collar or corporate crime—like consumer fraud and industrial pollution—and victimless crime—like drunkenness—appear far less often on the screen than in the real world.

Moreover, according to Haney and Manzolati, TV criminals typically sweep in from nowhere, with no history, personality, or relationships to help explain their actions. In nearly 40 percent of the shows the researchers analyzed, for example, the crimes occurred in the first three minutes. When the shows do sketch motives, criminals are shown as crazy, rich and greedy, or both. The rich-and-greedy stereotype might ring truer if more white-collar crime were shown, but studies of convicted criminals consistently find that most convicts are poor and that their rates of mental illness are not significantly above the rates for comparable groups who have not been arrested. Although recent studies by Harvey Brenner, an economist at Johns Hopkins, have shown that when unemployment rises, crime does also, unemployment ap-

[3] Reprint of magazine article by Berkeley Rice, contributing editor, *Psychology Today*. 14:26+. Ag. '80. Reprinted from *Psychology Today* Magazine. Copyright © 1980 Ziff-Davis Publishing Company.

peared as a factor contributing to crime in less than 5 percent
of the shows the researchers sampled.

The unbalanced portrayal of crime on TV would not be
cause for much concern if the shows were merely entertainment. But in surveys of 350 TV watchers in northern California, Haney and Manzolati found heavy viewers (defined as
those watching TV more than four hours a day) much more
likely than light viewers to associate crime with psychological
abnormality and to discount unemployment as a possible
cause. To be sure, other researchers have shown (see "News-
line," July 1979) that the variables of age, sex, education, income, or neighborhood may be as influential in shaping attitudes toward crime as is TV watching. Haney and Manzolati
did not study the effect of such variables.

Television crime lets viewers avoid a relevant question,
the researchers say: "How would we behave in circumstances
like those experienced by most people who commit crimes?
Since television rarely shows us these circumstances, it fails to
promote this kind of awareness. Moreover, it diverts our attention away from these 'criminogenic' situations and their
consequences."

Television shows avoid other crime issues too, the researchers found. While most real police work is routine—
drunkenness and other victimless crimes make up about one-
third of all arrests nationwide—TV cops and detectives spend
most of their time out in the field on exciting investigative
work. And they seldom make mistakes. In most shows, the
first suspect proves to be the true culprit and a wrong suspect
is rarely arrested. Moreover, TV cops "blatantly" infringe
upon Constitutional rights by assaulting witnesses or breaking
into suspects' homes to steal evidence without a search warrant. "On television," say the researchers, "only the 'bad
guys' are roughed up and harassed, while the truly innocent
and uninvolved are treated justly and with dignity." Citizen
complaints about police indifference and brutality are rarely
mentioned.

The video aura of certainty about the correctness of police conduct seems to affect heavy viewers, who, in the study,

were much more likely than light viewers were to presume that real-life defendants "must be guilty of something, otherwise they wouldn't be brought to trial." The researchers add, "It is not too farfetched to speculate that juries composed of heavy television watchers begin with a presumption of guilt and are thus more likely to convict. Indeed, as increasing numbers of Americans watch more and more television crime drama, juries may become generally conviction-prone—based on the false reality of television criminology."

Haney and Manzolati concede that in 50-minute dramas, "it may be difficult to develop the sensitive and complex crime stories of a Charles Dickens or a Victor Hugo." But the researchers do not rule out "the possibility that corporate and industrial crime may be difficult to portray on television when the bills are being paid by companies that may be engaging in it," or that television writers, in a self-confirming circle, may be "playing to the popular stereotypes."

PEDDLING PRIME TIME[4]

Sonny Fox, a former NBC vice-president and currently an independent TV producer, dropped the first shoe. "The salient fact," he announced at a lecture series sponsored by the Annenberg School at USC, "is that commercial television is primarily a marketing medium and secondarily an entertainment medium."

If you wonder how so many dreary programs eventually find their way to the tube, it is important to remember that comment. The people who run the networks do not perceive of television as primarily a conduit for information, enlightenment, or amusement. To them it is first a marketing medium.

---

[4] Reprint of magazine article "Television: Peddling Prime Time," by Peter Andrews, contributing editor, *Saturday Review*. 7:64–65. Je. '80. Copyright © 1980 by Saturday Review. All rights reserved. Reprinted by permission.

Watching the pathetic performers in *Three's Company,*
Vegas, Love Boat, and *Fantasy Island* slog by like members of
an overdressed chain gang, one can easily fall into the trap of
thinking that programming executives at ABC are somehow
stupid. But they know precisely what they are doing.

The second shoe was dropped on the parquet of a New
York office by an advertising executive who has spent the
better part of the last 20 years selling detergent. "Anyone
who tells you television is anything but an efficient cost-per-
thousand advertising vehicle is kidding," he said. "I get tired
of hearing about quality programming for upscale audiences.
If I want to brush up a corporate image, I'll buy time on PBS;
and don't think PBS isn't under the gun to produce numbers,
too. But my business is selling a high-volume, low-ticket item,
and I tell you television was made to sell that kind of product."

A situation under the control of people who are interested
only in numbers and who do not consider themselves to be in
the entertainment business anyway, is not about to make any
giant strides toward superior programming. It is, however, a
controller's idea of heaven on earth because every rating
point taken away from the competition is worth an estimated $2.8 million in profit for every single hour that point
holds up.

Money like that has a way of making programmers cautious. Paul Klein refined this theory at the USC conference
when he dropped the third shoe (this being a column about
television, everything is greater than life). Klein, a former
program chief at NBC, is an impassioned believer in the
"least objectionable program" theory of scheduling. The LOP
theory holds that most viewers just want their eyeballs mas-
saged for a while and will watch whatever bothers them the
least.

Klein maintains that programming must be built on a
solid defense. Assuming each network starts out with approximately 32 percent of the viewing audience, the programmer's
first responsibility is to make sure that his shows do not lose
any of those $2.8 million-an-hour points. The emphasis is less

on building an audience than on not having one fade away because of any provocative element that might cause a viewer to tune out.

"Thought is a tune out," Klein said. "So is education. Melodrama's good. A little tear here and there, a little morality tale. That's good." Then, warming to his theme, Klein described his basic programming criterion. "One of the qualities I look for is fake realism, the illusion you're getting something meaningful. Then you overlay that with what I call trash. . . . It's the ideal content to fit the nature of 'waste time,' which is what people use the media for."

Klein's tenure as NBC's programming chief was a ratings disaster, leading Johnny Carson to quip the network's letters stood for "Nine Bombs Canceled." Klein lost his job in the wreckage of *Supertrain*, but his basic philosophy is still a fundamental of programming.

Now we're getting there. The majority of network programming is vapid not because the people in the business don't know how to develop interesting shows, but because the industry deploys squads of well-paid, highly skilled craftsmen whose specific task it is to keep the programs dull. Interest, except for the kind generated by automobile accidents and naked women, is usually the result of some kind of thought process requiring the active participation of the audience members. But activity is contrary to the requirements of a medium as narcomatous as network television. An active viewer is likely to switch to another channel. It is much better to keep him heavily sedated between the inevitable commercial breaks.

The fourth and final shoe was NBC president Fred Silverman's heavy brogan. He actually dropped it five years ago, when he was at ABC, but its clattering has been echoing through the industry ever since, and today it is the overriding theme of prime-time network television programming. Simply put, Silverman's idea is that virtually all television is children's television. Perhaps Silverman came to this understanding during his early training recutting old *Jungle Boy* movies for a local Chicago station, or perhaps it was when he sensed that the national television set was now being ruled by kids whose parents were willing to watch anything that kept the children quiet. Led by *Charlie's Angels*, which its own staff freely admitted was aimed at the mentality of a 12-year-old audience, ABC (under Silverman) quickly flounced from last to first place in the network standings.

Now the broad outline is taking shape. Most reasonably intelligent adults can find so little in the way of entertainment on network television because the networks don't care whether they watch or not. By pandering to a youth market, the networks can generate both numbers and a young, unsophisticated market, the one most prized by TV's principal advertisers.

The basic approach of this marketing strategy is easy enough to figure out, but the detailed execution of programming is more difficult to discern. Few adults know with any certainty what adolescents like. To get an idea of what I mean, go out tomorrow and comandeer a 13-year-old to whom you are not already bound by ties of blood or affection. The child can be selected at random, although to get a sense of the depth of the problem, the little nipper should be of a particularly phlegmatic stripe. Now sit down and have a long, detailed discussion with the child for six straight hours, which is about the average daily viewing time for heavy viewers. At the end of the session you will either have truly come to know the meaning of the word boring or have displayed the makings of a network programmer.

Now up the ante. Imagine that if you can entertain the tyke for seven days a week, you will become a millionaire many times over. But if his attention span begins to wander for any reason whatsoever, you will become unemployed. Perhaps you can now understand what a challenging job the programmer has. Of course most middle-aged programmers have no more idea of what goes on in the mind of a teenager than they can comprehend the intellectual processes of a Canadian snow goose caught in an electrical storm. But they manage. Preview House, the most powerful show-testing facility in the television industry, compared an audience's reac-

tion to a pilot to its appreciation of an old Mr. Magoo cartoon. That's right, an old Mr. Magoo cartoon.

Some glorious entertainment does, of course, slip through
the net. But such programming is not really the business of
television. Or at least it is not the business as perceived by the
people who run the networks. Which is why the adult pleasures of watching television often seem so furtive, like sneak-
ing a drink in the kitchen during a children's birthday party.

II. POLITICS AND RELIGION

EDITOR'S INTRODUCTION

It is not surprising that television's ability to reach large numbers of people has made it an important tool of politicians and religious evangelists. Without TV most Americans would never get a chance to see presidential candidates speak. Likewise, TV evangelists have acquired many more followers and contributions than their predecessors who depended on tent revival meetings.

But TV changes the relationship between speaker and audience when the speaker addresses a camera instead of live, flesh and blood people. There may be a "live" audience at the rally or in the studio, but the number of people present at the event is insignificant compared to the numbers who view the broadcast. Viewers are presented with a package—the picture and sound they see on their sets at home. In this context, power to affect public opinion shifts to the packagers, the technicians who construct the TV program.

Ward Just, a contributing editor to *Atlantic Monthly*, compares a Ted Kennedy speech he attended in person, with the version presented by TV network news. "What I heard at Faneuil Hall bore scant relation to what I saw in my living room." He complains that the TV report disemboweled the event and that the viewer lost a sense of "reality, which is at best unsober and disheveled."

In an article from the *New York Review of Books*, Tom Wicker, associate editor of the *New York Times*, examines the presidential primary system with regard to television and campaign reform laws. He states that "Presidential politics today, it is reasonably fair to say, *is* television." But while he admits that TV has destroyed the power of political parties and changed the kind of men elected to office, he is against governmental control of television's political functions. "I have strong First Amendment reservations about regulating their [politicians'] use of television."

The new political power of technicians is the subject of Michael J. Arlen, contributing editor to the *New Yorker*. Arlen makes the point that the people who mix the videotape that gets on TV news have the ultimate power over the minds of the public. The vision they create on their mixing board is America's vision of reality. "These engineers are the new creators, our political kingmakers."

Russell Baker, columnist for the *New York Times*, writing at the height of the 1980 campaign, also sees today's political power in the hands of technicians, advertising men who package the candidates like "competing beers and scouring powders." According to Baker, this kind of climate works against any candidate ambitious enough to want to say what's really on his/her mind. "Candor is a violation of the rules. It is upsetting."

Evangelists on TV is the subject of Edwin Diamond's report from the American Film Institute. Diamond, head of the News Study Group at MIT, finds that the TV preachers too often succumb to the corrupting lure of money and power found on the small screen. He warns: "In an uncertain time of energy shortages and inflationary pressures, oversimplistic appeals from telegenic operators may take hold and grow in the darker ground of the American spirit.

NEWSPAPER DAYS: POLITICS—WE ARE THE HOSTAGES[1]

There is nothing like an old-fashioned political rally to begin the day, so when Senator Kennedy announced his candidacy for the presidency one morning last fall in Boston, I was there. It was the first political speech I can remember attending voluntarily, as a citizen, not as a working journalist.

[1] Excerpted from magazine article "Newspaper Days: Politics—We Are the Hostages," by Ward Just, contributing editor. *Atlantic*. 245:99–101. Ap. 80. Used by permission.

No need for the protective coloring of notebook and pencil (the M-16 and flak jacket of the trade); I stood outside Faneuil Hall with a thousand or so other citizens and listened to the speech over a loudspeaker. Most of those in attendance that morning were Kennedy supporters, but there appeared to be a number who, like me, were there out of curiosity or a desire to hear the rhetoric in person.

I did not think it a very good speech. He seemed uncertain in his themes and hesitant in his approach; the old Kennedy brio was lacking. In a word, I thought it false in some way I could not define. In the old days there would have been three or four colleagues to try the theory out on; but that morning I was alone with it. There were questions following the speech, and one of them concerned Kennedy's wife. Would she campaign? When the Senator said he'd let her answer that one, a little gasp went through the crowd outside. Someone near me murmured, "Oh, no." A man said, "That bastard," meaning the reporter who had asked the question. But all conversation ceased when Joan Kennedy took the microphone, and when she concluded, her amplified voice firm and steady, saying yes, she would campaign, and, yes, she would hold a press conference to answer *all* the questions, the crowd outside burst into spontaneous and heartfelt applause. Everyone was pulling for her; she had come through, taken a high hard one and pounded it out of the park.

I had seen none of this—Faneuil Hall was well packed by the time I arrived—but I had heard all of it. I stayed to watch the Kennedys and their entourage leave the building, working the crowd in the special carnival style of political campaigning; then I walked back to my apartment. I was pleased that I had gone to hear it in person. I had a vague sense of having fulfilled some civic duty. I turned Kennedy's speech over in my mind. I didn't think it augured well for the campaign. The Thomas Wolfe quotation at the end was forced and out of harmony with what had gone before, the result of a tour through Bartlett's or some southern speechwriter's memory, not of Edward Kennedy's experience. (Indeed, it developed later that the quote was inaccurate; with unerring instinct for tampering with other people's ideas, Kennedy's speechwriters had bowdlerized the passage, rewriting Thomas Wolfe to conform to feminist sensibilities.) Kennedy himself seemed distracted, and I believe that a careful reading of—or listening to—the speech would confirm this. I think that anyone not blinded by Kennedy-love or Kennedy-hate would feel roughly as I did, had he heard the whole speech and the Q & A that followed. But it was interesting, and it was certainly one of the two most important public statements of Kennedy's long, surprising, conspicuous, and turbulent political career.

I was careful to watch the seven o'clock news that night, momentarily seduced by the trendy notion that the camera's "perception" was as important as my own "perception." But I was puzzled, then angered, by the account. The reporter summarized it in his own words, allowing—as I remember— only a few brief excerpts from the candidate himself. Then there was Joan Kennedy's statement—she looked more flustered than she sounded—and that was that. The reporter acted bored, perhaps because the announcement came as no surprise. No question that the speech was predictable, mild in its criticism of President Carter and promising little more than fresh leadership. Still, I thought, the manner of delivery, the priorities implicit in the diction . . . it was worth hearing, and whether or not it contained surprises seemed to me beside the point. The announcement of candidacy is roughly similar to the opening paragraph of a novel, and deserves to be read with care. What I saw on television was a minor political melodrama with a beginning, middle, and end, and lest we miss any of the obvious points, the reporter was there to explain them. And explain and explain and explain, until the explanations overwhelmed the events. It was less an interpretation of what Kennedy said than a precis of it, against the background of the then-immutable political realities. The reader will recall them. This was the period when very few reasonable people believed Jimmy Carter had a chance at renomination, let alone election. The candidacy was launched in an atmosphere very different from that in which it would continue.

Broadcasters do love the sound of their own voices. It is as if the networks believe that to present a candidate *en clair* is somehow to give him a free ride. A voter cannot be trusted to hear the words as they are actually spoken, and to draw whatever conclusions seem reasonable. I suppose it is the identical impulse that causes Kennedy and his speechwriters to interfere with the prose of Thomas Wolfe. The arrogance is breathtaking.

No one is safe. . . .

What I heard at Faneuil Hall bore scant relation to what I saw in my living room. The core and rhythm of the speech were missing, and I wonder why this has to be. The event seemed to me arranged by television for television, and the reporter was in the middle of it in the way a newspaper reporter seldom is. I suppose this is hopeless naiveté on my part; the symbiotic relationship between the politicians and the electronic mediators is so close as to resemble the chummiest of marriages: scratch one and the other bleeds. They speak to each other in shorthand and then to us: "momentum," "perceptions." But I wish the mediators would get out of the way so the rest of us could see the action and listen to the words as the candidate chooses to speak them. My complaint is not that the reporters are biased or stupid but that they are present always, omniscient narrators in what is often a first-person tale, interfering in the fashion of the bore at the end of the table who interrupts every thirty seconds to demand that you define your terms or, better, accept his.

So we have a plausible three- or four-minute segment on the evening news, the helter-skelter of a candidate's day made coherent. But in war or politics, reporting that is too coherent is unfaithful to the situation. Disorder and mystery lie at the heart of both conditions, so beware any neatly wrapped-up version of a battle or a political campaign. It does not reflect reality, which is at best unsober and disheveled. However, it serves the purposes of journalists and politicians to appear both sober and organized, so every event has an explanation and every explanation its various "perceptions." Einstein's random throw of the dice has been firmly rejected by the mediators, hence the confidence and spurious predictability of political reporting. . . .

Of course the explanations and comments that one hears on television are not necessarily the same as what one reads in the newspapers. Thus, John P. Sears, then Ronald Reagan's campaign manager, on Senator Kennedy's January speech, to David Broder of the Washington *Post:* It was wise for Kennedy to "move to the left of Carter domestically, but I would think internationally he'd want to be to the right of him. That way he could strip him from both sides." That's cynicism approaching misanthropy, which is not to say that it's incorrect. But I would find it hugely enjoyable to watch John Sears, grinning and steepling his fingers no doubt, explaining to David Broder how Kennedy had only to talk like John Connally in order to "strip Carter from both sides."

Reporting a political campaign intelligently is demanding work, requiring at once the instincts of a gumshoe, the fastidiousness of a historian, and the liver of W. C. Fields. Also the attention of a scorekeeper, because one way or another the fans want to know the score—what inning is it, and who's ahead—as if the United States in a political year had the symmetry of Frank Chance's diamond. The political reporters have it one up on the war correspondents because they have polls to tell them what the voters think, who's up and who's down on Day Whatever of our national campaign. If one poll contradicts another, that's fine; it's a news story. The polls are buttressed by a caucus here and a primary election there, and it cannot be said too strongly or repeated too often that the momentum of this or that candidate is entirely media-created. In the Vietnam War, we called this the body count.

The admirable *60 Minutes* is capable of presenting a fifteen-minute profile of George Bush without once seriously examining his views on public policy. The most arresting section of the profile, or the one that appeared to be the most carefully reported, was an account of a hoked-up television commercial, something to do with whether or not Bush actually arrived in some Iowa cornfield in an airplane, as his commercial attested, or in a car, where the *60 Minutes* camera crew found him. The commercial showed him alighting from a plane, like Lindbergh. The idea, I guess, was that

George Bush's truth-in-advertising did not meet the highest standards of the profession. There was a time when people over the age of ten assumed that advertisements were what they appeared to be, pitches. One could take them or leave them alone. A candidate or a soap company bought time and made a pitch, and one assumed that the standards of accuracy were not those of a philosopher king.

It occurs to me that in any campaign there's room for both the mediators and the candidates. The best examples I know have to do with Senator Kennedy. Roger Mudd's interview late last year was vintage stuff, again and again catching the candidate off guard and inarticulate, posing questions that were not particularly difficult or abrasive, simply those that had to be asked, and Kennedy somehow unable to answer them convincingly.

But there's another cut to that cloth, and it came in late January, when the Senator bought half an hour of television time to talk to New England. This was a version of the speech that John Sears found unsatisfactory. It began with a five-minute statement on the death of Mary Jo Kopechne. ("I alone feel in my conscience the loss of Mary Jo Kopechne's life and the failure to report the accident immediately. I carry that burden with sorrow and regret.") But the heart of the speech was a detailed criticism of the foreign and domestic policies of the Carter Administration. This speech had been carefully advanced, and there's no question that one's interest in it was heightened by the loss in Iowa, Kennedy's dismal standing in the polls, and the confused nature of his campaign. But it was a serious speech, seriously delivered, and I found it fascinating—not because it conformed to my own views but because it was genuine, the candidate saying what he had to say at length and in his own words. I suppose the objection would run, "But it's what he wanted you to hear!" And my reply is, Of course! I'm eager to listen to what they want to tell me, and then decide. There's nothing preventing any of us from actually attending a speech or rally: in person, them and us, unmediated.

THE ELECTIONS: WHY THE SYSTEM HAS FAILED[2]

One week to the day before the New Hampshire primary last February 26, Representative John Anderson of Illinois, his daughter, his traveling staff, and his trailing press corps drove through sunny weather and a strangely snowless countryside from Manchester to Hanover—all in one van. Mr. Anderson, then exciting more public interest as a character in "Doonesbury" than as a Republican presidential campaigner, was looking forward to what he considered a big event in his campaign: he was to be interviewed by an ABC News television crew. For a contender buried in the pack of seven "major" candidates, a network TV spot was a rarity indeed.

But one of the two reporters accompanying Mr. Anderson heard the news of the ABC interview with a sinking heart. He was not sadistic enough to tell the elated candidate the cruel truth—that the ABC crew was working on a documentary, which would not be shown until summer, a little late to influence the New Hampshire primary.

Two days later another Republican hopeful, Senator Howard Baker of Tennessee, appeared for an early morning rally at the fire station in North Londonderry, a small community not far from Manchester. At that time, primarily because of his prominence as Senate Minority Leader, Mr. Baker was considered one of "the top three"—or, as John Anderson enviously termed them, "the charmed circle"—which also included Ronald Reagan, the leader in national polls, and George Bush, the surprise winner of the Iowa caucuses.

The main advantage of being among the top three was the attention of television crews, which cost the networks something like $2,000 a day to deploy; at those rates, and considering the scarcity of time on thirty-minute evening news shows, the cameras were seldom pointed at the lowly likes of

[2] Excerpted from magazine article by Tom Wicker, political columnist and associate editor of the *New York Times*. *New York Review of Books.* 27:11–15. Ag. 14, '80. Reprinted with permission from *The New York Review of Books.* Copyright © 1980 Nyrev, Inc.

Mr. Anderson or Representative Philip Crane. But at the North Londonderry firehouse, that chilly February morning, a total of seven cameras, network and local, filmed Mr. Baker's typically low-keyed speech—while, at most, perhaps two dozen laconic Hampshiremen and women listened with no great enthusiasm.

That lack of local interest in Howard Baker foretold his fate; within a week or two, he was not only out of the top three but out of the race. On the other hand, Mr. Anderson, with a surprising second-place finish in the Massachusetts primary, sprang right out of Doonesbury and into the "charmed circle" he had so envied—ultimately, of course, into the national spotlight and an independent presidential candidacy that has both major parties looking over their collective shoulders.

At least two conclusions suggest themselves from these cautionary tales. One is that in presidential politics, television can neither redeem an otherwise lifeless campaign (Baker signally lacked organization, an issue appeal, or the kind of victor's aura Iowa had given Bush), nor kill by inattention a campaign that has a real base of public support (which Mr. Anderson as "the only moderate in the race" only needed opportunity to demonstrate).

But the other conclusion is that nothing, any more, is quite so important to a presidential candidate as television coverage. Television made Jimmy Carter in 1976, it gave George Bush his brief fling into notoriety in 1980, it has carried John Anderson—a national unknown in January of this year—into serious contention for the presidency, and it is the primary instrument by which Ronald Reagan will reach the White House, if he does.

Presidential politics today, it is reasonably fair to say, *is* television. Party politics in America has given way to media politics, and the full consequences of that momentous shift probably are yet to be seen; among them, surely, is the loss of function of the traditional parties and the widening gap between the media arts of running for president and the grinding politics of governing the country.

But it is not just television that has changed the way we choose presidents almost beyond recognition—hence changed the kind of presidents we are likely to elect, and what they will do with the office when they win it. When Hubert Humphrey won the Democratic nomination in 1968 without winning or even entering a single primary, a reaction centered in the Democratic Party led to "opening up the system" for nominating presidential candidates; and when the vast sums raised for Richard Nixon's re-election in 1972 were shown to have been tainted by scandal, steeped in influence, and poured into Watergate, another reaction—this time in Congress—produced a complex federal subsidy scheme to "take the money out of politics."

Both reforms succeeded—succeeded so well, in fact, that they turned the nominating system upside down and inside out and raised in the process the questions whether the system is not now *too* open on the one hand and too constrained on the other by federal restrictions on fund-raising and spending. Like most reforms conceived in committee cerebration, moreover, these produced side effects foreseen by none but the longheaded.

The new system produced, for 1980, the apparently certain nomination of President Carter by the Democrats and of Ronald Reagan by the Republicans—a pair of ex-governors, one of whom had in late June only 30 percent public approval for his handling of the presidency, and the other of whom had been rejected twice by his party and lacked, at age sixty-nine, any demonstrable experience in foreign policy, national security, or congressional affairs.

"This is what reform gets us?" a reader wrote to me last spring. And when I published in the *New York Times* the rather snide conclusion that Carter's record of ineptitude was the worst since Warren G. Harding's, several letters informed me that this was a slur on Harding.

In one poll, 58 percent of the respondents termed themselves unhappy with the choices offered them by the two parties; and John Anderson and his managers freely concede that his independent campaign was made possible only by the unpopularity of the Reagan-Carter match-up, which left many a voter in both parties looking for an alternative and gave Anderson roughly 20 percent of the vote in pre-convention polls.

It is not clear, however, that the system inevitably produced Reagan and Carter, or that other nominees would have emerged from a different system—say, the old, pre-1968 method—of separating wheat from chaff. Reagan, for instance, was a front-runner and won; Carter was an underdog (last fall) and won.

Both, it's true, were veterans of the 1976 campaign, the first under the new dispensation, and presumably took advantage from that experience. But it seems unlikely that if nominations were still dominated by party leaders and professionals, an incumbent president would have been challenged for renomination, as Carter was. On the other hand, the necessity to run in primaries, which Gerald Ford did not want to do, foreclosed his chances and kept Reagan's most formidable foe off the field.

Aside from the end product in any one year, however, sharp questions about the new nominating system are now being raised by many students of politics—practitioners, academics, journalists. And though one and a half elections— 1976 and the primary half of 1980—provide limited experience by which to judge, a number of cogent criticisms seem to be emerging already, from the relatively obvious (thirty-six state primaries are too many) to the comparatively subtle (is proportional selection of delegates as fair as it seems?). Naturally, proposals to reform the reforms (regional primaries, for example) are being heard.

Here, in summary form, are the major problems—at least as I see them—of the way we nominate now:

The Early Primaries and Caucuses. Something has to come first, of course; if not the New Hampshire primary, then the Iowa caucuses, or whatever. But in a nominating system in which *public contests* between two or more candidates are largely determinant, the first such contests—particularly the very first—are bound to draw press coverage out of all proportion to their intrinsic importance. Iowa and New Hampshire may have only eight and four electoral votes apiece but if they provide the arenas for the first victories and the first defeats, the press will descend in numbers more appropriate to a national convention.

Editorialists as well as press critics can and do argue that this should not be so, that editors and political reporters ought to discipline themselves to give coverage to the early campaign events in proportion to their intrinsic importance. But a happening that is first of many *does* take on outsized even if momentary importance, particularly when candidates have been organizing and campaigning for months and when the public—the press must assume—is hungry for some measure of who's doing well and who's not.

Besides, in a free and highly competitive business, does the *Washington Post* ask the *New York Times* what kind of coverage it plans for the Iowa caucuses? Does NBC ask CBS? Of course not. They all assume the other fellow will go all out, and they plan to match or outdo him. And if newspapers and television *did* try to restrain coverage generally, they might lay themselves open to the charge they least want or need— that of collusion to affect public opinion.

The result in a contest-centered system and a media age is that the first "winner" reaps a disproportionate harvest of publicity; television, in particular, quickly stamps him (or maybe some day her) as a front-runner and parlays his name, face, and foibles (Carter's teeth, Bush's jogging) into national familiarity. Carter, up against a relatively faceless field in 1976, was never headed after gaining such a media advantage in Iowa and New Hampshire; Bush, facing the famous Reagan in 1980, was boosted into his most persistent Republican challenger.

The Proliferation of Candidates. The availability of all those primaries, plus the provision of federal financing even for unknown candidates who meet a relatively low threshold of fund-raising, ensures a big field of contenders in the out-party and makes likely a challenge even to an incumbent. That's fine for giving new faces a break, offering the voters a variety of choices, and keeping a president on his toes.

The problem is that it means somebody can come in first

in a multi-candidate primary, and thus be declared a "winner," with perhaps as little as 28 percent of the vote, as Carter did in New Hampshire in 1976. Less than a third of the voters of a minority party in a state with four electoral votes is not representative of much of anything, but the resulting press "circus" took the Georgian a long way in 1976—which is why some critics say that primaries plus federal subsidies plus television have taken the nomination away from one small and unrepresentative group (party leaders and pros) and given it to another such group (a few New Hampshire or Iowa Democrats or Republicans).

Primary Spending Limits. Not only can someone with a small percentage of the total party vote in a small state be catapulted by omnipresent media into national prominence and front-runner status. But no other candidate—including some who might have finished only a percentage point or two behind—can rush out to his supporters, beg or borrow an infusion of funds, then outspend that "front-runner" the next time out in order to catch up. Acceptance of a federal subsidy also means acceptance of federal spending limits for each primary.

This is a classic example of how a reform meant to preclude any candidate from having a financial advantage over another instead can give a huge advantage to the winner of the first public contest. Those who fall behind at the outset are, in effect, penalized by restrictions on what they can spend and where.

'John B. Connally, Jr., tried to get around this problem in 1980 by raising huge sums privately (about $14 million) and refusing federal subsidy, thus entitling himself to ignore the spending limits. He then took South Carolina and Florida as the targets for intense efforts—a scheme that might have worked for a more appealing candidate. It produced a total of one delegate for Big John before he went home to Texas.

Proportional Selection of Delegates. In the Democratic Party, and to a somewhat lesser extent in the Republican, unit rules and winner-take-all primaries are now prohibited. A candidate entered in a primary or competing for delegates at a convention, if he or she reaches a minimum level of support, is entitled to a number of delegates proportionate to his or her final share of the vote.

What could be fairer than that? Nothing, on the face of it, and in fact this was one of the more eagerly accepted Democratic reforms, following the contentious 1968 campaign. But in both of Carter's winning campaigns, proportional selection gave him a considerable advantage—again derived from getting out front early.

Once an early front-runner takes a delegate lead, and assuming a few victories or at least a decent showing in all remaining primaries, he has a good chance to maintain or add to that lead even when he comes in third or fourth. With the delegates being divided among all candidates, no one is likely to win so many more than the early front-runner in any state, or group of states, as to catch up or go ahead. The front-runner goes on piling up his total.

Thus, even though Carter lost numerous primaries in the late 1976 race, the early lead he had established was never seriously challenged. And in one brief early stretch in 1980— March 11 to March 18—encompassing five primaries (three in the South) and seven state caucuses (almost all in states favorable to him), the president took such a huge lead over Senator Edward Kennedy that he was all but guaranteed victory no matter what happened the rest of the way.

Even after Kennedy won New York and Connecticut on March 25, he would have had to capture about 60 percent of all remaining delegates—which meant defeating Carter nearly two to one in each primary thereafter—to overcome the early Carter lead. Merely beating the president by, say, fifty-one to forty-nine, would yield almost no change in their relative delegate strength. So even though Kennedy later carried Pennsylvania, New Jersey, and California, his margin of victory was never large enough to yield many more delegates than Carter won even while losing.

Tightly Pledged Delegates. When John F. Kennedy smashed Hubert Humphrey in the West Virginia primary in 1960, it wasn't the delegates he won that mattered; rather,

Kennedy proved that a Catholic could win in a non-urban, semi-Southern state. When Nelson Rockefeller defeated Barry Goldwater in Oregon in 1964, he kept his candidacy alive not with Oregon's handful of delegates but by underlining doubts about the conservative Goldwater's electability.

Under the post-1968 system, however, candidates enter most primaries because that is the best way to accumulate delegates—as Gerald Ford quickly found out last spring when he tried to make the race outside the primaries; and the rules provide that delegates won in primaries or picked off in convention contests are tightly pledged for at least one ballot. That prohibits the old evil of party leaders snatching delegates away from candidates who might have shown themselves "the people's choice," if not that of the leaders.

But it also makes reconsideration, negotiating, compromising, and maneuvering, in the classic presidential style, difficult if not impossible. A delegate pledged to Carter from the New Hampshire or the Florida primary, back in February and March, conceivably might have concluded later that the president's economic policy was a disaster and his rescue effort in Iran a fiasco; but he would still be a pledged Carter delegate, his only option to resign in favor of another pledged Carter delegate.

Together with proportional selection, irrevocably pledged delegates make it unlikely that there will be late entries into the presidential race, or that any such entries can succeed. They tend to make the later primaries irrelevant, or at least less important than the earlier, even though the most populous states, as things now stand, come along in the later part of the program. That has a depressing effect, in the late primaries, on public participation and voter turnout—not what the reformers had in mind.

Finally, if a candidate like Jimmy Carter can win a majority of delegates, all tightly pledged to him on the first ballot, by early May or thereabouts, what remaining value do the national conventions have? Why call the roll, if the outcome is inevitable a month before the gavel falls? If in these traditional arenas of compromise and maneuver, there can be no compromise or maneuver—no consideration of changing circumstances or late developments—what is the purpose of holding a convention at all, other than for blather and ballyhoo?

If the consequences of delegate-selection and fund-raising reforms have been extensive in themselves, they have been magnified many times over by the rising dependence of presidential campaigners on television—a dependence which seems to me essentially unreformable in an era when the networks have become a sort of national nervous system.

When a candidate must compete in all or most of thirty-six state primaries, the home screen obviously is the most effective instrument with which to reach so many voters so widely dispersed. When the amount of money that may be spent is restricted by federal law, the high cost of television time dictates that most of the funds available will be spent on the ubiquitous "tube."

Thus, what most voters in, say, Illinois knew of that state's primary last March 18, they learned from what they saw on television—either in candidates' paid advertisements, or in the news broadcasts and talk-show interviews that all candidates sought desperately to break into, or in the Republican candidates' forum sponsored by the League of Women Voters. Personal appearances before live audiences were insignificant by comparison; and in fact most such appearances were staged in the hope of television news coverage, then immediately restaged in some other television market in the hope of further coverage.

There's nothing inherently wrong with this; voters see more of candidates via television than they ever saw of them in person, in the old days. In practice, however, media politics tends to heighten the puffery, pretense, and downright deception that have always been part and parcel of politics—which is the art of persuading people to think and do what you want them to think and do. *What* the voters see of candidates, not how much, is the problem.

More than ever before—in my judgment, anyway—television campaigning puts the emphasis on a contrived image of the candidate—what he and his media whizzes can persuade the public to think about him. And what they want the public to think about the candidate often has less to do with what the candidate is or believes than with what public opinion polls have disclosed that the voters would like to think he is or believes. Armed with that kind of precise information, television campaign specialists—a thriving new industry—can design and produce a series of ads to create exactly the desired effect. And these ads, ranging from thirty-second spots to five-minute or thirty-minute productions and televised to enormous numbers of poeple, not only have the ability to convince for which TV is justly famed (who is more "real" in American life than J. R. Ewing of *Dallas* and why did even the American Bar Association once invite Perry Mason/Raymond Burr to address its convention?) but also have the advantage of great flexibility and immediacy. Ad campaigns can be put together just for, say, Pennsylvania, where unemployment is high, while an entirely different series is presented in Texas, where oil and gas questions dominate. For candidates, television is a dial-an-image godsend, with which reporters— even when they try to get at the truth—can rarely cope.

Thus, candidate Carter bore down heavily, in post-Watergate 1976, on homely images of a peanut farmer in clodhopper shoes communing with the old values on a Georgia farm; this was a man who was not a lawyer, hardly knew where Washington was, and would never tell us a lie—now would he?

Thus, in 1980, bold John Anderson went before the gun buffs in New Hampshire and advocated gun control, damned if he didn't—with the television cameras that recorded the dramatic moment for the national audience failing to explain that since there were few Anderson votes in that New Hampshire crowd anyway, the candidate was risking little locally to make a big score nationally.

Thus, too, Carroll O'Connor appeared in a series of ads for Edward Kennedy, not only throwing his own popularity behind the senator but implicitly suggesting that the blue-collar views of Archie Bunker were shared by the candidate, Chappaquiddick or no Chappaquiddick.

Politics, of course, always has been illusionist, to a certain extent. Television merely extends the possibilities and yields greater returns for the superior magic show. But the heavy modern reliance on television imagery, like procedural reforms, also tends toward unanticipated side effects—for example, a creeping disparity between the ability to get elected and the ability to serve well after election.

There is no necessary distinction between these abilities but obviously there may be quite a gap—perhaps more often than not. Divining what the public would like to hear and what kind of leader it thinks it wants in particular circumstances, then calculating a campaign to satisfy those desires, is no doubt an art and not a despicable one, either.

The problem is that this art does not have much to do with the ability to govern, as the Carter Administration demonstrates. In fact, the successful projection of an image in a campaign can bring on serious trouble later, if the image can't be realized or sustained under the pressures of office—again, witness Jimmy Carter.

On the other hand, a successfully established image can sustain a candidate even when his perfomance in office might normally mandate a change. Carter—obviously the most prominent product of media politics so far—kept winning 1980 primaries with the votes of Democrats who deplored his record but who nevertheless still regarded him as the honest, moral family man of the 1976 peanut-farmer ads, in sharp contrast to the Chappaquiddick-laden Kennedy.

At the same time that presidential campaigning was changing, moreover, so was the presidency. After Vietnam and Watergate, the prestige and authority of the office declined, while congressional independence rose. The combination of single-interest politics, independent legislators, and sohisticated lobbying made it more difficult to put together effective coalitions. Even the major issues—energy and the economy—are more complex than they were a decade ago.

So if the arts of winning elections have less and less to do with governing, it's the other way around with the qualities important for a chief executive trying to surmount such difficulties—experience in government, a solid background in party politics with its emphasis on alliances and compromises, an intricate network of associations with other political leaders, a deep sense of the way the system works or can be made to work. These have little relevance to the problems of winning a presidential nomination or election in the media era.

Another "side effect" of media politics and electoral reforms has been the diminished functions of the American political party. Ever since Thomas Jefferson invented this strange beast its main purpose has been to bring various factions and leaders together under what Lyndon Johnson called "one great tent," and to unite them, however uneasily, around an issue or a personality for just long enough to register a national majority. To choose candidates who could unite such a majority, or articulate an issue that could do so, was a prime party responsibility.

When most voters could neither see nor hear candidates, moreover, the parties gave them their identities; an Arkansas farmer might not know much about a presidential hopeful, but if the Democrats nominated him he must be all right—or at least better than a bloody-shirt Republican. The parties also raised funds and financed campaigns and their platforms more or less defined the issues, if for election-day purposes only.

Television alone takes away or diminishes most of these party functions. Candidates now are identified more decisively by widely perceived television images than by party labels. Expensively appealing to mass audience, they are unlikely to target on Democrats or Republicans alone, but to present themselves in less partisan guise. All candidates, especially national candidates, it follows, are more nearly independents now than partisans, no matter what their ideologies and party labels; and voters, too, are more likely to take an independent attitude as against traditional party loyalty.

For all these reasons, the unifying factor in a momentary national majority now tends to be the candidate's television image, rather than his party. Proliferating primaries, moreover, have handed to the general public—at least that part of it involved in the early primaries—the old party function of choosing candidates. Even the party's fund-raising chores and its influence on campaign spending have been largely usurped in national elections by federal subsidies.

And when most of the money available to the presidential nominees has to be spent on waging the central, all-important television contest, those participatory functions which the parties once organized and supervised—storefronts, canvassing, registration, and get-out-of-the-vote drives—take a back seat, and the parties along with them.

But all of these criticisms don't seem to me to constitute an indictment of the new system; certainly, they don't mean that the nation should return forthwith to the 1968 model. Despite the advantage conferred on the early front-runner, for example, by proportional delegate selection, who would want to re-establish the unit rules, winner-take-all devices, smoke-filled rooms, wheeling and dealing, and outright skulduggery by which delegates used to be apportioned about as the Mayor Daleys and Boss Flynns and Mark Hannas decided?

There may well be too many primaries; thirty might make more sense and be easier on the health of candidates and reporters. But that's essentially a matter for the states to decide and no method by which the parties or Congress might try to dictate a more orderly system appeals to me. Similarly, regional primaries—states in a particular region holding primaries at the same time—might be an improvement; but the states seem to me to be moving into this arrangement by usage. The New England, southern, and northwestern primaries were identifiably grouped in 1980, on one or consecutive Tuesdays.

The campaign subsidy law would be improved, I think, if the individual contribution limit were $5,000 instead of $1,-000, and if the subsidies and spending limits were increased; in general, we spend too little, not too much, on political education, which, at its best, is what campaigning is. And the experience of John Anderson, like that of Eugene McCarthy in 1976, raises the real question whether a federal subsidy law ought to be used to shut out independents and third parties and build in the Democrats and Republicans as official parties just at the time when they have become less useful than ever.

As for television, nothing can or should be done about its reach and impact, or to prevent candidates from taking advantage of it. I have strong First Amendment reservations about regulating their use of television—by prohibiting their use of spot advertisements, for instance, or restricting them to blocs of free time extorted by government from the national networks.

One welcome development, however, is increased attention by the political press to the use candidates make of the home screen. Numerous newspapers now assign reporters to cover the television campaigns exclusively, reporting not only on what the public sees but on what messages the candidates are trying to get across, why, and by what means or trickery. That television documentary for which John Anderson was interviewed in February was about the impact of television on politics, a subject getting increased attention from self-conscious networks and local stations. Still, probably no news institution as yet pays anywhere near as much attention to the television campaign as it does to the candidates' personal appearances.

THE MODULATING OF THE PRESIDENCY[3]
by Michael J. Arlen

Our Presidential candidates are lost somewhere out there in America. They've been lost for weeks, for months, maybe for years—two mainstream candidates, one independent candidate, a baker's dozen of peripheral candidates. Bill Moyers found some of the peripheral candidates the other evening— wandering bleakly like trappers in the dark woods, where the media sun never shines—and warmed them briefly in the glow of public television's lights; but soon they wandered off again (their faces pink and glowing) and are lost once more.

[3] Reprint of magazine article by Michael J. Arlen, contributing editor, *New Yorker*. 56:172–177. O. 27, '80. Reprinted by permission; © 1980 The New Yorker Magazine, Inc.

Of course, our independent and peripheral candidates are always lost—trappers trudging through the wilderness, stubbornly trapping for extinct or near-extinct species. But in this autumn of an election year, in a nation whose politics (so virtually everyone agrees) have been taken over, veritably subsumed, by television, our mainstream candidates are also lost—not entirely out of view or altogether out of mind, for they pop up constantly on the news, addressing factory workers here or chatting with Hispanics there, but nonetheless as good as vanished, *perdu*, lost from sight, and right in front of the all-seeing, all-powerful eyes of the mighty network cameras.

To listen to the political people and the network people talk about the election coverage, you'd think that there was nothing wrong with it that a little more fiddling with the controls and components wouldn't cure. If there's a problem, it is apparently a problem of *modulation;* at any rate, these days everybody is bent on fine-tuning. Some weeks ago, when the networks were riding hard on Governor Reagan for a careless remark he'd made about our China policy (in other words, they were modulating their coverage of the Reagan campaign so as to bring out the special vibrato of his China statement), a Reagan aide observed to a correspondent—in the manner of one engineer talking shop with another—that henceforth Reagan's campaign staff would be "doing a little more fine-tuning" of the Governor's press encounters; in short, they'd be modulating *their* controls so as to excise unplayable Reagan statements before they got locked into the soundtrack.

There are times, of course, when the modulation problem is mainly in the video side of the equipment, as took place the other day when an unexpected visual malfunction occurred over at CBS News—a problem of graphics overload, as it might be described. What happened was this: In an attempt to clearly demonstrate (i.e., fine-tune) candidate Reagan's penchant for changing his mind, CBS News flashed little white Xs over an image of the Governor while a voice-over tracked the candidate's about-faces on the issues. The network's modest foray into early newspaper-art design seemed inoffensive enough at the time, and scarcely the point at issue compared with the Governor's record of rhetorical instability. But clearly the network's efforts at visual fine-tuning had taxed the system. (Doubtless, good Republicans in the television audience, close in spirit to primitive peoples in their concern for the well-being of the soul, had feared that those little white Xs presaged an X'ing out not only of their leader's discarded enthusiasms but of their leader as well.) Alarm bells rang. Red lights flashed in secret control rooms. *Graphics overload on Channel 2!* The next evening, no less a totemic figure than the venerable Walter Cronkite, sage and elder of CBS News, apologized on camera for the mistake—not a mistake of accuracy or reporting but a mistake in graphics. The red lights blinked off. Gradually, the system returned to harmony—sputtering, fizzling, steaming, cooling. Only the Governor and what he stood (or didn't stand) for were left somehow out of focus.

Most of the time, however, the modulation trouble seems to lie in the audio components: problems of sound mixing, so to speak. For example, when President Carter (who had visually fine-tuned himself out of the primaries by staying in the White House) attempted to fine-tune himself into the campaign by criticizing Reagan, his criticisms made news less for their substance than for what might be thought of as their audio qualities—qualities that were measured and noted by the press on a daily basis, and whose generally perceived "harshness" soon became the principal journalistic point of reference for the whole Carter campaign. As a result of poor audio notices, Carter then decided to change the sound of his campaign—or at least the sound mix. This new audio-engineering decision to sound less harsh (which was announced appropriately by the candidate in a Barbara Walters interview) then became the next press reference point for the President's efforts to retain the Presidency. In fact, Carter had probably meant what he had said in his attacks on Reagan, in his admonitions to the effect that Reagan would divide the country, would turn "race against race," and so forth. That was Carter talking, but the press didn't seem to be listening to what he was saying—only to the sound of what he was saying: a "harsh" sound, a *bad* sound. Perhaps Carter shouldn't have put the word "race" into the soundtrack; the sound of the word "race" seems to grate on everybody's ears this year. Perhaps he should have introduced a little sociology into the mix, thereby providing that kind of soft, blurry, statesmanly sound that makes for easy listening. One imagines, however, that some savvy Carter media strategist—one of the President's fine-tuners—had heard somewhere of the terrific sound produced years ago by Harry Truman in his "Give 'em hell" campaign, and thought, Hey, if we could just get President Jimmy to put on the bib overalls and raise a little hell and play some of that down-home music, we'll be at the top of the charts by Halloween. The Harry Truman sound! The sound of the once and future country-and-Western Presidency! *Good* sound! It was the right general idea but with the wrong particulars. What they got instead was that *other* country music: that dry-lipped Appalachian sound—quavering reeds and sombre, God-fearing plainsong: harsh, albeit authentic.

Similarly, when Governor Reagan, early in the campaign, was making all those discordant sounds about China and the Ku Klux Klan and God knows what else, those were *his* sounds, too. They weren't nice sounds, either, of course, and this posed a special kind of problem. The video equipment indicated the Governor to be a uniformly nice fellow, but the audio equipment registered an awkward mixture: a lot of bad sounds were coming through. Evidently, the equipment was at fault; it was another problem of modulation. Audio engineers were called in to fine-tune the Governor after the China sounds played poorly, but there are some sounds so sharp and strange that they can't easily be mixed. Possibly the equipment is still primitive in certain ways; it amplifies some things when you least expect it. For instance, your candidate is being cool, just bopping along in the recording studio, laying down a little warm and easy candidacy music, doing his thing, figuring that if there's a real soft spot somewhere the engineers can always put in a couple of mariachi tracks after the session, or maybe some echoes, or church bells, or a whole defense-department percussion section, but then suddenly—whoooee! *Ku Klux Klan!* Oh, man. *Ku Klux Klan?* A very bad sound. Just about jams the machine. More alarms. Red lights everywhere. *Bad-sound overload!* No engineer can wipe that kind of sound once it gets on the track. You have to cancel the recording session. Delay the tour. Send everybody back to Malibu and figure out how to get that bad sound out of there.

Sooner or later, nowadays, the bad sound disappears, even if you have to fine-tune the candidate out of the campaign to do it. Television anchormen, like the great stone heads on Easter Island, have had their day. This is the day of the modulating engineers: the cutters, splicers, mixers, editors, and so on. Listen to the hum of our modern political campaigns: the whir of tape on editing and mixing machines—forward, stop, reverse, snip, snip, splice, forward, stop, snip, whir: our new montage actuality. The candidates wander the country, like trappers—or perhaps like rock bands, in full view of everyone but seen by no one. Who are those men behind the painted faces and fright wigs onstage, and what actual music is buried in their wires, cables, consoles, and amplifying systems? Today, both the politicians and the networks are caught up in the same dance of technology. The real power is the power of the men and women who control the montage effects—the technologists who instinctively understand the truth of Eisenstein's statement: "The basic fact was true, and remains true to this day, that the juxtaposition of two separate shots by splicing them together resembles not so much a simple sum of one shot plus another shot as it does a *creation.*" One shot plus another shot; one sound plus another sound: *Creation!* These engineers are the new creators, our political kingmakers. The other day, President Carter was on a speaking tour in Nashville, in the course of which, for a brief moment, he criticized the three networks for not having shown on their news programs a few nights before that part of a Reagan interview where the Governor strongly disavowed the SALT II treaty. Carter, in other words, was speaking to the issue of network

editing, fine-tuning—scolding them for having declined to
transmit a more creative Reagan montage. In rebuttal, however, the CBS technicians employed montage on Carter.
They fine-tuned his Nashville remarks so that, in their presentation, the President seemed to have little on his mind beyond attacking the three networks. Then they employed
montage on one of their earlier news broadcasts and thus ex-
tracted a brief CBS reference to Reagan's disavowal of SALT
II. Now they put it all together: a new montage—a new creation. How clever, one thought. Such energy of technique! It
was more than an interesting example of television byplay.
What we had witnessed was a journalistic-political dialogue
entirely focussed on montage—on the technology of video-
and-sound modulation. The only thing missing, of course, was
a coherent sense of the candidate: of either one, or of both
candidates, for that matter, who seem destined to dart per-
petually through factories, airports, slum-housing projects,
municipal parades, etc., always beneath the camera lights—
beautifully framed, expertly recorded—but somehow never
seen. It's as if the love that politicians once bore the public
has been transferred to the new machines, and the machines
have lost sight of the one thing about these strange, complex,
and driven people that anyone ever really cared about: *who
they are*.

A FEW WORDS OF HIS OWN[4]

Ronald Reagan's early campaign flounderings disclose a
severe case of McKay's Syndrome, a deadly political affliction
named for Douglas McKay, an Oregon car dealer who ran for
the Senate some years ago.

McKay's case became terminal during a rousing campaign
rally in which he delivered the customary speech stuffed with

[4] Reprinted from newspaper column "Observer," by Russell Baker, New York *Times*.
p. A19. S. 3, '80. © 1980 by The New York Times Company. Reprinted by permission.

the customary banalities, evasions and bromides, to the customary applause from the party claque. Not content to quit while he was behind, McKay then laid aside his prepared text, looked over the audience and said, "Now I'd like to say a few words of my own."

Needless to say, McKay did not become a United States Senator, and if Ronald Reagan continues to insist on saying a few words of his own while dispensing the gruel cooked up by his campaign technicians, he stands an excellent chance of not becoming a United States President.

On four occasions during the past fortnight Mr. Reagan has yielded to the impulse to say more than his technicians prescribed and each occasion has gladdened the man of Georgia. In two of these cases—Mr. Reagan's reaffirmation of the belief in the nobility of the Vietnam War and his elevation of the Carter recession to the status of "depression"—the candidate penciled in the troublesome phrases on his own behalf after the technicians had armed him with safely bland material.

The comic march up the hill and down again on China policy and the inflammatory suggestion that divine creation theory might also be taught in the public schools both seem to have been adventures wandered into by a haphazard impulse to work the jaw before the brain, or the technical brain trust, had been consulted.

Mr. Reagan's urge to say a few words of his own is not without a certain quaint beguiling charm. It has been a long time since we have had an important politician willing to expose himself so candidly during a campaign. There is something old-fashioned about campaign candor nowadays, however, which may trouble a generation of voters bred to think of political campaigns as exercises among masked men.

Presidential campaigns nowadays are perceived by most of us, though we might not phrase it this way, as a form of marketing. Americans are a race whose intuitive understanding is shaped by television. They know, if only intuitively, that successful marketing requires a highly skilled group of technical experts capable of measuring the market's whims and coming up with a sales campaign which emphasizes their product's ability to gratify those whims while obscuring its less attractive side effects.

The tip of this iceberg is the TV commercial, and we are all television-wise now; we know the rules of commercials. We know they do not deal in candor, and the commercials know that we know, and since we are all playing by the same rules, there is not a great deal of unhappiness about it.

Presidential politics having become essentially a TV commercial campaign, we tend to think about the candidates in much the same way that we think about the competing beers and scouring powders which campaign on the same stump with the Reagans, Carters and Andersons. In short, we do not expect candor.

Candor is a violation of the rules. It is upsetting. Candidates are not supposed to tell us what they think or to say a few words of their own. They are supposed to have technicians who find out what we desire to hear and copyreaders to compose messages that will satisfy that desire and performers—Reagans, Carters, Andersons—who will read the lines like professionals and not monkey with the script.

Mr. Reagan's habit of saying a few words of his own disturbs some sense of fitness bred into us by our television habit. It is a violation of the rules that may be more damaging to him than whatever he says when he breaks away from the technicians and begins operating as an individual, ignoring the professional market manipulators.

This is one error President Carter rarely makes. When his market surveys tell him to lie low in the Rose Garden, he lies low. He can change policy three times in a year in response to his ever-shifting market surveys, and continue to survive because of a public perception that though he may flit quixotically all over the political spectrum, he is flitting at the command of the best professional and technical advice available.

President Carter never says a few words of his own, and for good reason. Saying a few words of his own leaves the impression that a candidate thinks he is smarter than the technicians who run him instead of being merely the tip of the

iceberg doing his predetermined number with appropriate
conviction right there on the parlor tube.

If elected, you suspect, a man like that might ignore his
technicians and do something terribly upsetting. Mr. Reagan
has been creating the disturbing impression that, if elected, he
might do a few things of his own. Perhaps he should find a rose
garden and bunker down there for the next several weeks.

GOD'S TELEVISION[5]

It's pledge month. The mistress of ceremonies, a fortyish
blond whose bubbly manner and pert good looks remind the
viewer of a young Debbie Reynolds, admonishes the television audience: "This is the time of year when we've got to
raise the budget." The toll-free 800 number is superimposed
on the screen as she explains how a "$15-a-month partnership
pledge will help keep PTL on the air in your area. . . . Sixty
telephone operators are standing by. . . . Some people are
writin' us and tellin' us that they're watchin' television and
can't find us, and we have to explain that without money we
can't stay on the air. . . ."

The studio band riffs into upbeat music. The phones ring,
a floor producer signals for studio applause. The Debbie
Reynolds look-alike—her name, in fact, is Tammy Bakker—
beams over the gifts that a partnership pledge will bring: a
PTL stickpin, the PTL newsletter, a PTL Bible, and, for a
one-time gift of $1,000, an Heirloom Bible, illustrated, with
"a stamped antique gold cover" and the donor's name printed
on it.

PTL is not the public television station in Louisville, despite Tammy Bakker's down-home accent and the all too familiar sound of the pledge month pitch. PTL stands for Praise
the Lord, a television production and distribution service run

[5] Reprint of magazine article "God's Television," by Edwin Diamond, head of the
News Study group at MIT and a lecturer in political science. *American Film.* 5:30–35. Mr.
'80. Reprinted with permission from the March 1980 issue of *American Film* magazine, ©
1980 The American Film Institute, J. F. Kennedy Center, Washington, DC.

by a former tent preacher—and Tammy's husband—named Jim Bakker. Jim Bakker, Tammy Bakker, the PTL singers, and the PTL pledge operation are all part of the biggest, arguably strangest, and certainly least discussed new development in our popular culture—God's television.

God's television manifests itself in many forms around the dial: Bakker's song, dance, and prayer "PTL Club," beamed by satellite to scores of stations in the United States and Canada; Oral Roberts's evangelical Bible-teaching sessions and his prime-time variety specials; Robert Schuller's "Hour of Power" from Garden Grove, California, with its inspirational message of "possibility thinking"; and Pat Robertson's fast-paced "700 Club" from Virginia Beach, Virginia, part of the Christian Broadcasting Network that also uses satellite to reach Robertson-owned stations in Atlanta, Boston, Dallas, and Norfolk, as well as other television markets.

There are also Rex Humbard, Jerry Falwell, Jimmy Swaggart, Ernest Angley, and a host of others, small-town evangelicals and UHF preachers, often known no further than the modest range of an ultrahigh frequency television signal from a heartland station. The association of national religious broadcasters claims some 1,000 members, and a recent survey indicated that 38 television stations and 66 cable sytems across the United States—as well as 1,400 radio stations—specialize in what the FCC counts as "religious broadcasting."

Bakker, Roberts, Schuller, and Robertson are the big four of Christian television; they're in the major television markets, with yearly broadcast budgets of up to $50 million or more. Oral Roberts, the founding father of God's television, is now sixty-one. He began his television faith healing and Bible preaching in 1954, in television's infancy, when, he says, "I could buy prime time every week, whenever I wanted it." Today, Roberts's large staff says it needs $10 million a month to operate the Oral Roberts television ministry, the Oral Roberts University, and the Oral Roberts City of Faith medical complex, all in Tulsa.

Pat Robertson began broadcasting in 1961 with one UHF station in Virginia. Today, he boasts, his Christian Broadcasting Network (CBN) is "America's largest syndicator of programs via satellite." (A relay channel for CBN was aboard RCA's Satcom III, the ill-fated communications satellite launched last December.) Jim Bakker, who used to work for Robertson, started his own television program just five years ago, borrowing a sound-alike name and variety show format from Robertson. "Our broadcast budget in 1974 used to be $20,000 a month; now it's a million dollars a week," Bakker says. Fifty-two-year-old Robert Schuller, the only mainstream minister of the big four—he belongs to the Reformed Church in America—organized his first congregation in 1955, using a drive-in theater for six years. Schuller now says his "Hour of Power" is on 142 television stations in the United States and Canada, plus the 82 outlets of the armed forces network.

God's television—the phrase was used on one of Robertson's programs—may not catch the eye of the critics for the *Washington Post* or the *New York Times*. (One exception is the estimable Elizabeth Hardwick, who wrote brilliantly about evangelical television in an essay last summer in the *New York Review of Books*.) But God's television is a big and booming industry, one that may be changing traditional notions of television, and of religion.

Since its inception, television has been in the business of crowd collecting, normally for the sake of advertisers who want to reach specific audiences. Over the years television served certain audiences—for example, the consumers of comedy, or sports, or children's programs, or news and public affairs, or "Masterpiece Theatre," or old movies. But it apparently was ignoring the interests of other audiences. About the time of candidate Jimmy Carter's rise from southern obscurity four years ago, the political experts and cultural savants did a double take. From the vantage point of midtown Manhattan, *Time* magazine had already proclaimed that God Was Dead. But God was not dead for the fifty-five million Americans who were telling public opinion samplers that they were born-again Christians with a fundamentalist—that is, literal—belief in the Bible. It turned out that popular culture was ignoring twenty percent of the population, an over-

looked demographic group, if you please. These fundamentalist Christians had special meaning for television, our most
pervasive medium for popular culture.

From the first days of radio, religion has been a staple of
broadcasting. By the late fifties, although television had dis-
placed radio as our chief attention getter, the evangelists and
faith healers had not yet moved in force into the new medium. The audience was there, however. "By the mid-seven-
ties it was clear that . . . there were people out there who
weren't interested in Charlie's Angels or the Super Bowl or
rock'n'roll stars or show business talk on Merv Griffin," says
Stuart Zanger, a documentary filmmaker in Memphis. "These
people wanted sincere, fundamentalist Christian programming, and now they're getting it."

The matter of sincerity immediately occurs to any skeptic
who watches the big four of God's television. Their programs
are so slickly produced in the most glitzy Hollywood "variety
show" manner; the performers—the star preachers, gospel
singers, guest healers, and inspirational figures—are so neatly
turned out in their blow-dry hair, capped teeth, thousand-
watt smiles, banker's gray suits, and flowing robes; the format
is so artfully stage-managed (one black face invariably inte-
grates Tammy Bakker's backup singing group or Robert
Schuller's massed choir); the pledge numbers and pay-for-
prayer messages are so insistently presented—that God's television inevitably evokes images of the charlatan preacher, of
the Elmer Gantrys and the Reverend Ikes: *I wear $400 suits
because the Lord wants me to wear $400 suits.*

Stuart Zanger has been putting together a documentary
on the big four for Scripps-Howard Broadcasting, and he prefers to let his film, due to be aired this spring, speak for itself.
Still, he thinks it's wrong to view these programs as, strictly
speaking, "religion." "They're a hybrid," he says, "a combination of gospel values and television values."

In fact, the physical church has been all but abandoned on
God's television. PTL, "The 700 Club," and the Oral Roberts
program all take place in television studios with sweeping
stages, banked seats for the audience, an orchestra stand,

conversational sofas (in the manner of Carson and Griffin), and cameras that dolly, zoom, and do close-ups and deep focus shots just like the cameras on a Bob Hope special. If steeples and stained glass are symbols of traditional religion, then God's television is distinguished by satellite transponders, phone banks, and direct-mail follow-up campaigns. Viewers who phone or write become part of computerized mailing lists, which can be used for further solicitation of funds or for marketing a whole line of "Christian" consumer goods, like the Heirloom Bible. The computer lists themselves may also be sold to other organizations, in the manner of modern direct-mail selling. The $5 and $10 pledges add up; but so do the expenses for production, for satellite time, for staff and phone counselors and letter answerers. On God's television yearly budgets range from $15 million for Schuller to $50 million for the Christian Broadcasting Network.

Religion of course, is not exactly a stranger to production values, or to business values. For centuries churches have understood the appeal of soaring cathedrals and the full sensorium of sermon, ritual, music, lights, and incense. The collection box is older than America. So the question of sincerity versus shuck has to be answered individually for each preacher. While Jim Bakker in Charlotte, North Carolina, for example, has been the subject of an FCC investigation and articles in the Charlotte *Observer* about possible diversion of funds in his television empire, out West Robert Schuller has been riding high and handsomely. Eminent architect Philip Johnson is designing Schuller's new "crystal cathedral," a spectacular, $15 million, all-glass "studio" for the "Hour of Power."

Perhaps the more appropriate questions about God's television might be: What is the content of these programs, and what images come across on the screen, explicitly and implicitly? What do viewers get from these programs, and what does this tell us about ourselves, as a television audience and as a society?

God's television presents a cluster of mythical stories involving faith, folksiness, and family. One image we see on the screen is the American ethos about the poor boy who makes good through hard work and the love of his wife and children. Jim Bakker is the poor kid from Muskegon, Michigan, who went on the road for the pentecostal Assembly of God. Oral Roberts is the poor kid from Oklahoma who founded and named a university after himself and now lives the millionaire's life in Palm Springs, on the edge of a golf course. (His son, a Pat Boone look-alike, serves as emcee on the program and introduces him as "author, educator, evangelist, and my father.")

While Robert Schuller is the only one of the big four who belongs to a mainline Protestant denomination, he, too, presents himself as the indigent "farm boy from Iowa." Schuller tells how, twenty-five years ago, he came to California with $500 in cash and an organ in a rented U-Haul trailer, went door to door in search of a congregation, and finally started his drive-in church. Even Pat Robertson, son of the former U.S. senator from Virginia and a Yale graduate, had to become "poor" again in order to begin to serve God. His saga is that of the secularist who moved out of his Manhattan apartment—with its wealth, but emptiness—eventually to go back to Virginia to study the Bible.

A second image is one of brisk, no-apologies materialism. It's not just that everyone on God's television looks so television-commercial squeaky clean and expensively turned out. Nor is it just that so much attention has been lavished on "production values" like the studio set and the multiple cameras and the lighting. It is that on God's television one prays for God's help to get a new car or a higher paying job or a better apartment, and that the unremitting faith in getting the world's goods often makes these programs resemble "The $20,000 Pyramid" or other television grab shows. A game show host like Bob Barker appears interchangeable, in looks and manner, with gospel show hosts Bakker or Robertson.

Jim Bakker is up front about making it. He wanted to get ahead in the world, and he thinks that good Christians should have the riches of the world as much as anyone else. "Diamonds are made for Christians, not Satan," he says. Not surprisingly, God's television emphasizes happy endings, just like prime-time television. And, like television commercials, it stresses getting things. On God's television there is no virtue in solitude, or poverty, or humility. This is a worldly Christianity. Its motto could be lifted directly from a beer commercial: Go for It.

When Schuller, who keeps his mouth turned up in a perpetual Kewpie doll smile, interviews Ray Kroc, the founder of McDonald's, it sounds like Hope and Crosby, or Carson and McMahon, each comparing his various successful business enterprises:

Schuller: What do you think people know about you?

Kroc: Hamburgers . . . ?

Schuller: You started with $1,000 . . . and you've grown since then?

Kroc: Quite a bit.

Schuller: How many retail outlets do you have?

Kroc: Five thousand.

Schuller: All over the world?

Kroc: All over the world. Japan, Hong Kong, Germany, Austria, Holland, Sweden, New Zealand.

Schuller: How old are you?

Kroc: Seventy-six. How old are you?

Schuller: Well, I'm fifty-two.

Kroc: Well, you've started something, too [laughter and applause].

Schuller then asks Kroc the secret of his success, and Kroc replies that he had good parents, that he worked hard, and that America is the greatest country in the world. *Sure enough, we're just poor little old boys up here, but we know how to make that buck by satisfying our customers.* Or, in the words of the Fats Waller song: *Find out what he wants and give it to him just that way.* Waller is the spiritual father of modern marketing strategies, with their focus groups and demographic research aimed at identifying audience interests in order to raise sales or ratings. And Schuller is in the same ministry: *Find the hurt and heal it,* he says.

The dominant image of God's television, then, is that of

entertainment: rich, visual pleasures, simple story lines, Christian success driving away Satan's worry. If there is adversity in life, a cancerous growth, or a meddlesome FCC, then that's part of God's story line, too: Every situation must have complicating action before the dramatic resolution. ("If I weren't a Christian, the FCC would have driven me out of my mind," Tammy Bakker lamented during the time of the troubles.) But, above all, every television show must have a star, and Roberts, Schuller, and their brethren are consummately telegenic.

A producer connected with fundamentalist television programming once told Stuart Zanger that any number of ministers had come to him and pleaded, "Get me on television." They had seen Oral Roberts's great success on television, and they figured, *What worked for him will work for me.* But the producer says he told the would-be performers that the field was overcrowded. Then he reflected to Zanger: "Think about it. Why are these men on and not others? It's not their great deeds or their great intelligence. How can they be worth a $50 million-a-year operation? The answer is, because they're great television performers."

Viewers of a certain kind are entertained by the fundamentalist big four performers and the gospel beat, just as some viewers are entertained by "Saturday Night Live," or Bogart movies, or Catskill comics. When Zanger talked to viewers around the country, they told him, in effect, that they go to church on Sunday morning and to prayer meeting on Wednesday night, but that isn't enough. They want the Christian message in between times as well, from the television set if necessary. They feel the need for God's television as surely as they need food or sleep.

The big four and the smaller regional ministries take aim at this spiritual hunger (as well as at materialistic and entertainment cravings). Oral Roberts, until recently, called his program "Oral Roberts and You." A recent Rex Humbard prime-time special was called "You Are Loved." Pat Robertson's "700 Club" reminds viewers that "telephone counselors are standing by to talk to you because *you are impor-*

tant." God's television makes many viewers, perhaps most viewers, believe that they are not alone, that somebody likes them Up There—and down here, right here, on television. Zanger, for one, thinks that God's television, with its offerings of Christian love and spiritual entertainment, does some people some good. Whether it is the good that formal religion aims at is another matter. Whatever the judgment, it's clear that millions of Americans haven't found, or can't find, love in their own everyday lives, or need more than they're getting.

Are the big four just another form of special audience programming? In that sense, I suppose, a lot of God's television is "sincere." The fundamentalist reads his or her Bible and hears the command to go forth to the corners of the earth and preach the gospel. What better way to carry God's message than the medium of television, linked to satellite transponders and direct-mail campaigns? Is no harm done even if, in carrying out the biblical command, a few of God's messengers happen to enrich themselves a bit? In mainstream religion, contributors help pay for the parish house, the organ, and the clergy. On God's television, the pledge dollars go for satellite time, telephone lines, the studio set, and the producers' salaries. Isn't it all the same?

Such a benign vision is in keeping with those pluralistic notions of American society so beloved by the political scientists: *Feed and let feed.* But some star performers on God's television now face the temptations of wider audiences. Some evangelists want to organize around Pat Robertson for political action. Robertson's Christian Broadcasting Network already offers a newsletter, *Perspectives.* The sincere-looking pitchman on CBN's television commercial promises us that *Perspectives* "relates current events to the Scriptures."

The tent preacher or sawdust-trail evangelist who aspires to a more powerful pulpit has long been a staple of the American novel and melodrama. Soon you may be watching it on the dial, in real life. In the thirties, a time of great unrest and social change, the demagogic voice of Father Coughlin, the radio preacher, came out of the Midwest with its mixed messages of populism, faith, and hate. The eighties may be a time of change and unrest once again, with more people pursuing fewer resources. In an uncertain time of energy shortages and inflationary pressures, oversimplistic appeals from telegenic operators may take hold and grow in the darker ground of the American spirit.

III. THE NEWS

EDITOR'S INTRODUCTION

A great number of Americans have abandoned newspapers for television. This means that the nightly network news, interrupted by commercials, is the primary source of information about national and international events for many citizens. On these news shows, complicated situations and issues are necessarily reduced to blurbs spoken by network anchormen. Because of the constraints of time, many stories cannot be covered. This means that the editorial policies of a handful of people, those in control at the networks, determine which "facts" reach the consciousness of America.

Television news also conveys an "illusion of verifiable reality," according to Peter Funt, the editor of *On Cable* magazine. This means that an editor or cameraperson can give us a picture that reflects a reality that doesn't exist. What America sees on the screen isn't necessarily an accurate reflection of what occurred. Funt, reporting in the *Saturday Review*, cites TV's reporting of turmoil in Miami and Teheran to show that "television's coverage was not so much a window on the world as it was a peephole."

The distortions of TV news reporting reach epic proportions on what Joe Saltzman, writing in *USA Today*, calls nonfiction variety shows. Saltzman, coordinator of broadcasting and chairman of undergraduate studies at the University of Southern California School of Journalism, says that these entertainment shows, which use real-life situations as their starting points, are "abnormally happy, upbeat, positive, funny, unusual, optimistic, silly, often meaningless . . . funhouse reflections."

Michael Novak, a columnist reporting for *National Review*, objects to the long-term impact of TV news. He argues that it creates an environment that leads the viewer to surrender his sound judgment to emotionality. "To watch television news is to submit to wallops in the solar plexus. The moving pictures on the news are . . . chosen for power." He considers these nightly wallops to be bad for the mental health of the country.

Edwin Diamond is optimistic about the television audience's ability to resist the hype and distortions of TV news. Again reporting in *American Film* magazine, Diamond claims that TV news reporting badly underestimates the audience when it "aims at punching through no higher than the groin and the gut." He points out that members of the TV audience have been watching the tube for an average of 25 years and can see through the distortions and hype on the screen and recognize it for what it is.

Growing popularity among viewers and the relatively low cost of production have aided the growth of informational programming on TV, says an article by Laurence Bergreen in *American Film*. Bergreen, author of *Look Now, Pay Later: The Rise of Network Broadcasting*, examines TV's voracious appetite for programming material and finds the networks relying heavily on the news to fill the open spots on their television schedules. He doesn't think that audiences should use television as a primary source of information, but concludes "If reality has become the only programming source big enough to keep television indefinitely supplied, so be it." He quotes Fred Friendly to the effect that "the real world may be turning out to be an escape from escapism."

SEEING ISN'T BELIEVING[1]

History, other writers have noted, is what observers and historians choose to record. In centuries past, if no one wrote about an event—or passed on an oral tradition (of question-

[1] Reprint of magazine article "Seeing Isn't Believing," by Peter Funt, editor of *On Cable* magazine. *Saturday Review.* 7:30–32. N. '80. Copyright © 1980 by Saturday Review. All rights reserved. Reprinted by permission.

able reliability)—the event might just as well never have happened.

But in the age of video, it seems impossible that significant world events will ever escape objective preservation, since TV pictures never lie. Or do they? The taking of pictures, of course, is as subjective a process as selecting words: Which shots should you take, and which should you skip? The photographer, the moment he aims his camera, is performing an editorial function.

During the early stages of the hostage crisis in Iran, there were daily demonstrations outside the U.S. embassy building in Teheran. And night after night, American television viewers saw footage of the anti-American protests. The pictures themselves were not distorted, but some reporters who covered the story now believe the image was. Less than two blocks from the embassy, they note, there was business as usual in Teheran. Yet American viewers might have easily imagined that the entire city was in turmoil.

When rioting occurred in Miami early this summer, exactly the opposite seems to have been the case. Several critics have observed that all three networks made a determined effort to avoid televising the full extent of the trouble, perhaps out of fear that such coverage would spark more rioting, or perhaps due to sensitivity about television's mishandling of riots back in the Sixties. In both cases, Teheran and Miami, television's coverage was not so much a window on the world as it was a peephole.

But whatever the extent to which television pictures can by themselves betray a news story, there is far greater danger of distortion when the film and tape images are subjected to the editing process. Editing of TV news material ranges from virtually nil—on live programs such as *Meet the Press*, or *Face the Nation*—to moderate—on the three networks' evening newscasts—to heavy—on "magazine" programs such as *20/20* and *60 Minutes. Sixty Minutes* relies more on the editing process than any other program on television, both in ratio of film shot to film actually used, and in the restructuring of questions and answers so that bits of one comment are strung together with pieces of another. As a consequence, it is probably harder to distinguish objective reality from editing on *60 Minutes* than on any other program.

To illustrate what can happen in the editing room, let us go back to one *60 Minutes* segment, first broadcast on November 12, 1978—a close-up on the Franklin Mint titled "Limited Edition." In the report, co-anchor Morley Safer carried on at length about two fairly simple points. The first was that Franklin Mint collectibles—coins, plates, books, and the like—are not very good financial investments, particularly over a short term. The second point was that Franklin Mint customers are often misled about the first point.

As is often the case with *60 Minutes* segments, there was nothing revelatory here—both of Safer's major contentions had already been explored at length by print reporters. Still, none of the print pieces had so devastating an impact as the segment "Limited Edition." As it happens, Franklin Mint's chairman, Charles L. Andes, thought to have his own staff videotape the entire interview with Safer, thus providing a complete transcript against which the final *60 Minutes* segment can be measured.

One interesting fact that is immediately clear is that the entire interview, when typed single-spaced, runs 20 pages, while the final *60 Minutes* version takes up less than two. When Safer introduced the interview on the air, he said: ". . . we went to Franklin Mint, to their chairman of the board, Charles Andes, to hear their side of the story." That introduction alone might lead viewers to believe that what followed on film actually occurred shortly after Safer walked into Andes's office. In fact, what is shown first in Safer's finished piece actually appears on page 17 of the 20-page transcript.

Here is the final portion of the interview between Safer and Andes, exactly as presented on *60 Minutes:*

Safer:—The fact is that something like, what, more than 75 percent, to be conservative, of all Franklin Mint issues have decreased massively in price, in value.
Andes: Yes. Well, now, Morley, you're—you're absolutely right

that there is a difference, and I was just going to point out, that there is a—there is a difference between the selling prices which are listed in here [a book] and the prices sold by the dealers—
Safer: But that—that—that's what we're talking—
Andes: —and one must realize that if you are going to sell to a dealer in the after-market—Franklin Mint medals or any kind of products in the—to a dealer—that the dealer will, of course, buy it wholesale and sell it retail. But what a collector must do then, if he's not willing to—to—to sell through a dealer, is to sell directly to another collector through ads placed in classified sections of newspapers, or in the numismatic sections of major papers, or in *Coin World* and *Numismatic News.*
Safer: Well, let me tell you something. We went to *Coin World,* and we have a number of people who went to *Coin World,* and they found that when they advertised their collections in *Coin World,* they were offered roughly—either they were offered nothing or they were offered the spot bullion price for their collections.
Andes: But that is not necessarily the case in every case. We have many instances where collectors have sold to other collectors, and know of many instances in our—from our monitoring of the market—
Safer: At above the—at above the issue price?
Andes: —where—where they sell it—no, not necessarily. In many—in some cases they are sold above issue price. There are a number of products that are sold above issue price.

End of interview. Safer then cut directly to an interview with a Franklin Mint customer and informed the astonished buyer that the Franklin Mint product is often sold back to dealers who in turn "sell it for scrap," and the scrap is "in many cases, or some cases, sold back to Franklin Mint."

Now let us return to the raw interview between Safer and Andes and edit it differently. By using portions never aired, but without changing any of the quotes by either man, we can create an interview that might just as well have been aired on *60 Minutes:*

Safer: So far, what would you reckon that Franklin Mint has sold, roughly a billion dollars' worth of collectibles?
Andes: Yes, that is about the figure, yes.
Safer: And mainly in precious metals?

Andes: Not mainly now but I suppose the sum total since the beginning of the company—the majority would be in silver.

Safer: And even though the price of silver has gone up since you started selling, the price of Franklin Mint material has not gone up with it.

Andes: No, no. For the most part it is not so. That 62 percent of what the dealers report they sell, they sell above the original issue price.

Safer: Would you say that investing in Franklin Mint collectibles would be a bad investment?

Andes: We do not recommend investing in Franklin Mint products as a financial investment and we don't recommend—we don't believe—that people should invest in any kind of collectible or luxury product as a financial investment.

Thus might the interview have ended—perhaps no more fairly than in the actual CBS version, but certainly leaving the viewer with a vastly different impression of Franklin Mint.

The *60 Minutes* library is littered with such examples of the power of television editing. And those who have fallen victim to the *60 Minutes* techniques, regardless of their culpability in whatever is being "disclosed," invariably express surprise at how a recorded TV segment is put together. First, they are unnerved by the film-to-air ratio of about 10-to-one, claiming, in some cases, to have been worn down by the process and lulled into a false sense of security. Then, they are often startled when the interview ends and the camera is turned around to shoot so-called "reverse questions." With the camera aimed at him, the reporter rerecords all of his questions so that they may later be spliced together with the answers. Although all the networks insist that reverse questions match the original questions as closely as possible, there is no denying that the reporter is allowed to polish his performance, while the interview subject's answers must stand as first delivered.

Reverse questions, along with other random shots of the reporter nodding his head or writing in his notebook, are also used to camouflage edits in the final film or tape. Known in the trade as "cutaways," these devices make a segment look smooth and neat while at the same time doing the viewer a serious disservice. When an interview subject begins a sentence, then in the middle of that sentence a cutaway is inserted of the reporter's reaction, followed by what seems to be the remainder of the subject's sentence, chances are it was never one complete sentence in the first place. The sentence was probably patched together from two parts of the interview, with the cutaway covering the break.

A producer who has worked on *60 Minutes*—who requested anonymity—says that on more than one occasion he watched Mike Wallace record an interview during which Wallace smiled and encouraged the subject to continue talking, only to insert cutaways in which Wallace has a stern, doubting expression, in effect changing the mood of the piece.

Such ploys can even trip up such broadcast veterans as Daniel Schorr, the former CBS correspondent who now works for the Cable News Network. Back in September 1976, Schorr decided to leak a secret House committee report on the CIA to the *Village Voice* newspaper. While under suspension from his job at CBS, Schorr agreed to tape an interview with Wallace for use on *60 Minutes.*

The full interview runs over 40 pages in double-spaced transcript form, but only a fraction of it actually went on the air. Among the portions *not* aired was Wallace's on-camera opening: "Dan, you have my profound admiration and that of your colleagues here and elsewhere I know, for the eloquent and persuasive case that you made for the protection of a reporter's sources." But the edited version belittled and humiliated the "admired" Schorr.

"What bothered me most about the interview," says Schorr upon reflection, "was not only the editing, but the way they set me up. Because they taped so much more than could have ever been broadcast, they recorded an entire story about reporters' rights before even touching on what they intended to use.

"At one point when I was discussing with [my lawyer] whether I would go on—and he was warning me about what might happen—I said 'I can take care of myself if we do this thing live.' [The executive producer of *60 Minutes* Don] Hewitt talked me out of that. He said, 'No, we never go live because too many things could go wrong. But don't worry.' Well, my answer is that the man with the scissors is the man with ultimate control."

Politicians and other famous figures are increasingly demanding live interviews or none at all. Last spring, for instance, Richard Nixon decided he was ready to talk about his new book. Don Hewitt of *60 Minutes* was quoted as saying he turned down a Nixon interview because Nixon insisted it be done live. According to Hewitt, the editing pencil—or scissors—is one of a journalist's most valuable tools, and should never be surrendered. Barbara Walters of ABC felt differently, however, and agreed to interview Nixon live on *20/20*.

"If you do a recorded interview," she says, "one of the advantages for the reporter is that he always comes out on top, he's always right. You've never seen a *60 Minutes* interview, or any taped interview, in which the reporter gets the worst of it. Doing live interviews has credibility."

Still, it is clear that filmed, taped, or live, the televised image is never more accurate or precise than the cameraman, editor, or reporter allows it to be. The same is true, of course, for the written word. But television's illusion of verifiable reality is so powerful that it is continually necessary to remind oneself that, even with television "news," seeing is not always believing.

THE "REAL" WORLD ON TELEVISION[2]

They call them "informational entertainment," "docutainment," and "non-fiction variety shows." Whatever the

[2] Reprinted from magazine article "The 'Real' World on Television," by Joe Saltzman, coordinator of broadcasting and chairman of undergraduate studies, University of Southern California School of Journalism. *USA Today.* 109:61. S. '80. Reprinted from *USA TODAY*, September, 1980, p. 61. Copyright 1980 by Society for the Advancement of Education.

name, the cross-breeding of news and entertainment, the careless mixture of reality and show business, is cause for alarm.

It is one thing for "60 Minutes" to combine good journalism with villains, heroes, happy endings, and melodrama; for NBC's "Prime Time Saturday" to turn Tom Snyder into a Johnny Carson cum information; for ABC's "20/20" to jazz up its reporting with show-biz trappings (as critic Tom Shales of the *Washington Post* put it, "Even when there is a report of some substance, it is usually wrapped up as cheaply as a carnival kewpie doll. To call it a news magazine is like calling Rona Barrett an investigative reporter.") However, it is quite another to take real-life situations and transform them into circus.

George Schlatter's "Real People" is that kind of hybrid. Schlatter hired some of the best non-fiction people—documentarians—in Los Angeles, who produced segments featuring real people doing real things that were at times unusual, funny, poignant, and occasionally even enlightening. Schlatter then spiced up these slices of life with the flavor of "Laugh-in." The result is a curious one—the pieces occasionally have that quality of truth that makes fragments of broadcast news, pieces of documentaries, local TV magazines, and "60 Minutes" so wonderful to watch; but it's as if you were looking at real people through distorted lenses, as if the bits and pieces of people's lives were chopped up, rearranged, and thrown out in disarray—all done to a background of audience laughter, applause, and happy music.

The latest addition to non-fiction network variety shows is ABC's "That's Incredible!" The show features a trio of friendly, good-looking, nice people who take turns telling you about people who feel no pain, or are visited by ghosts, or can break bricks with a water glass, or have been hit by lightning seven times, or can foresee air disasters, or. . . . Pieces of reality are squeezed into compartments marked incredible and shipped across the airwaves. Any beginning writer will tell you that you should use exclamation points carefully—use it too often and no one will take you seriously. The boy who cried wolf learned the hard way. The way televison goes, it will take considerably longer for the popular "That's Incredible!" to learn its lesson.

Both programs are soaring in the ratings, so more such programs will undoubtedly be produced in the future. Where is all this taking us?

It seems that, in the 1980's we're moving toward an uncomfortable blending of information and entertainment programming. When television executives discovered that broadcasting the daily news could be a profitable venture, they also decided that it was too profitable an operation to let the broadcast journalists who made it profitable control it. That's one of the reasons local television news has degenerated into what it is today. The same thing is happening with the non-fiction TV magazine format.

The most prevalent way Americans formulate pictures in their heads about the world in which they live is through television—primarily prime-time network television. The new non-fiction variety shows, like the "docudramas" that preceded and now surround them, are in many ways a fake; they utilize reality and all the importance and appeal of reality, but share none of the responsibilities of bringing reality to a mass audience. When news and public affairs people bring the real world to the public, they do so under certain specific ground rules (a mission to be fair, to be truthful, to tell as many sides of the issue as possible). These ground rules occasionally may be violated, but at least they are the starting point, not an afterthought. The non-fiction entertainment producers have no such duty. Their programs look real and sound real, but reality has been changed, subjugated, and subordinated to fit the dominant needs of entertainment; everything becomes slightly unreal—abnormally happy, upbeat, positive, funny, unusual, optimistic, silly, often meaningless. These are not pictures of the world in which we all survive; these are funhouse reflections, oddities that have little impact on our lives and the lives around us, and those that do are so trivialized as to become impotent.

Someone pointed out recently that these new network

non-fiction variety shows are beginning to look suspiciously like Paddy Chayefsky's nightmare in "Network." Indeed they do—but no one seems to be mad as hell about it. These shows are doing beautifully in the ratings, the profits are pouring in, the stations are happy, the advertisers are happy, the public seems happy.

Who's unhappy?—almost anyone concerned about those people who claim to get more than 70% of their information solely from television. The thought of what kind of world they imagine they are living in boggles the mind. It even might cause one to say "That's Incredible!," if the phrase hadn't worn out its welcome weeks ago.

DANGEROUS TO YOUR HEALTH[3]

Institutions do not retire, one thought—until Walter Cronkite, admitting mortality, did so. Dan Rather, his designated replacement as anchorman on CBS, is now to become one of the most important presences in American life, at a salary (it is said) of $8 million over five years, the better to complain about the profits of the oil companies.

There are 261 weekdays in a year, and allowing Mr. Rather thirty vacation days in each 261, I compute that Mr. Rather will be paid $6,927 for every telecast he makes. This is considerably less than the cost of each commercial.

The networks use public air. It is difficult, indeed, to know why public officials (or aspiring candidates) should have to pay for time on public airwaves. If candidates did not have to buy television time, they would not need nearly so much money in order to run for office. To wipe out monetary corruption, halt payments to television.

That, actually, is my moderate proposal. I have a more radical one: Do away with television news altogether; it is dangerous to public health. If you don't believe this, try

[3] Reprint of magazine article "Dangerous to Your Health," by Michael Novak, columnist, *National Review*. 32:358. Mr. 21, '80. Used by permission.

omitting the television news from your daily life. Rely on newspapers. You will notice an immediate improvement in your physical well-being. It will do more for you than jogging.

The reason is obvious. Television does not *tell* you anything you could not learn more fully and in context from the papers and the best magazines. What, then, does television add? In a word, *impact.* To watch television news is to submit to wallops in the solar plexus. The moving pictures on the news are not pruned from reels of tape for the sake of calmness and objectivity. They are chosen for power. A "good visual" conveys every drop of emotion possible. What has emotionality to do with sound judgment?

In addition, certain kinds of emotion are customarily preferred to others. Television news is drenched with the desire to do good. The good guys are fairly easily spotted on television, and also the bad guys.

It is my happy duty every year, serving on the jury for the DuPont awards in broadcasting journalism, to screen the best of each year's submissions from news departments, including documentaries and segments (or wholes) of daily newscasts. At the end of each day's viewing, one feels that one has been punched again and again with *impact,* almost always in a good cause (reform the prisons, fight for better care in the mental hospitals, halt nuclear energy, loathe padded defense contracts, etc.). Reformers are the Alka-Seltzer of television news.

The fault is not television's alone. The fault—and the virtue—lies in ourselves. It is part of the American metaphysic, as it is not (say) of the Southern or Eastern European metaphysic, to anticipate, nay even to *demand,* after some confrontation with evil, that the question be posed: "What can be *done* about it?" The soothing answer must include something effective, like starting a committee.

Whether effective or not, the ritual within our psyches demands hope for improvement. It would be intolerable simply to be shown a grievance or an evil. Our sense of reality could not bear it. *Something must be done about it now.*

Not for us resignation, the wisdom to accept what cannot

be changed. "You'll never know until you try." It is a lovely failing, this terminal *felix culpa interminabilis.* Television is dangerous to the public health because it nourishes what is adolescent within us, blocking out the wisdom of maturity.

The third way in which television is unhealthy is that the camera always lies. It is not just that the camera sometimes lies. It is in its essence a mechanical instrument of mechanical illusion. Great camaramen are masters of artifice; their art is composition artlessly effected. To begin with, the studio walls and studio desks are fake. Then, too, meeting in reality someone one has seen only on television is, invariably, a shock. Television personalities once out of the lights are disgustingly ordinary. Dan Rather without CBS would be just another handsome Texas lawyer, full of whatever Texas lawyers are full of. For CBS he seems, well, clean, acceptable at Harvard, and official. Authority speaks through him.

The camera lies. Dan Rather's opinions are lifted up out of the crowd and become part of the consciousness of the entire nation-state. What gets through his skull gets through, what does not does not. *Televisatores inimici rei publicae,* so to speak: *Television figures, enemies of the Republic.* Their range constrains us. What they say is, is, even if it isn't.

Television is not faithful, either, to human presence. Wholly admirable persons are not attractive on television. Certain qualities of intelligence one loves face-to-face seem ugly on television. The camera does not permit every quality of human presence to show through. Some persons are telegenic, some are not. The camera—heaven forbid!—*discriminates.*

In a nice touch, the camera makes black faces seem more attractive, more radiant, less penetrable; it is harsher on white faces. The camera sees through white faces often; through black faces never. Black faces seem more gentle, more lovable, more supple, even when they glower as Jesse Jackson's does.

Television, in a word, alters what it transmits.

Try and see. Not watching television news reduces noise in one's soul, screens excitement and impact from the news, permits reflection, invites further questions. Compared to reading the news, watching television news quickens heart, blood, and passion. That is good for network profits. It is not good for the Republic.

I'm ready to join those whose inner sense of ritual demands the further question: *What can be done about it?* Something must be, lest we perish.

ALL THE NEWS THAT ISN'T NEWS[4]

It's not a new question. In his autobiography, Lincoln Steffens wrote that Theodore Roosevelt, when he was police commissioner of New York City in the 1890s, complained about newspaper reports of a "crime wave" sweeping the city when the crime rate had actually dropped under his regime. What had happened was that there was an increase in newspaper reporting about crime, to increase street sales.

The news hype we see on television is not as blatant as the practices of the advertising industry or the record or book-publishing or motion picture businesses. These methods, however, are amiable free enterprise excrescences involving no more—and no less—than the separation of dollars from wallets. When hype comes to the news, something more is at stake; news hype affects our politics, our public dialogue, our ways of perceiving the world. A different level of danger is involved when bad movies or records succeed than when bad candidates succeed.

When Walter Cronkite told his CBS audience watching the Republican convention on the night of July 16 that there was "a definite plan" for a Reagan-Ford ticket—"an unparalleled, unprecedented situation"—Cronkite wasn't just getting the story wrong. He was also creating an aura of importance

[4] Reprint of magazine article "All the News That Isn't News," by Edwin Diamond, head of the News Study group at MIT and lecturer in political science. *American Film.* 6:74+. 0. '80. Reprinted with permission from the October 1980 issue of *American Film* magazine, © 1980 The American Film Institute, J. F. Kennedy Center, Washington, D.C.

for the media process. In this hothouse atmosphere, the hype
lives on after the story dies. *Newsweek*'s superheated account
of the television coverage of the Reagan-Ford mismatch went
beyond "unparalleled, unprecedented" to declare: "The
Veepstakes set off a media stampede that may have changed
history." History? Well: Ford didn't become the GOP vice-
presidential candidate, because television influenced Reagan,
who offered the job to Bush, and so if they're elected and if
Reagan dies, Bush becomes president, and if Bush responds to
some crisis in a different way than Reagan would have, then
history has been changed. Get it? That's how hype works.

What makes news hype of immediate concern is the way
it has taken hold and proliferated, like a kudzu vine, in the
medium of television. While newspaper front pages have become more responsible, even sedate—the *New York Post* ex-
cepted—the jazzed-up style of twenties journalism flourishes
on the nightly news: tabloid television. William Randolph
Hearst, the story goes, used to cite approvingly the kind of reaction he sought in the old *New York American:* You look at
the first page and say, "Gee whiz"; you turn to page two and
say, "Holy Moses"; you move to page three and say, "God Al-
mighty." Now, an evening of television news watching produces the same reactions.

News hype, I think, grows out of three factors, each interrelated but still possible to discuss separately.

First, there's technology. News gatherers and news producers now have equipment that enables them to do more to
the news, to make presentation as exciting as content, or
more exciting. In the fifties and sixties style of newsreel television, the form for presenting a story was fairly rigid: Anchorman introduces news film (received by packet and edited on
Moviola) of dignitary descending airplane steps; anchorman
then reads short items before introducing next film. Today,
live remotes, split-screen hookups, and computer graphics
make the television screen more visually stimulating. A dull
Gallup poll that may reveal nothing more than that one-third
of the electorate is still uncertain about its presidential
choices suddenly comes to life as electronic digital numbers

spin out and color bar graphs are generated before our eyes. In addition, the use of lightweight cameras, the shift from film to easily processed videotape, and, above all, the easy availability of satellite transponders for live transmission have speeded up the news process. As it becomes possible to get stories on the air faster, there's less time for the editing and the organization of the news. Thought takes a backseat to speed and technical skill. *Thinking*, in fact, sounds musty, the enemy of television-style *action*.

For example, perhaps the major event of the year in television was the emergence last summer of Ted Turner's Cable News Network (CNN). (That sentence may sound like hype, but June 1, 1980, is as good a symbolic date as any for the birth of the new multichannel information-entertainment cablecasting system in the United States.) Cable stations and satellite technology make possible the Turner network, bringing news programming into more than two million homes twenty-four hours a day, seven days a week. Now, no one has to wait until 7:00 P.M., or even until the hourly newsbreaks, for reports on the latest happenings. One June night, early in CNN's infancy, one of the anchors came on around 9:30 P.M. EST after a commercial to tell CNN watchers that "bottles were thrown at the press bus during President Carter's visit to Miami [the Liberty City area, scene of riots in late May]." The anchor went on: "Here is what it looked like, the unedited tape. . . ."

Sure enough, viewers saw surging crowds and running police on videotape shot from an accelerating bus, some of which seemed to be recorded as the camera operator crouched on the bus floor. It was certainly exciting stuff, but no accompanying narrative told of injuries or arrests, if any, of the denouement, the upshot of this event. There were no facts or thoughts to help make sense of the visceral thrills. On the contrary, CNN seemed proud of the raw reality presented ("Here is . . . the unedited tape . . ."). The coverage turned traditional journalism on its head. Not: *Here's the story as selected, shaped, and edited by our competent news processors, given the familiar constraints of time and space.* But: *Here it*

*is, right off the satellite transponder, get the news while it's
still sizzling, hot enough for you, have an exciting day. [Break
for commercial.]*

The second reason for hype centers on time, which is another way of saying money. Not only does today's television
news come at us faster, but there's also more air time for the
news. Leaving aside Ted Turner's round-the-clock operation,
local newscasts now run as long as two hours in the early evening in some cities. ABC has just added "ABC News Nightline," a twenty-minute late-night newscast. When the morning shows ("Today," "Good Morning America," "CBS
Morning News," "CBS News Sunday Morning") and the evening informational shows ("PM Magazine") are added, a typical station may be offering as much as five hours of news a
day. This programming is not necessarily done out of a belief
in a more informed society. Rather, the news has become a
money-maker in recent years, less expensive to produce than
prime-time entertainment.

Third, the news has become popular as well as profitable.
"60 Minutes" was the top-rated regular series in the 1979–80
season. With the news, television sees itself delivered from
mediocre sit-coms and action series, derivative story ideas,
and writing by hack committee—as long as the news itself
can be made lively and "interesting." That is, as long as the
news is more entertaining than the entertainment shows. But
news producers aren't willing to depend entirely on the quo-
tidian events to be exciting, any more than entertainment
producers can depend on their writers to be Chekhov every
week. Provisions have to be made for slow news days; techniques have to be developed to spark interest on moderate
news days. Attention has to be commandeered even on big
news days; having yelled hype so often, television has to have
alerting devices for a real wolf at the door. Along with the
usual methods of voice modulation and facial expression, television has borrowed, from the carnival midway, the tease:
"Coming Up Next: A Perfect 10" (translation: The weatherman says tomorrow will be nice). But the real innovation in
news hype recently has been the newsbreak.

The newsbreak is an art form in itself—a thirty- or sixty-second package consisting typically of two ten-second news items wrapped around a commercial, usually run between the early evening and late-evening newscasts. Do news producers think viewers cannot bear to wait between 7:30 and 11:00 to find out what happened after Walter Cronkite told us, "And that's the way it is . . ."? Are they worried viewers will switch to CNN? Perhaps, but they also realize that the newsbreak form gives both the networks and the local stations another program in which to insert commercials. Granted, it is a sci-fi sort of program: the Incredible Shrinking Newscast, like the Incredible Shrinking Man, who, as Tom Wolfe points out, doesn't shrivel but grows smaller and remains perfectly formed and smartly dressed. Very smartly dressed. One station manager told me that his outlet carved out its own minute around 9:00 P.M. and sold the commercial seconds for $1 million a year.

The benefits that newsbreaks bring to the viewer are mixed. Headlines can inform, or move audiences to tune in the late news, where information may be forthcoming. But more and more the ten-second newsbreak leads to a twenty-second tease that leads to a ninety-five-second item that does nothing more than set our antennae quivering. "Chemical Fire in New Jersey" . . . "Missing Girl's Body Found" . . . "Hijack in Progress in Kuwait." Hype to hype to hype; a lethal double-play combination on the viewer's nervous system.

If the above propositions were put to most of the people who produce the news, they would dismiss me as some sort of cranky traditionalist from print, or from sixties television (the exception would be the networks, where older, print-influenced producers still have a foothold, though a fast-slipping one). That there is a new generation of television persons operating today is well known. Somewhat less understood is how the new breed affects the news product, particularly the amount of news hype per thirty-minute news program.

The hype approach is intuitive rather than systematic. Generally, the new breed prefers the visual over the analytic, excitement over explication, stimulation over talking heads—as the television medium itself does. The new generation is form rather than content oriented; content, facts, the hard nuggets of the news, have relatively less interest for this generation than for earlier generations of journalists. In the fifties and sixties, there was a commitment among television journalists to principles, some good, some wrongheaded (democracy, the free world, the cold war). The television of the late seventies and early eighties concerns itself with television as television. When young producers want to praise a piece, they say, "It's good television," not, "This will rattle them at city hall." From "good television" to hype is little more than an automatic glide shift.

Boston, for example, is the sixth largest television market in the country, and a not unsophisticated city. The age of the active news producers averages around thirty-one. These people are bright, quick, tough; don't expect to discuss Graham Greene, or even Tom Wicker, with them, but rely on them to produce fast-paced, entertaining news to a disco beat that disorients. A few months ago, a young homosexual in Rhode Island decided to take another young man as his date to the high school prom. The Boston television stations treated the story as if it were the first lunar landing:

"It's one week to the prom and young. . . ."

"For tomorrow's prom the school principal plans. . . ."

"Tonight's the prom. Our reporter is on the scene."

"Rhode Island prom . . . details at 11:00 P.M."

"Here's a special report on the prom."

For a cynical viewer to say that the prom story was hyped for the sake of ratings during a slow news time is to miss the real cause for cynicism: The news producers think it's good television. To play tricks with the news for ratings is a form of prostitution; but it's hardly a victimless crime. News hype inflames an already complex and confused society.

In the end, news hype exists because news producers have a condescending attitude toward the audience. The news producers of the eighties, for all their disco news ways, picture a fifties audience Out There: short attention spans, zero political interests, unschooled in visual techniques, Joe Six-Pack and Harriet Housewife. So this doltish audience, it's said, has to be teased, tickled, and jerked around.

Around newsrooms there's a certain kind of story known

as a "grabber." In his new book, *The Whole World Is Watching*, Berkeley sociologist and former SDS activist Todd Gitlin recounts how the SDS story was handled by the networks in the mid-sixties. Stanhope Gould, a "young, long-haired, brash" associate producer for Walter Cronkite, proposed going with a grabber. Gould wanted to do the story of "SDS in the high schools," expecting to draw the reaction "What? Those jerks are in the high schools?" Gould, says Gitlin, "wanted to stoke up public anger, thinking that whatever 'punched through' the public apathy would produce a *reasoned* anger."

Back in the sixties, Gould had a political purpose as well as a journalistic one: making people think. Whatever his politics, his news instincts were true. Today's apolitical newsroom generation aims at punching through no higher than the groin and the gut.

I believe, of course, that today's news producers are wrong about the audience. The average thirty-year-old viewer has been watching television for twenty-five years now; he or she is not stupid, visually or politically. No amount of news hype on television's primary nights could get people excited about Ronald Reagan or Jimmy Carter. A year after the Three-Mile Island media overkill, polls show a majority of Americans will accept nuclear power as a transitional energy source. On prom night in Rhode Island, the fabric of society did not fray. Only television became unraveled, twisting in its own hot-air draft.

NEWS: TELEVISION'S BARGAIN BASEMENT[5]

Television programming is changing right before our glazed eyes. The steady trickle of hard news and feature—or "informational"—programming has swelled to a flood, with more on the way. While most of the new entries exist outside

[5] Reprint of magazine article by Laurence Bergreen, the author of *Look Now, Pay Later: The Rise of Network Broadcasting. American Film.* 5:37–40. Jl.-Ag. '80. Reprinted with permission from the July–August 1980 issue of *American Film* magazine, © 1980 The American Film Institute, J. F. Kennedy Center, Washington DC.

the prime-time limelight, their number and variety are impressive. The new crop includes "CBS News Sunday Morning," a ninety-minute electronic Sunday newspaper; "Nightline," the ABC late-night news update anchored by Ted Koppel; "Universe," CBS's forthcoming half-hour science series anchored by Walter Cronkite; and a gaggle of television magazine shows, including the weekly "30 Minutes" and the monthly "Magazine" on CBS, and, more prominently, Westinghouse Broadcasting's daily syndicated "PM Magazine." The latter program made its debut in New York and Los Angeles last month after several successful years' exposure nearly everywhere else. Group W hopes "PM Magazine" will continue to erode the dominance of schlock game shows as a low-cost programming staple.

Lest the viewer feel tempted to cancel all subscriptions to newspapers and print magazines, it is worth noting that, television being what it is, not all the new informational programs are destined to last, and, more alarmingly, many of them contain as much ingratiating fluff as the entertainment programming they replace. Just because a program is based in reality does not mean it is genuinely informative.

The networks, especially CBS and ABC, have continued to schedule increasing amounts of informational programming for what appear to them to be two very good reasons. First, they detect an increased appetite for reality-oriented material. Two newsmagazines, CBS's "60 Minutes," the granddaddy of the news programs, and ABC's recent imitation, "20/20," are among the most watched prime-time series. Furthermore, audiences of all three network evening news broadcasts have reached record levels in recent months. Second, and of even greater importance to network executives, informational programming is, minute for minute, far cheaper to produce than entertainment programming. Information has become television's bargain basement, and programmers are drawing heavily on it to refurbish the worn and tattered parts of the broadcast schedule.

The cost of an hour of prime-time programming these days runs anywhere from an estimated $450,000 invested in a single installment of "The Misadventures of Sheriff Lobo" to $620,000 for the hit "Dallas," and a fantastic $800,000 for an hour of "Buck Rogers in the 25th Century." In contrast, an hour of "60 Minutes" is said to cost but $140,000, "20/20" about $160,000. Yet both these informational programs earn as much in advertising revenue as their entertainment competition. No wonder the networks prefer them to an expensive sit-com.

But the real bargain in informational programming is "Sunday Morning," whose budget for a full year of weekly broadcasts, seventy-eight hours of programming, comes to slightly more than $2 million; in other words, less than the cost of four episodes of "Dallas." Informational programming does carry a significant liability, however. It lacks what is known in the industry as "shelf life," whereas sit-coms, cop shows, and other filmed or taped entertainment series can be rerun ad infinitum, earning residuals with each showing. It is possible that "I Love Lucy" will be with us in the year 2000, long after the seemingly durable Walter Cronkite has faded from memory.

The reason for informational programming's low rates has to do with the manner in which networks acquire programs. In the case of entertainment, they purchase the product of Hollywood producers, paying top retail dollar for it. But in the case of news, the networks can get it wholesale. They employ their own personnel, studios, and cameras. As Bill Leonard, president of CBS News, put it, "We own the factory." This cozy situation makes for stable overhead costs, and the expense of producing individual programs declines even further as their overall number rises. Thus Leonard can justifiably point to "60 Minutes" as television's "biggest bargain today."

Once upon a time, the scheduling of more news served as a useful ploy to attract publicity and prestige. Now networks look to low-cost information as a way of surviving in an increasingly competitive marketplace, where conventional broadcasting, ever-increasing cable systems, videocassette recorders, and videodiscs all compete for viewer attention.

Fred Friendly, a former head of CBS News, who is now a television advisor to the Ford Foundation, noted, "Television uses up resources faster than any other enterprise in America. [It has] no other place to look for new material but the world of reality." He predicted that in five years half of the prime-time schedule will be reality based (including sports), and that networks will supply an hour of evening news.

Already Bill Leonard has begun urging CBS affiliates to accept a forty-five-minute evening news built around Dan Rather. . . . Similarly, he wants to extend the network's long-running "Morning" news broadcast from sixty minutes to ninety minutes. And if CBS, which was the first network to increase evening news from fifteen minutes to thirty minutes back in 1963, makes these new commitments, the other networks are sure to follow.

In the meantime, news division chiefs, accustomed to pleading with their bosses for more air time and coming away empty-handed, sense a shift in the programming winds in their favor. Says Leonard of the available entertainment programming: "There isn't enough mediocrity to go around." So networks look to their "factories" and star correspondents such as Rather, Tom Snyder, and Barbara Walters to remain lucrative attractions for years to come. After all, Rather's much-ballyhooed $8 million contract gives CBS his services for five *years*, while the same amount supplies NBC with only ten *hours* of "Buck Rogers in the 25th Century."

So much for the economics that has triggered the boom in informational programming. What about the new programs themselves? Granted they're cheap, but are they truly informative? And how valuable are they compared to the programming they replace?

Probably the most valuable of all the informational programs is "Sunday Morning," but even this program raises difficult questions. CBS News launched the broadcast with a minimum of fanfare in January 1979, assigning it the highly improbable time period of Sunday mornings from 9:00 to 10:30 in New York. It is seen even earlier in many other areas. In scheduling "Sunday Morning," CBS sacrificed the long-running and respected religious and cultural affairs programs "Look Up and Live" and "Camera Three"; the latter found a new home on PBS. Neither carried advertising, while "Sunday Morning" does. Furthermore, the affiliates, committed to lucrative religious programming, were reluctant to pick it up. "Sunday Morning" still can't be seen in Boston, Miami, or much of Texas.

The anchorman of "Sunday Morning," Charles Kuralt, serves as an acceptable early morning presence, but the best thing about the show is its veteran executive producer, Robert "Shad" Northshield, who qualifies as an auteur of news production. He gives the correspondents time for languid, eccentric, and moving reports and closes each broadcast with a silent nature study. Regular features include a television critic, Jeff Greenfield, who talks quickly but wittily, and a music critic, harpsichordist Frances Cole. If there can be such a thing as an avant-garde network news program, then "Sunday Morning" is it.

Though informative and engaging, "Sunday Morning" is no substitute for a Sunday paper, and even Northshield is candid about the limitations of television journalism. "The race is over," he said this spring of presidential politics. "Iran we can't cover. The other big story is inflation, and how do we cover that? Everybody is poised to kill each other, and one of the great stories of the year is Dan Rather replacing Walter Cronkite." It is, lamentably, a foregone conclusion that television cannot do justice to economic stories. "Anything that is an abstraction, that is basically intellectual rather than emotional, is very difficult to do," he said.

If "Sunday Morning," with all of its ninety minutes, can't cope with abstractions, then no one else can. However, CBS's glossy new science series, "Universe," will be forced to try. The network has committed itself to broadcast six half hours. The pilot contained enough flashy graphics, miniquizzes, and reading lists to hold the most jaded nine-year-old's attention. Abstractions did appear to come to electronic life. Nevertheless, the half hour lacked a sense of immediacy. The absence of reference to science stories in the news contributed to an unreal atmosphere. People watch television for many of the same reasons that they read a newspaper—to find out what's happening in the world now. If an informational program is not current, then its reason for being is diminished. Already "Universe" has undergone a change of producers, hinting that alterations may be forthcoming. Beyond such transient problems, science, as an informational programming subcategory, is clearly a growth industry. Even before the returns on "Universe" are in, ABC has put a science adventure series of its own in the works.

In fact, the highly competitive, aggressive, flexible ABC News organization borrows more than just ideas from CBS. Since 1977 ABC has enticed no less than a dozen key personnel away from CBS on the theory that, according to one ABC executive, "there was no benefit in spending ten years" to train its own. On this basis, CBS News, far from cornering the market on informational programming, has proved to be the best thing that ever happened to its upstart rival.

Give ABC credit for at least one innovation, though: "Nightline," a welcome addition to insomniac television. As the by-product of a political crisis, "Nightline's" genesis was considerably different from the CBS informational programs. Where stuffy CBS News grooms new programs for months before daring to air them, the ABC late-night news updates began overnight in November 1979 as an opportunistic reaction to the crisis in Iran. As an ABC executive described it, the coverage was "not created around a conference table, but grew out of something that happened."

However, the crisis approach, though topical, does have drawbacks, namely, what to do when the crisis dies down and how to cope with the risk of exploiting the news. ABC solved the first problem in March 1980 by converting its Iran specials, with the rabble-rousing title "America Held Hostage," into the regularly scheduled 11:30 P.M. "Nightline." But as for the second problem, critics pointed out that ABC's relentless coverage of chanting Iranian mobs served no useful purpose, but only fanned the flames of irrational hatred. ABC News at times appeared to be both serving a useful news function and exploiting American-Iranian rancor.

Networks are not the only shoppers raiding the informational bargain basement. What works for them can work just as well for smaller entities. In September 1978, Westinghouse Broadcasting began syndicating the half-hour "PM Magazine," a light amalgam of feature stories and "how-to" tips. Perhaps "PM Magazine's" greatest value lies not in what it is but in what it attempts to replace. In most markets (New York being an exception) it is seen at 7:30 P.M., the infamous prime-time access slot created by the Federal Communications Commission in 1971 with prodding from Westinghouse. Though designed to attract worthwhile non-network offerings, the access period became, much to Westinghouse's chagrin, the home of "The $1.98 Beauty Show," "The Newlywed Game," and so on. By September 1980, "PM Magazine" will be seen in eight markets, where it often competes with and usurps such nonsense. While "PM Magazine" is no "60 Minutes," it is at least a distinct improvement over game shows.

Favorable ratings demonstrate that "PM Magazine" is an example of an idea whose time has come, and by offering stations that carry it considerable assistance, Westinghouse is shrewdly marketing it. Risks are at a minimum, as they are with all the aforementioned programming. News is just too respectable to be risky, except in the hands of the Atlanta-based entrepreneur Ted Turner. Where others are adding a little more informational programming here and there, Turner has inaugurated a cable network supplying nothing but news, round-the-clock. If Turner's Cable News Network succeeds financially, then it could trigger an information boom that makes the current one look like a sixty-second news update.

But the nagging question remains: Can the viewer be truly informed by learning about the world from the tube? Certainly more people than ever have come to rely on television for their information. Av Westin, a veteran news producer who now develops informational programs for ABC, said, "We are dealing for the first time with an audience that has grown up with television, absorbing information through glass rather than through paper." Does the thought make him cheer at the triumph of television? Not exactly. "I get very disturbed," he told me, "when I hear that over sixty percent [of the audience] relies on us as a primary source of information. Unless they read, they are going to be uninformed. You can't substitute a headline for a full account. We are *always* leaving things out."

For a network executive, Westin is unusually candid in admitting that there may be any flaw in the new informational programming. He senses the danger of conditioning viewers to become too dependent on television news programs for information. Television all too often conveys the lulling illusion of being in touch with reality when, in fact, it is highly selective and artificial. Though proving itself as a learning accessory, television cannot function as the primary source of information. There just aren't enough hours in the broadcast day.

Most programmers, however, are not thinking as far ahead as Westin is. They are simply grateful to have discovered a cheap and successful new programming formula. If reality has become the only programming source big enough to keep television indefinitely supplied, so be it. They are learning that, as Fred Friendly put it, "the real world may be turning out to be an escape from escapism."

IV. EDUCATION AND CHILDREN

EDITOR'S INTRODUCTION

Perhaps the heaviest viewers of television are children. Parents often welcome TV into their lives as a babysitter who works long, cheap hours. Kids don't seem to mind. Many seem willing to stay glued to the tube forever. But there are many disturbing and unanswered questions as to what effect long hours of watching television does to the developing mind of a youngster. Does the violence on TV make children more violent? How do commercials change their view of the world? (The average child sees 20,000 commercials per year.) What happens to children's ability to concentrate after being exposed to the never-ending TV rhythm of ten minutes of simple-minded narrative punctuated by raucous advertisements? Although there are no definitive answers to these questions, it is hard to see how the average child's TV megadose could be beneficial.

That there can be no definitive answers to television's effect on youngsters because of the impossibility of setting up controlled, scientifically valid studies is one of the conclusions of an article from *Psychology Today* written by Howard Gardner, a psychologist at Harvard University. Gardner warns that children heavily exposed to TV may be growing up with world views substantially different from preceding generations, because "the ways [they] conceptualize . . . experience may reflect the kinds of media with which [they] have been engaged."

Two other articles from *Psychology Today* debate the pros and cons of the TV shows "Mr. Rogers' Neighborhood" and "Sesame Street." Two psychology professors, J. L. Singer and D. G. Singer, feel that the fast pacing on "Sesame Street" defeats the show's educational purpose by making mush out of children's attention spans. They find more value in a show

like "Mr. Rogers' Neighborhood" that employs "longer sequences, slower pacing, and more personal communication."
G. S. Lesser, chief psychological adviser to the producers of
"Sesame Street," feels that both shows are of value to children. He defends "Sesame Street's" quick tempo on the
grounds that there is "little research evidence to support the
claim that any possible negative effects of such techniques
outweigh the positive learning benefits."

The need to develop children's critical viewing skills is a
main theme of Terry Herndon, chairman of the National
Council for Children and Television, in an interview from
Today's Education. Herndon believes that the schools should
teach children how to deal with TV and interpret what they
see. "The public schools . . . are about the only institutionalized safety valve capable of preventing television programming from intellectually dominating the public."

C. D. Ferris, chairman of the Federal Communications
Commission, sees hope for more varied and better programming for children in the development of new broadcasting
technologies. Writing in *Today's Education,* he says, "Instead
of only a few broadcast outlets . . . new delivery systems such
as satellites and cable will provide us with easily accessible,
highly specialized types of information . . . [These] new communications technologies [will] make more children's programming options widely available."

An article from *USA Today* examines governmental rules
affecting children's television and discusses proposed regulations. In the article, James Roman, assistant professor of communications at Hunter College of the City University of New
York, finds merit in the proposal to "cluster" commercials,
making them appear all together instead of interspersed
within the shows. "The advantage of such a practice would
be to give parents more control over what their children are
watching."

The last two pieces in this section look at television's
changing relationship to modern education. Daniel Boorstin,
the Librarian of Congress, writes in *U.S. News & World Report* that the growth of television and information increases

the need for a populace well educated in the "heritage of our whole, long past." Otherwise, perspectiveless, we'll drown in the current flood of information, convinced "we were born yesterday, or with the last 7 o'clock news."

Fred M. Hechinger, education editor of the *New York Times*, looks at the attempts to set up a nationwide University of the Air, an American "Open University." Proposals to start up this kind of college by TV have met resistance from established institutions of learning. "The ultimate test of these plans may well be whether America's Open University can become a supportive new link in the nation's shaky and frightened system of higher education, instead of a victim of that system's panicky determination to stonewall any attempts by a competitor to gain a foothold."

REPROGRAMMING THE MEDIA RESEARCHERS[1]

During its early years, a new medium of communication characteristically conveys the content of older, entrenched media. Thus, movies at first presented a celluloid version of the theater, radio initially carried vaudeville shows, and television was for some years a visual version of radio. Scientific research in a new area often follows this pattern as well. It is hardly surprising, then, that when researchers turned their attention to studying media, the same trend emerged. The first cadre of researchers to probe a new medium of communications has typically proved insensitive to the special qualities of that medium.

As an occasional viewer of television—and an observer of those who study television—I looked forward with considerable anticipation to reading *Television and Human Behavior*, a new book that offers the most exhaustive assessment to date

[1] Reprint of magazine article by Howard Gardner, psychologist at Harvard's Project Zero, a study of children's artistic development. *Psychology Today.* 13:6+. Ja. '80. Reprinted from *Psychology Today* Magazine. Copyright © 1980 Ziff-Davis Publishing Company.

of the influences of TV on our lives. Compiled by George Comstock of Syracuse University and a group at the Rand Corporation, the book reviews more than 2,500 reports done in recent years, covering everything from how many sets exist in the country, how many hours various segments of the population spend watching them, and what their preferences and dislikes are, to sorting out what the research literature tells us about issues that especially arouse the public.

Although the book is a scholarly and thoughtful compendium, I read through it with a mounting sense of disappointment. Take, for example, a set of issues that has exercised the public—the effects of violent programs and of commercial messages on children. The millions of research dollars spent on these controversial issues in the last two decades seem to have yielded only two major findings, each of which might easily have been anticipated by the experimenter's proverbial grandmother.

As the authors constantly remind us, it has now been "established" that children will imitate behavior they see on television, whether these actions be aggressive, violent, or benignly "prosocial." Moreover, it has also been "established" that the younger the child, the more likely he or she is to believe the commercials, to confuse them with programming fare, and to pester parents for advertised products.

To be sure, Comstock and his colleagues include a few newer "cognitive" approaches to the young viewing audience. For instance, some researchers in the Piagetian tradition regard the child as sort of a fledgling anthropologist whose task is to understand the mysterious lands that unfold before him on TV, starting virtually with infancy. These pioneering studies reassure us that, much as children pass through stages in the other realms of existence probed by psychologists, they also pass through "stages of television comprehension." But again, the studies do not reveal much that would surprise an observant parent.

Why do we know so little? Why have the thousands of studies failed to tell us more about the medium of television per se and about the minds of the children who view it?

A number of answers spring to mind. First of all, as I noted, the initial lines of television research largely imported methods—and raised questions—that were applicable to older media, or unmediated behavior. Another dimension that is limiting has been the practical orientation of most television research. Because society has been justifiably vexed about exposing children to excessive violence or bombarding them with commercial messages, it has twisted researchers' arms to grapple with these issues.

But probably the chief stumbling block to reaching any definitive conclusions is that almost everyone (and his grandmother) has a television set. Thus, the crucial controlled experiment—comparing individuals who have televisions with those who do not—cannot be done. The few eccentrics who don't have a set are too different from their viewing counterparts to serve as a meaningful control group. When social psychologist Stanley Milgram was asked to study the effects of televised violence on behavior, his first impulse was to divide the country in half, remove all violence on television west of the Mississippi, enact laws so that no one could move from one part of the country to the other, and then observe what happened over a period of years. "It turned out not to be practical," he wryly admitted.

I have recently encountered a few strands of research that address more directly the distinctive features of television. Appropriately, they have been done for the most part by a younger generation of researchers, reared on television and McLuhan.

Trying to determine which aspects of TV compel children's attention, Aletha Huston-Stein and John Wright at the University of Kansas have focused on the medium's "formal features"—the quick cutaways, zooms, and frenetic tempo in which commercial television revels. Huston-Stein and Wright have demonstrated that the younger the child, the more likely he or she is to attend to these dazzling techniques of television, regardless of program content. In contrast, older children will watch a program for extended periods even when such formal features are not heavily exploited. Huston-

Stein and Wright make the interesting suggestion that violence or aggression are unnecessary for capturing the attention of preschool children. As long as a show is fast paced and laced with interesting visual effects, as, for example, is much of "Sesame Street," the youngsters will be hooked. (Whether or not such "hooking" is beneficial remains controversial. . . .)

Another innovative researcher, Gavriel Salomon of the Hebrew University in Jerusalem, has paid special attention to such features as the zoom, which begins with a panoramic overview and rapidly moves closer up to focus on a telltale detail. According to Salomon, children who have difficulty attending to relevant detail can be greatly aided by frequent use of zooms: the medium, in effect, supplies a skill that, for one reason or another, they have not yet developed. Yet even these promising new directions do not tell us much about the effects of television vis-à-vis other media.

One line that does, however, was initiated by Laurene Meringoff, a colleague of mine at Harvard Project Zero. Along with Hope Kelly and Mary Holt, Meringoff has been studying, with as much precision as possible, what children learn from story content when it is presented on television compared with when it is presented in picture-book form. Using materials dveloped at Weston Woods in Connecticut, a leading producer of stories for children, the Project Zero researchers have prepared book and television versions that are virtually identical.

For example, the researchers have worked extensively with a story by Tomi Ungerer called *The Three Robbers*. In this tale, three ferocious bandits abandon their violent ways after stopping a stagecoach that carries the charming orphan Tiffany. Turning their backs on a life of crime, the robbers go on to help abandoned girls and boys throughout the land. In a typical study, one group of subjects hears the story read by an experimenter and sees the accompanying pictures—the "book version." Another group of subjects views a film of equivalent length, based on the book, on a television monitor; in this "television version," the specially recorded sound track uses the voice of the book narrator and the animated film presents the same illustrations that appear in the printed text. Thus, while respecting the essential properties of each medium (movement within the image in the case of television, discrete static imagery in the case of a picture book), the two versions are about as similar as can be imagined. (Of course, reading a book oneself is different from having it read aloud to one at a preordained rate, but we were interested in attempting to simulate the latter experience.)

Four studies of this sort carried out with children in Watertown, Massachusetts, thus far reveal a consistent and instructive picture. Clear differences are attributable to the medium of transmission; and the younger the child, the greater the differences.

Adults who watch the television program remember about as much of the story on their own, and score about as well on a series of multiple-choice questions about it, as matched adults who have had the picture book read to them. Only when the TV group is asked to make inferences that go beyond the text—when asked, for example, to evaluate how difficult it was for the robbers to carry out an action—are modest effects of the medium found. Adults who saw the story on television are more likely to make inferences based on the visual portions of the story (for instance, the expression on a character's face), while those exposed to the book are more likely to rely on the plot they have heard (although both groups heard the same voice telling the story and saw a similar set of visual images, one static and the other dynamic).

With children, the differences are far more dramatic. Compared with the television viewers, the book children remember much more of the story on their own and are also better able to recall information when they are cued. The differences in recall of precise wording and figures of speech are especially significant: the book children are surprisingly skilled at repeating just what they have heard (for example, phrases such as "visit her wicked aunt"), while the TV children, when they remember verbal information at all, are more inclined to paraphrase.

The most intriguing media differences concern the ability

to make inferences about the material. Both groups of children tend to reach the same conclusions; for instance, an equal number of each group concluded that the robbers' axe was "easy to wield," or that Tiffany "felt happy." But the lines of reasoning used to buttress the inferences were different. Television children relied overwhelmingly on what they had seen—how difficult an action looks, how someone appears to feel. They rarely went beyond the visual information, either to attend to what was said, or to draw on their own experience. In contrast, book children were far more likely to draw on their own personal experiences or to apply their own real world knowledge ("It's hard for me to hold an axe—it's way too heavy"). Estimates of time and space are also more constrained for those watching television. That is, when asked how long an action takes, or how far apart two locations are, television children make more modest estimates; this finding suggests a reliance on the superficial flow of information (how much TV time elapses), rather than on consideration of what is plausible (how long an action usually takes).

In all, television emerges as a much more self-contained experience for children, and, within its boundaries, the visual component emerges as paramount. The book experience, on the other hand, allows for greater access to the story's language and suggests greater expanses of time and space. Books may encourage readers to make connections with other realms of life—just as some bibliophiles argue.

One possible outcome of such studies is to comfort the critics of television. But it would be premature—and misleading—to suggest that this research establishes the superiority of one medium over another. For one thing, the largely verbal measures used thus far could well be charged with being "pro-book." It could be that other, more visual, measures (for instance, asking the child to draw scenes) might have favored television; or it could be that the kinds of skills actually fostered by television (for example, being able to create or recreate in one's mind a visual sequence) cannot be tapped by our methodology.

Rather, the importance of the research may be that it

demonstrates qualitative differences in the effects of the media. Exposure to television apparently highlights a different line of inference than experience with books. Thus, the child who views many hours of television, day after day, may well develop different kinds of imaginative powers, or, as McLuhan might claim, a different "ratio among imaginations," from one weaned on books.

We are left with an even more intriguing thought. It has been assumed by most philosophers since Immanuel Kant that individuals perceive experience in terms of certain basic categories—time, space, and causality. Indeed, one has no choice but to conceive of life in such terms—they are "givens." While psychologists do not necessarily accept these categories as given at birth, they assume that all normal individuals will come to share similar concepts of them.

An alternative perspective, however, is that some of our knowledge of time, space, and causality comes from the media of communication that happen to predominate in our culture. In other words, the ways we conceptualize our experience may reflect the kinds of media with which we have been engaged. And so, the temporal and spatial outlooks of the TV freak and the bookworm may differ in fundamental respects, as may the quality of their imaginations. Such a finding would have far-reaching educational implications. For instance, the teaching of history (with its time-frames) or geometry (with its spatial components) might vary in different cultures, depending on which medium the children were raised on and have available to them in the classroom. The findings may also reveal something about our own era. Based on comparisons between two pervasive cultural media—print and television—the results can perhaps suggest how people today differ in their thinking from previous generations—and which differences are due to TV alone.

COME BACK, MISTER ROGERS, COME BACK[2]

No sane parent would present a child with a fire engine,
snatch it away in 30 seconds, replace it with a set of blocks,
snatch that away 30 seconds later, replace the blocks with
clay, and then replace the clay with a toy car. Yet, in effect, a
young child receives that kind of experience when he or she
watches American television.

As psychologists who have been investigating television
for the past decade, we have become concerned about the
ways in which television's rapid-fire delivery may be affecting
young children's capacities for imaginative and reflective
thought. Our research on imaginative play in early childhood
suggests that private fantasy has significant benefits for a
growing child. Children of three or four who engage in pretending or make-believe play not only appear to be happier
but also are more fluent verbally, and show more cooperation
and sharing behavior. They can wait quietly or delay gratifi-
cation, can concentrate better, and seem to be more em-
phatic and less aggressive, thanks to their use of private fantasy.

Can television enhance or inhibit imagination in young
children? We think the latter is true, and are increasingly disturbed about the emphasis in American television on extremely short action sequences, frequent interruptions, and
drastic changes in the visual field. Producers—even the producers of "Sesame Street"—argue that they need rapid
change to hold children's attention. Yet it seems possible that
they are actually creating a psychological orientation in children that leads to a shortened attention span, a lack of reflec-
tiveness, and an expectation of rapid change in the broader
environment. The pacing of television itself may be stimulating an appetite for novelty and lively action, as well as an ex-

[2] Reprint of magazine article by Jerome L. Singer and Dorothy G. Singer, codirectors
of the Yale Family Television Research and Consultation Center. *Psychology Today*.
12:56+. Mr. '79. Reprinted from *Psychology Today* Magazine. Copyright © 1979 Ziff-
Davis Publishing Company.

pectation that problems can be resolved in a very short space of time.

The development of young children's imaginative skills requires that they periodically shift their attention away from a rich visual environment—television—and assimilate new information or engage in their own mental imagery. Television, with its constantly changing sequences, may well prevent the elaboration of such private images, and preclude the inner rehearsal that is critical in transferring material from the short- to the long-term memory system.

In effect, the major result of watching television may simply be to train children to watch the screen in a fashion that permits surprisingly little subsequent retention. Learning numbers and the names of letters by rote may be a useful outcome for children who watch "Sesame Street." But, according to psychologists Donald Meichenbaum and Lorraine Turk, children need to learn thinking strategies that will provide them with a variety of active learning attitudes for coping with new material. Fast-paced shows like "Sesame Street," "The Electric Company," and, of course, most commercial children's shows, leave little time for the response and reflection that are important ingredients of such strategies.

Children also need adult models who are thoughtful, who seem to listen, and who ask youngsters to think or to express themselves as part of a total learning process. One of our favorite programs for preschoolers does just this: "Mister Rogers' Neighborhood." Unfortunately, it has been limited to reruns for some years now. Mister Rogers' show is perhaps the best-thought-out program for young children, from a psychological standpoint. It does not focus primarily on cognitive skills, but attempts to reassure children about their own uniqueness and to convey to them a sense of security and personal worth. Significantly, Mister Rogers' manner is slow and he repeats himself often. His sugary style irritates many parents. They feel his pace is too slow and that he is perhaps not sufficiently masculine in his manner. *But Mister Rogers is not talking to parents.* He is talking to three- and four-year-old children who are still having lots of trouble making sense of the complexities of the outside world. Children seem to benefit enormously from his relaxed rhythm, the way he follows a subject over a period of days, his reassuring attitude, and his willingness to ask a question and then, in defiance of most television conventions, to say nothing for a few seconds—while children answer for themselves.

Independent research studies have shown that children exposed to about two weeks of watching "Mister Rogers' Neighborhood" become more willing to share with other children, more cooperative in their play behavior, and more imaginative. In addition, our own study, carried out with Roni Tower and Ann Biggs, found some interesting patterns in what young television-watchers recall from Mister Rogers' program.

We compared the behavior of nursery-school children watching "Sesame Street" with that of children watching "Mister Rogers' Neighborhood." The children watching "Sesame Street" kept their eyes glued to the set, while children watching "Mister Rogers' Neighborhood" allowed their eyes to wander from the TV screen and occasionally walked away from the set. Nevertheless, when we measured recall of particular details from both programs, including story content, the children watching "Mister Rogers' Neighborhood" did as well as those watching "Sesame Street." There seemed to be distinct advantages in watching "Mister Rogers' Neighborhood" for children who were less intellectually gifted and less imaginative. Those children could follow Mister Rogers' material better than children of comparable intellectual capabilities who watched "Sesame Street." After two weeks of watching "Mister Rogers' Neighborhood" every day at school, they increased their level of imaginative play and showed more positive emotional reactions to the other children than did children who watched "Sesame Street" or a group of control films.

We are not plugging a specific show. Rather, we feel that the research evidence and an analysis of the cognitive properties of the television medium suggest that it would be far more useful for children if producers of children's shows learned the lesson of "Mister Rogers' Neighborhood" and began providing children with longer sequences, slower pacing, and more personal communication.

Children can actually learn a good deal from television and acquire some constructive social habits. But children, particularly preschoolers, need relatively simple material that lends itself to imitation in action or words. They need bits of time to "talk back" to the TV set. They need to be able to walk away from it, develop pictures in their minds, or try out for size something they have just watched by playing it out on the floor for a few minutes.

Currently, hearings are going on under the auspices of both the Federal Trade Commission and the Federal Communications Commission that deal primarily with commercials directed at children, but that also are raising fundamental questions about the overall impact of television on children's information-processing.

We think that, rather than attempt to ban commercials, it would be helpful if the networks and producers could use a larger percentage of the huge income derived from advertising to children to generate creative and imaginative programming. There should be continuous consultation with child-development specialists and careful research on children's reactions to programming and the clustering of commercials.

We think Mister Rogers had the right idea and we'd like to see more of him. But there could be even better shows that would reflect a genuine awareness that three- and four- and five-year-olds need the chance to sort out the complexity of images and to elaborate the information they must process. If television for preschoolers might become "boring," it's worth the chance. As a matter of fact, so powerful is the medium that if all of the networks agreed on a massive graduated slowdown of material being presented, preschool children would still watch, and would adjust to the new rhythm.

One might well ask whether all Saturday-morning television should be paced so slowly, but maybe one hour of such a morning's fare is all a child ought to be watching anyway! Above all, children need time with parents or other "live" care-givers who talk with them, listen to what they say, and encourage their imaginative development by telling stories, singing songs, or playing pretend games.

STOP PICKING ON BIG BIRD[3]

The Singers say there is a single best style of television for young children. I believe we serve children better by providing a variety of styles. I cannot find the logic in the Singers' "either/or" argument that for young children, slower must be better than faster, longer better than shorter. In an effort to sustain the attention of preschoolers and to teach them effectively, "Sesame Street" mixes fast and slow segments, long and short ones, human as well as animated characters, and puppets. Surely there is room for programs with a variety of styles, as well as for "Mister Rogers' Neighborhood."

The Singers are not the first to express dismay concerning what they see as American television's increasing emphasis on "extremely short action sequences, frequent interruption, and drastic changes in the visual field." But so far, I have found little research evidence to support the claim that any possible negative effects of such techniques outweigh the positive learning benefits.

Let's look first at the clinical evidence, based on children who were brought to a child-guidance center for a variety of behavior symptoms. Werner Halpern, director of the Children and Youth Division of the Rochester Mental Health Center, reported in 1973 that he had observed cases of a "revving up," or disorganized hyperactivity, in young children, which he attributed to viewing the "stimulus-rich, highly focused" programs of "Sesame Street." However, to check his original observation, Halpern continued his study during the

[3] Reprint of magazine article by Gerald S. Lesser, chairman of the board of advisors of Children's Television Workshop. *Psychology Today.* 12:57+. Mr. '79. Reprinted from *Psychology Today* Magazine. Copyright © 1979 Ziff-Davis Publishing Company.

following year and, by 1974, reported that for unclear reasons, "the number of two-year-olds who manifested hyperactivity and echoic speech related to 'Sesame Street' dropped to the vanishing point in our clinic population."

Experimental research evidence also runs counter to the Singers' arguments. At the University of Massachusetts, Daniel Anderson, Stephen Levin, and Elizabeth Lorch compared the reactions of 72 four-year-olds to rapidly paced and slowly paced segments of "Sesame Street." The research team observed the children watching differently paced versions, tested them after viewing to measure their impulsive behavior and their persistence in completing a puzzle, and then observed them during a 10-minute free-play period. They concluded, "We could find no evidence whatsoever that rapid television pacing has a negative impact on preschool children's behavior. We were unable to find a reduction in 'sustained effort'; nor . . . an increase in aggression or in 'unfocused hyperactivity.' "

Anderson, Levin, and Lorch's research alerts us to another dubious distinction made by the Singers, who not only claim that slow and long are better than fast and short, but also imply that fostering imagination is somehow more important than teaching young children the intellectual skills that will help them in school. Testing assertions made earlier by the Singers and other critics, Anderson and his colleagues declared that "if the 'Sesame Street' critics' assertions [about reduced attention span, aggression, and hyperactivity] have any basis, then the effects would seem to be small, subtle, and insignificant in comparison with the program's demonstrated educational benefits."

When the Singers and their colleagues conducted their own experimental comparison of children's responses to the "fast-paced" "Sesame Street" and the "low-key" "Mister Rogers' Neighborhood," they also failed to find evidence of the shortened attention span that they fear will result from rapidly paced programs: the tables in their 1977 paper reporting the results of their work do not reveal significant differences in concentration.

However, when the Singers looked at the entire group of

children they studied, and not just at the subgroup that was less intellectually gifted and less imaginative, they reported two other significant findings: while "Mister Rogers' Neighborhood" viewers increased significantly in "imaginativeness," "Sesame Street" viewers also increased, but not as much; "Sesame Street" viewers increased significantly in positive interaction with adults, while overall, "Mister Rogers' Neighborhood" viewers declined on that variable.

The Singers' research reveals another important distinction between "Mister Rogers' Neighborhood" and "Sesame Street" that they fail to mention in their present analysis. In comparing the two programs, the Singers guessed that the "simple, direct" format of "Mister Rogers' Neighborhood" would be better at teaching facts, while the "complex" format of "Sesame Street" would help a child learn to make inferences (". . . which requires the child to abstract meaning from situations . . ."). Their research showed that the guess was correct: "Mister Rogers' Neighborhood" was better at teaching facts, such as the way a pitch pipe works; "Sesame Street" was better at teaching inferences.

Since I prefer not to regard different types of learning as competing alternatives, I will not claim that learning to make inferences is more important than learning factual information. Clearly, both are important to the young child. The Singers' data thus provide another convincing argument for diversity of television programs for children.

I share the Singers' sadness over the loss of "Mister Rogers' Neighborhood" in anything but reruns. The variety and quality of television programs for our children must be expanded, not diminished. But let us not assume that one style of television program is best for all young children. Don't we have enough ingenuity and commitment to children to provide programs in different forms, styles, and moods? Can't we give children and their parents the opportunity to watch "Mister Rogers' Neighborhood," "Sesame Street," and any other educational programs that we care enough to invent? Let's leave room to experiment, to discover the range and variety of programs that will most benefit our children.

SCHOOLS AND THE POWER OF TELEVISION[4]

What is the background of NEA's involvement and concern with television?

Television has been a scapegoat for almost every adult's anxiety about what's happening to children. The 1.8 million teachers who are members of the National Education Association experience daily the anxiety, frustration, and trauma in the lives of children. They, like much of the rest of the population, think that television viewing is at least a partial explanation for the often difficult behavior of children today.

This criticism of television probably contains some truth, but it is not nearly so valid as many people believe it to be.

What is the NEA doing about the situation you describe?

The NEA has looked for ways to become a constructive influence on television programming. One thing we are doing is calling to the attention of America's teachers the television programs that might be useful in classroom activity. Research on a number of programs we have recommended this way suggests that classroom use of a television program significantly increases the audience for that program.

Further, through recommendations released to the general public, we make children aware of quality programs on television. A number of years ago we started recommending certain programs for viewing. Gradually the networks became convinced that an NEA recommendation significantly increased the audience for a program. Naturally enough, they now seek our recommendations.

Recommending programs no longer demands a great deal of initiative on our part, but rather judgment and the willingness to take some risks. We are interested in exposing children to quality programs; the networks are interested in increasing their audience. Those interests sometimes coincide.

[4] Reprint of an interview of Terry Herndon, NEA executive director, by Maria Robbins, associate editor, *Today's Education.* 69:48–52. S.-O. '80. Used by permission.

Do teachers actually recommend that kids watch the programs?

Selectively. It's up to the individual teacher. When *Roots* and *Holocaust* were shown, many teachers built classroom activities based on those programs into their curriculums and assigned the programs as homework. In other cases, teachers merely call attention to a scheduled program. I'm sure some teachers ignore programs that are recommended.

Have you come across much resistance from parents when teachers assign children to watch certain programs?

Some. But a high quality program that deals with contemporary issues and attracts a lot of public attention would be seen in many homes anyway. Moreover, most American parents are very cooperative about assignments that children bring home from school.

A great deal of work is now being done to develop curriculums in critical viewing skills. What do you think about the need for this?

It is absolutely essential that we find ways to increase the ability of children to use television selectively and view it critically. A curriculum in critical viewing skills is worth experimentation in this area.

The power of television as a communications medium is awesome, and control over the medium inexorably tends to gravitate into the hands of relatively few corporate interests. Any situation in which economic power is the principal qualification for controlling such a medium is dangerous. Anyone with enough money can skillfully present an ideology to great numbers of people, and such concentrated control over programming could lead to intellectual tyranny.

The public schools, which are decentralized by law, are about the only institutionalized safety valve capable of preventing television programming from intellectually dominating the public. The schools need to inculcate into children a disposition toward critical thinking, an ability to evelute alternatives, and a habit of consciously making decisions rather than passively accepting the messages delivered by this pervasive medium.

Our children need to be taught the skills of challenging, hypothesizing, inquiring, documenting, evaluating, and making intelligent choices. As I see it, they need these skills even more than they need critical viewing skills. They must be encouraged to create and not just absorb.

Qube, an experiment with interactive television, plans to bring secondary and college-level courses into the home by means of the television set. What do you think of that approach to teaching?

I think it has considerable potential. Interactive television can be a very powerful instructional device. The NEA and I tend to think about television in two ways: on the one hand, as the sum of the programs that enter almost every home and some classrooms; and, on the other hand, as a technology. Obviously, linking television with computers to provide sophisticated interactive capacity makes it possible to do many things in the classroom that could never have been done before.

Television has great potential as instructional technology. It may be used for good or ill. There is, after all, a great deal of flexibility in what one does with any technology.

Then you are not worried about the prospect of a child's sitting at home and learning from a television set rather than learning in the classroom?

No. I'm pretty realistic about that. There are thousands of influences other than schools in the lives of children. Television is one. Interactive television might be another. The schools' challenge is to deal with children as they come to school, realizing that they are exposed to many influences outside of school. I expect that in the life of a child, the neighborhood, the community, even the family can be a far more destructive influence than an afternoon with television, interactive or otherwise.

What do you think about the tentative connection between heavy television viewing and declining English and math scores?

I know that television is at least a significant distraction in the lives of children, but there is some rather impressive evidence that television can be used to stimulate reading and to raise the level of interest in reading—albeit very selective reading. The effects are probably mixed.

We simply can't isolate television as a variable and describe its impact on children's behavior. I am regularly impressed by the profound changes in the social environment in which children live. Television is one part, but certainly not the whole. The typical child in our society has many, many choices of what to do with his or her time.

Life is much more complex than just going to school for a few hours, coming home to work for a few hours, playing for a few hours, and going to bed. Children today have access to transportation that enables them to escape easily from a community in which they are known to a world of anonymity. They have money to spend and places to spend it. They have television to watch. They have families that don't function in the way that families used to function. Twenty years ago it was quite realistic for children 10, 11, 12 years old to believe that once they mastered certain fundamental skills they would be employable. It is now virtually impossible for children to think realistically about employment until they are 17, 18, 19 years old, and even then it's difficult.

All of the incentives to master those fundamental skills have changed. The goals and rewards are abstract and long-range rather than concrete and immediate. I expect that these changes are more profound influences than the availability of television.

In some ways, I think children's attraction to television is an effect rather than a cause, although many people believe that television is the cause and all else is the effect.

One of the most often-heard criticisms of television is that it presents an unrealisitic picture of life. Many people think that as a result of watching television children are unable to distinguish between fantasy and reality.

Television certainly miseducates. The land of television in which major problems arise, unfold, and get solved in 25 or 30 minutes is a fantasy land. But I'm very cautious about reaching simple conclusions about causes and effects. I'd like to know why some children are more susceptible to delusions

than others. I'd like to know what it is in the social environment of some kids that makes them so susceptible to influence
by fantasy.

More than any other medium, television makes fantasy
available readily, easily, inexpensively, and uniformly. Maybe
many children have crossed the threshold of tolerance. But I
think that the vast majority have enough experience with reality to offset their experience with television. Again, I consider the attraction to television to be an effect, not a cause.

*Where do you feel the responsibility lies for monitoring
how much television children watch?*

There is only one place where it can be done—in the
home. That does not mean that it *will* be done. The current
direction of our social structure suggests that children will be
subject to fewer and fewer adult controls at earlier and earlier
ages. That's the way things are going.

There's no way the schools can change that, because they
only have the children five or six hours a day. The schools can
be only a part-time control mechanism and perhaps a partial
antidote to whatever social pathologies children are exposed
to in the balance of a 24-hour day.

*What do you think government can do about the effects of
television viewing on young people?*

Here again, I don't think that government can be effective if it focuses entirely on the politics and economics of television distribution, fairness, and accessibility. Probably the
most constructive things that government can do are to bol-
ster the schools and to create opportunities for young people
to be productive outside of what we have perceived traadi-
tionally as the school day.

Our governments—state, local, and national—have never
really responded to the changes in society and the diminished
economic roles of young people. We have never posed the
question, "What does this mean in terms of governmental
services and social order?" Never having posed the question,
we have never discovered the answer.

*What about advertising to children? Should it be banned?
Is it really as harmful as some people say it is?*

My view on that is not terribly popular with many teachers or most reformers. I think the whole issue is a red herring. Available data suggest that children spend more time watching adult programs than watching children's programs. Therefore, if you are going to control what is perpetrated on children by means of television, you'll have to look at a great deal more than children's programs and the hours that are set aside for children.

Certainly the popularization of sugar-coated cereals is bad, but in my opinion it is not nearly so destructive as some of the other aspects of television. Narcissism, materialism, the quick and easy answer, violence as a solution to problems—all are of much greater concern to me than attraction to sugar-coated cereal and silly toys. If we don't deal with these larger issues, I think we have really missed the boat, certainly as far as children are concerned.

What about the Saturday morning ghetto?

I have said very often that my biggest concern about children and television is the values reflected in the way children use time. There is some real junk on Saturday morning television, certainly. There is some real junk on Friday night television. But television generally delivers an array of choices. Some programs are constructive, and some programs are destructive. The great mass are at worst simply inane. They're probably not going to do anybody any great harm; they're just wasting a lot of very valuable time.

The challenge for our society, particularly for parents and teachers, is to enable children to make constructive decisions about using their time. To sit in front of a television set for four hours on Saturday morning and expose oneself to the absurdity and the inanity of whatever comes along is probably not so harmful in itself, but the children who do that will not have done what they might have done with those four hours.

Let's talk about television within the schools: Do you think that a lot of television sets in schools are unused?

Yes. It isn't only television sets; it's hardware in general. The schools in many cases are not well managed or well directed. Decisions are often made by people who will have virtually nothing to do with carrying them out, that is to say, by people other than teachers.

Television is particularly difficult to use in the classroom unless the school has the resources to provide a wide array of programs that teachers can use on a flexible schedule. The typical elementary school teacher who is trying to lay out a flow of work over a 40-week period does not have any particular interest in, or need for, a piece of film at 10 o'clock on a Tuesday morning just because that's when it happens to be scheduled on ETV. If that particular program on Tuesday morning is not in some way related to what has happened in that class on Monday and what is planned for Wednesday, it is simply a distraction from the flow of events.

In most cases, a school can get some federal or private money to purchase a piece of equipment, but without a constant flow of money to support the utilization of that equipment, it will sit around unused.

When a school district is strapped for money, as most seem to be, where should the money go—television sets or teachers' salaries?

I think most people accept the fact that a real, live, breathing teacher is the core of any instructional program. However, when cuts are to be made, they generally are proportional. If the payroll for teachers is 65 percent of a $20 million budget and there is a $5 million budget reduction, the payroll will probably be cut to 65 percent of a $15 million budget.

That's the nature of the school, because it is essentially a social institution. It is people. You need supporting materials and supplies in direct proportion to the number of people using them. Relative costs have been very constant through massive fluctuations in spending on education. If spending goes up dramatically, relative costs don't change. Likewise, if it goes down, they don't change.

If I had my own way with federal money, all of it would be earmarked for two things: additional teachers and additional teacher training. I'd leave it for the local districts to find the best ways they could to finance discretionary materials as needed. The opportunistic acquisition of new hardware merely because there are federal dollars available for hardware has no effect on what actually happens in the school.

Let's go back to a point you mentioned earlier. Will you say something more about what you mean by intellectual tyranny in relation to television?

I'm talking about the regular, frequent exposure of the American people to a powerful and sophisticated medium controlled by a few people whose interests are primarily economic and who have the capital to be in business.

As I said earlier, I think the schools are probably the best opportunity that this society has to develop the intellectual capacity to cope with this dominant influence and place it in perspective.

Corporate influence on television has profound implications for education and freedom of thought. One of the major issues that we as a teachers organization have had to cope with over the last hundred years has been academic freedom. And probably the most significant challenges to real freedom to inquire, to study, to explore, and to read have been the very powerful economic interests in the United States, which often take a relatively conservative view of what ought to be happening in schools.

Now if those economic interests are able through their political influence to lay more and more strictures on the right to inquire in the schools, and if teachers continue to be in jeopardy for challenging traditional assumptions and traditional institutions, and if at the same time, television, which enters all the homes in the country, is promulgating a similar traditional orthodoxy, then I think the prospects for intellectual tyranny by corporate America become very real. Schools and teachers must be free.

THE FCC TAKES A HARD LOOK AT TELEVISION[5]

Educators are in a better position than any other group of adults—with the exception of thoughtful parents—to under-

[5] Reprint of magazine article by Charles D. Ferris, chairman of the Federal Communications Commission (O. 17, '77-Ap. 10, '81). *Today's Education.* 69:66–68. S.-O. '80. Used by permission.

stand television's impact on children. Thirty years ago, when television arrived, teachers found it to be potent competition for the attention of their students. That competition has only grown stronger.

Not surprisingly, the teacher's attitude toward television has often been a mixture of disdain, awe, and perhaps even fear. For how many of us look like Charlie's Angels or have the style of Miss Piggy or can match the zaniness of Mork? And how frequently can the classroom teacher serve up learning in simple, easily digestible lumps, like TV program segments, without the personal struggle that usually accompanies real intellectual growth?

Our hopes that our children or our students would benefit from television programming that is both culturally broadening and educational, as well as entertaining, have been disappointed. We have watched most of television become a daily round of predictable serials and melodramas, interspersed with an occasional program that is profound and moving.

Television executives point with understandable pride to accomplishments like *Roots* and *Holocaust,* programs that gripped the emotions and imaginations of both adults and children. While they were superior entertainment, they also served the higher purpose of enlarging the viewer's perspective on humanity's capacity for both love and hate.

Even when TV provides only formula entertainment, it still teaches children about the world and about social values with an immediacy that classroom teachers simply cannot duplicate.

Television, then, is more than the business of entertaining millions of viewers. It is also a teacher, shaping the values of our society. It teaches young people how we as a nation think about ourselves and our place in the world, and it affects the way we behave, both as individuals and as a nation.

History has taught us that innovations in communications methods have always radically changed social and political environments. Gutenberg's invention of movable type made the printed word available to entire populations. No longer was the flow of information limited to the social and intellectual elites. In a later era, radio tied the world together via electromagnetic waves. More recently, television has made people all over the world participants in a global community.

In the United States, television has influenced our national and international affairs—from civil rights, Vietnam, and Watergate to Afghanistan and Iran. Not a passive medium, television conveys events instantly from around the globe as well as within our national borders. It makes viewers participants in these events, and viewer reactions add another dimension to the events themselves.

While past changes in communications capabilities have vastly enlarged the numbers of persons reached, television's phenomenal power today lies in the fact that more people can have instantaneous access to the same event or artistic experience than ever before.

The still unanswered question is what the quality of such an experience will be.

Classroom teachers immediately saw the educational possibilities of dramatic presentations such as *Roots* and *Holocaust* and used them to their students' benefit. Likewise, they have recognized the value of children's programs with more explicit educational goals such as *Electric Company, 3-2-1 Contact,* and *Fat Albert and the Cosby Kids.*

Many teachers and much of the general public, however, still take a dim view of TV. I have received thousands of letters from disillusioned child viewers and their parents—all seeking more diverse and satisfying subject matter and better scheduling.

Recent surveys, such as one poll conducted for the Public Broadcasting Service (PBS), find that a majority of Americans today think commercial television falls far short of its potential. People are weary of television programs that seem like reruns even the first time they're shown.

In spite of a generalized dissatisfaction with TV, as a nation we have incorporated TV viewing as part of our daily routine. Its growth has been nothing less than phenomenal. Immediately after World War II, only 1 in 100 homes had a TV set. By the mid-fifties, 75 out of 100 homes had a TV set. Today the percentage of homes with one or more television sets roughly equals the percentage of homes with indoor plumbing, and I would guess if Americans had to choose between the two, many would find it nearly impossible to do so.

Young children, in particular, are devoted television viewers. In a recent documentary on television and the family, Bill Moyers of PBS asked children whether they would rather give up their toys, their fathers, or their television. The majority said that they would give up playing with their toys and even talking with their fathers before they would give up watching television.

If our children could have access to dozens of new networks, all vying for their attention, would this abundance simply add to the distraction level for our children, our students, and ourselves?

I think it would be a positive step. No longer would television be limited solely to those programs that attract over one-third of the total viewing audience. The new media will narrowcast rather than broadcast. They will provide more effective and satisfying programming to specialized audiences.

Today we are experiencing a wave of technological breakthroughs in communications that is almost as significant as the advent of television itself. This quantum leap will permanently change the structure of television programming. Instead of only a few broadcast outlets existing in each city, new delivery systems such as satellites and cable will provide us with easily accessible, highly specialized types of information and thrust us ever closer to an information-based society.

These new communications systems will provide now-restless television audiences with fresh and specialized programming. For example, the number of programs for children and college-age adults will markedly increase. The Appalachian Regional Commission, an agency servicing 13 Eastern states, has already established its television system, the Appalachian Community Service Network, as a separate nonprofit corporation. By satellite and cable communications, this network now offers 70 hours of nationwide programming each week. The programming concentrates largely on courses for college credit established in conjunction with more than 50 colleges and universities.

The rapid and dramatic explosion in multichannel television systems and in pay TV—both on cable and over-the-air—is itself a big step. But the future use of two-way cable communications to provide information on call and the keen interest by major corporations in combining computer and communications technologies are even more exciting possibilities. This will make all forms of knowledge—both entertainment and information—accessible, inexpensive, and convenient.

New technologies can make a teacher's job less difficult. No longer will the classroom teacher be limited by the straitjacket of centrally broadcast programming that is aired once and never repeated. New communications systems will make television as flexible as today's textbooks. Programming will be readily available on video cassettes and discs as well as in central program banks. Multiple channels will make all programming available on an "as-needed" basis.

These are not the "blue sky" predictions of an unrestrained optimist. They are a solid description of a reality that is already defining itself.

A recent count of specialized programming services available to cable television systems listed almost 40 new programmers, 25 of which began operating since the beginning of 1979. New networks range from movie, sports, and religious channels to specialized programming for Black audiences, the elderly, the Spanish-speaking, and children.

The instant success of C-SPAN, which provides gavel-to-gavel coverage of the deliberations of the U.S. House of Representatives, and the intense interest in Ted Turner's new Cable News Network, which provides 24-hour news, are evidence of the rapidity with which our assumptions about what television programming "people won't watch" are changing.

Clear evidence indicates that viewers are willing to pay for programming that is not available on commercial television. Revenues in cable and subscription television doubled between 1977 and 1978 and doubled again last year. Future revenue projections look equally promising.

Innovative programming formats are starting to develop in response to new communications delivery systems. The Public Broadcasting Service—the only television network to interconnect all its member stations by satellite—has begun simultaneous transmission of three program services. One of them is designed to carry a complete children's program schedule. This three-channel feed allows each public television station to select programming that is most responsive to the interests of its local audience.

A study of staff of the Carnegie Commission on the Future of Public Broadcasting recently concluded that a nonprofit pay cable network—providing the highest quality performing arts programs and entertainment—could also find a substantial market.

Yes, the future beckons with the possibilities we all anticipated when television sets first started glowing in the nation's living rooms 30 years ago. But in spite of the many new program proposals and future projects, the vast majority of children today continue to rely solely on commercial television for their information and entertainment. Here, unfortunately, the present still looks much like the past.

While commercial television has produced some important exceptions in the area of children's specials, it has not increased its daily programming for preschool and school-age children. A recent study by the staff of the Federal Communications Commission (FCC) concluded that during the last six years the programming and scheduling practices of children's television on commercial stations had changed very little, despite these stations' assurances to the FCC in 1974 that they intended to provide substantially more weekday programming to reflect children's special interests and needs.

The ABC *Afterschool Specials* and *Fat Albert and the Cosby Kids* illustrate how high quality programming that enriches and entertains can also teach. CBS still produces *Captain Kangaroo,* the pioneer in this field, but it remains, after 25 years, the only daily preschool-age program on a commercial network. NBC has announced *Project Peacock,* a new series of prime-time children's specials, to premiere in 1981.

But the unanswered question is whether having each television station in a community broadcast an occasional hour of age-related children's programming per week is sufficient for the millions of young viewers who are glued to the set for 30 hours or more each week. The new fall schedule that the three networks announced this spring contained no substantially new initiatives for weekday morning or after-school programs for children.

The FCC is continuing to review children's television policies. We are considering a broad range of options. These range from eliminating existing policies to insisting that each television station meet certain requirements to air a minimum amount of age-related children's programming each week. Any such requirements would, of course, be removed when new communications technologies make more children's programming options widely available.

Programming for children has always evoked strong reactions from parents, educators, and children. Because children are among the heaviest consumers of television at a point in their lives in which they have only limited abilities to place programming in a realistic context, concerned adults are closely scrutinizing children's television. We no longer debate whether children learn from TV; instead we argue over what it is that TV teaches them.

In recent years, teachers and parents—who see most directly the misuse of television—have begun to seek a more rational and informed use of this medium. For example, the national PTA develops program rating guides and gives awards for top quality family shows, and the NEA recommends informative programming of educational value.

The Office of Education of the [then] Department of Health, Education and Welfare (now within the Department of Education) has funded special children's programs that are available to all broadcasters for only the cost of mailing. It has also provided financial support for several projects to develop critical TV viewing skills in children. These programs will now be carried on by the new Department of Education. . . .

The real question in my mind is how long we can wait for the future communications abundance to meet children's needs. Programming designed for children and available throughout the day to most Americans will, I believe, be a reality 10 years or so from now. We will have advanced information systems that can recall information for the classroom or home study projects on demand—an electronic encyclopedia, never out of date. Narrowcasting, specialized program services, and instant access to information will, I believe, provide the technical breakthrough that will again put America at the forefront of innovation and creative growth.

Although no technology, by itself, will ever replace our need for a well-developed educational system, new technologies will offer educators many options in the future. Those new technologies will bring the world into the classroom and provide an inexpensive and efficient support system for schools.

We at the Federal Communications Commission are hopeful about these new developments. But we are also concerned about the present generation of children and the lack of services commercial television currently provides them. We must decide whether to simply await the future of programming abundance or to hasten its development or to affirmatively impose obligations on existing commercial TV broadcasters to meet the needs of today's school-age children and others who will reach their formative years over the next decade.

We look to educators, in particular, to provide us with their insights as we undertake this important task.

DEALING WITH THE CONTROVERSIES OVER
CHILDREN'S TELEVISION[6]

We are now into another season of network television. Each season produces a minimal number of successful new shows, a crop of midseason replacement shows, intense competition between networks during normal programming hours and "sweep" periods, and Saturday morning/weekly children's programs. While the prime time program competition receives most of the publicity, the battle for rating supremacy among children's programs is perhaps even more intense. Advertising in children's programs has evolved into a billion-dollar business where rating points quickly translate into higher prices charged for commercial messages. Industry critics decry the use of sophisticated selling techniques on defenseless youngsters and criticize children's programs for excessive violence and poor taste. While some of the criticisms are valid, it would be unfair to state that nothing has changed in the children's television market. The industry has responded to criticism by consumer advocates and the petitions of one group, Action for Children's Television (ACT), have made a significant difference. ACT has managed to effect the following changes in children's programs:

☐ removal of vitamin commercials

☐ reduction of the amount of commercial time to nine minutes and 30 seconds per hour weekends and 12 minutes per hour weekdays

☐ the forbidding of program hosts to endorse or sell products

☐ reduction of the frequency of commercial interruptions

☐ the requirement of nutritional messages to balance product announcements

☐ the requirement of the insertion of five-second separator devices (bumpers) before and after commercials, which will

[6] Reprint of magazine article "Dealing with the Controversies over Children's Television," by James Roman, assistant professor of communications, Hunter College of the City University of New York. *USA Today.* 109:62–64. S. '80. Reprinted from *USA TODAY*, September 1980, pp. 62–64. Copyright 1980 by Society for the Advancement of Education.

help children distinguish between program and non-program material.

In addition to various structural changes in children's programming, there have been some encouraging advances in program formats. CBS has developed several delightful programs for chidren under 12, as well as adolescents. "Patchwork Family" was an interesting live puppet program that covered a diversity of subjects. One program examined the different cultures of England, Greece, Japan, Italy, and France. "Marlo and the Magic Movie Machine" utilizes two engaging hosts (Marlo and the Machine) to take viewers on trips, play games, and present them with interesting bits of information. Another program that was similar in scope was "Razzmatazz." A unique feature of this program was the segment featuring Don Herbert, better known to many adults as the indefatigable Mr. Wizard. "Fat Albert and the Cosby Kids," created and hosted by Bill Cosby, exposes children to realistic problems and attempts to deal with many of the myths that children hold so dear. Like Aesop's fables, each program presents a didactic message.

ABC has also experimented with different children's formats, producing "Kids Are People Too" and "Hot Fudge." The former profiles children of famous celebrities, in addition to presenting other interesting segments; the latter nurtures a much-needed nutritional and health format.

Complementing the children's programs are a variety of short program segments that instruct, enrich and provide pro-social messages for children. These segments include news ("Ask NBC News"), instruction in the use of metrics ("Metric Marvels"), and various nutritional and safety public service announcements. Most are produced or provided by networks, advertisers, and government agencies.

While there has been some movement from the *status quo,* many critics feel that much more must be done before children's programming achieves a foundation of respectability and legitimacy. Perhaps the most emotional issue in children's television today is advertising. The FTC has been conducting hearings on a proposal to ban advertising in programs which are seen by children under eight, ban all commercials for sugared products where children under 12 constitute a significant portion of the audience, and require that commercials for all other sugared products be balanced by separate nutritional and dental messages.

The first proposal initiates a discussion of cognitive development and how young children perceive commercials. Do children under eight understand the intentions of commercials and do they perceive them as being different from the program they are adjacent to? Much of the research indicates that a child's distrust of commericals is positively related to age, while attention to them is negatively related. From kindergarten to third grade, children exhibit some confusion when asked to identify a commercial or explain its intent. Industry representatives claim that the research does not conclusively prove that children under eight are unable to identify a commercial. However, the research has proven that there is a reasonable doubt as to the ability of a child under eight to distinguish the commercial from the program and to understand its intent. While such doubt is expressed, precautions should be taken to shield youngsters under eight from the potential negative effects commercials may have.

The second and third proposals attempt to mediate between the child and commercials for sugared products. Presenting nutritional messages to counter commercials for sugared products is a legitimate device for presenting children with a balanced point of views. However, if such messages are to be effective, they require the same care and creative effort that go into the production of commercials.

Banning commercials for sugared products where audiences consist of many children under 12 is a naive attempt at regulation. Children will always be exposed to stimuli other than television that will encourage their use of sugared products. Television can best be used as a medium to instruct children in the dangers of excessive sugar consumption and provide them with sound nutritional information.

Industry representatives repeatedly express their distaste of those who attempt to curtail advertising and threaten the *laissez-faire* economy of broadcasting. They equate freedom of commerce and freedom of commercial speech and wonder why critics always choose television to fire their salvos at. Industry leaders readily point to advertising in comic books and magazines, quickly condemning the double standard that exists in regulating one medium and not the other. However, comparing television advertising to print advertising is like comparing computer technology and crayons—both differ greatly in frequency, length of exposure, and effect. Children of all age groups see more television than print advertising. Recent estimates indicate that children see about 20,000 commercials a year. Passive print advertisements are no match for the slick, flashy, colorful, action-packed television commercials, with their catchy musical phrasing and potential of unlimited repetition. Television is a more persuasive and powerful tool than any other medium and, as such, requires closer scrutiny by consumers, government, and industry.

Those that support advertising on children's programs argue that commercials offer children a wide range of options, thus allowing them to make choices based upon their personal interests. Are the choices that diversified? On Saturday morning, children see endless commercials for McDonald's and Burger King, both offering brand-name diversity, but very little difference in product. While children are making decisions about advertised products, for the most part their decisions are dictated by the artificial needs established for them by advertisers.

Of course, one of the most effective arguments of challenging government regulation of the children's television market is that parents should govern their children's viewing habits. Should there be a "national nanny" to prescribe adequate doses of viewing for our children? Recently, the FCC issued a staff report deploring the present status of children's programming and recommending that a quota of weekly instructional network programming be provided for children by the stations and networks. The FCC's prescription calls for seven-and-a-half hours of instructional network children's programs weekly—five hours for pre-schoolers and two-and-a-half hours for older children.

Should the FCC act as a "national nanny" or should we rely on parents to regulate television viewing? Unfortunately, too many parents are television abusers. They are not discriminating viewers and either choose to ignore or are unaware of the potential negative effects of the medium. Just as the government (FTC) has the responsibility to protect viewers from what they can't see (excessive set radiation), it also must have the option to regulate what they can see.

Beside the FTC and FCC proposals, other suggestions have been offered. Kenneth Mason, a concerned executive with the Quaker Oats Company, recommended that the networks pool their programming revenue to produce a schedule common to all three for Saturday mornings. Each network would rotate the responsibility for producing the shows and all three would broadcast them simultaneously. Most industry representatives have scoffed at Mason's plan and find it completely unworkable. They ask if Quaker Oats would pool their revenue with other cereal manufacturers to produce a single nutritional brand with a common label. One must give Mason credit for being a concerned and enlightened executive. However, his plan is terribly naive, considering the fiercely competetive nature of network television today.

The Heinz Bill

Another plan introduced to help upgrade children's television is the creation of a National Endowment for Children's Television, proposed as legislation by Senators John Heinz (R.-Pa.) and Ernest Hollings (D.-S.C.). The Heinz bill would create a 27-member national council to guide the endowment, headed by a chairman selected by the President. Heinz hopes that, if the bill passes, initial funding will approach $10,000,000. The money would be allocated for the development of new programming concepts and the funding for research on the effects of television. Programs created with endowment funds would be made available to both public and commercial television.

On the surface, Heinz's proposal seems attractive and realistic. However, most legislators will vote against it for some very sound reasons. Presently, the Federal government is contributing approximately $200,000,000 a year to the support of public broadcasting. In addition, various agencies of the Federal government have contributed funds to children's television production entities like Children's Television Workshop, the producers of "Sesame Street." To many, the creation of an endowment will appear to be duplication of spending. Another fault with the proposal is that most legislators will find it offensive to fund programming for the networks when network profits are at an all-time high. Many could justifiably argue that commercial television can readily support innovative children's programs.

While the Heinz bill advocates Federal support, other recommendations for external funding include grants from corporations and foundations. Institutional advertising on commercial television has attracted corporations like Hallmark, IBM, and Xerox. Other corporations that cater to children's needs (Health-Tex, Playskool, etc.) could help underwrite children's programming.

Program underwriting is a common source of funding programs on public television. By law, all underwriters contributing support to a particular program or series of programs must be identified both before and after the program is broadcast. While many observers have criticized underwriting announcements as another form of advertising, their format is more acceptable for children's viewing because the announcement, rather than attempting to sell a product, simply identifies the corporate donor.

Instead of prohibiting commercials on children's programs, some critics have suggested clustering them at a certain time of day. Commercial clusters have long been a part of many European broadcasting systems. The advantage of such a practice would be to give parents more control over what their children are watching. All commercials would appear at a specific time during the day and the parent would decide whether or not the child should watch. Under present circumstances, there is little control over program interruptions. While commercial clusters would not affect content, it could be an effective tool for parental monitoring. For clustering to be used effectively, however, an intensive promotional campaign would be necessary to make parents aware of the procedure.

With the introduction of new television technology, parents will have the opportunity to regulate their children's viewing from a wide variety of sources. Cable television is expanding its efforts in the area of children's programming. Warner Communications, a leader in cable television, is offering a full schedule of daily children's programs called "Nickelodeon," with notable scholars contributing to program development.

Along with cable TV, more homes soon will be equipped with video cassette and video disc players. Parents will be able to rent or buy programs they think suitable for their children and thus could become television "programmers" for their families.

While commercial broadcasters may be reluctant to respond to the criticisms outlined above, they can not ignore marketplace forces. If, in the future, more children are drawn away from broadcast television to the competing technologies, the broadcasters will be forced to change their approach to children's television. While the broadcasters might prefer to be insensitive to moral persuasion, they certainly can not afford to ignore the mentality of the marketplace.

AMERICANS ARE "HAUNTED BY A FEAR OF
TECHNOLOGY"[7]
Reprinted from *U.S. News & World Report*

"Man Is a Problem Inventor" by Nature

Today our nation is haunted by a fear of technology. But this fear, and not technology itself, is the real menace. The unpredictability of technology frightens us.

---

[7] Reprint of comments by Daniel Boorstin, Librarian of Congress. *U.S. News & World Report.* 88:70. Mr. 17, '80.

Yet this is our challenge. Contrary to the cliché, man is not uniquely a problem solver; other animals can solve problems. Man is a problem inventor. It's by technology that we make new problems and open up new possibilities that were never imagined.

TV "Helps Us Discover the Virtues of Reading"

People mistakenly assume that the new technology must displace the old. That's what I call "the displacive fallacy." Television did not abolish radio. That's not the way it usually works. Generally, new technology transforms the old, opening up unimagined uses for the old.

Radio and television help us discover a new uniqueness and new uses for the book and all other printed matter. There's something special and private, even secret, something personal and active about reading which distinguishes it from "watching." These virtues of reading can be plainer to us now than ever before.

Literacy: From "Menace" to Lost Art

Every group that makes its living or secures its prestige through one form of technology considers the new form to be a threat. At the time of the introduction of printing, professors accustomed to dictating to students from their precious manuscripts thought that the printed book was a menace. When you let people read books, they said, you couldn't be sure that they would read what you wanted them to read or draw the moral you preferred them to draw.

Similarly, in our time, many academics are troubled by the way television trespasses on the book. Of course, TV is "vulgar"—because it's not in their control. They object to its sex and violence. But they offered the same sort of objections against the spread of literacy and the book. In the 18th century, when women were taught to read, it was feared that reading novels would violate the chastity of female minds. And weren't they right!

"Populist Fallacy" vs. "Natural Aristocracy"

Unlike many, I do not see the decline of reading and writing skills as mainly a byproduct of television. Instead, I see this decline coming from the misapplication of our democratic ideals. There is really no necessary contradiction between democracy and standards.

Where we go wrong is by insisting that everybody is just as competent as everybody else, that no tasks are more complicated than any other. This is the Lorelei song of democracy, the Populist fallacy—and we have to resist it. Instead, we must insist on a modern version of Jefferson's "natural aristocracy." This means opening opportunity to everybody for a disciplined basic education. And then, after the freest competition—regardless of race, creed, sex or age—we must stand fast for high standards.

"Information Obsolesces, but Knowledge Endures"

With radio and television, we cross the continents and the oceans, but cannot cross the centuries. They conquer space, but not time. They flood us with what has happened—or what newsmen speculate may have happened—lately. We end up preoccupied with the problematic present. We think we were born yesterday, or with the last 7 o'clock news.

Our institutions of higher education, too, fill their curricula with obsolescent information and obsolescing skills when they should be concentrating on knowledge and the heritage of our whole, long past. Information obsolesces; otherwise there would be no market for today's newspapers or magazines like *U.S. News & World Report.*

Information can be *given* to us. But knowledge, which endures through the centuries, must be acquired by the autonomous learner. Educating in a democracy means giving everybody the opportunity and the incentive and the skills to acquire knowledge, to distinguish knowledge from news and to reflect on what it all might mean.

A citizenry saturated with today's information will always

be puzzled—and isolated in the present. What we need is a *knowledgeable* citizenry.

BIRTH OF A NATION'S ELECTRONIC CAMPUS[8]

The Open University of America, based on the irresistible idea of a higher-education network that would rely primarily on television, video disks and other electronic devices is struggling to be born.

The success of Britain's Open University, which recently celebrated its 10th anniversary and has 64,000 currently enrolled students and 21,000 alumni, has removed all doubts that it can be done. The remaining question is how to adapt the idea to American higher education, which already reaches more people than the traditional British universities.

There are two concepts for the Open University's future. The first, aimed mainly at adults past college age, is the brainchild of advocates of existing nontraditional education under the leadership of the University of Mid-America, a consortium of 11 Middle Western universities (Box 430, Owings Mills, Md. 21117).

The second concept is being pushed by Walter Annenberg, the publishing tycoon and former United States Ambassador to Britain, who has offered the Corporation for Public Broadcasting $150 million—in 15 annual $10 million installments—toward the establishment of a "National University of the Air."

The Annenberg plan would aim primarily at 18- to 21-year-olds. Mr. Annenberg is said to be convinced that great numbers of young people are not served by the traditional campuses largely because they cannot afford to attend college for four years.

---

[8] Excerpted from newspaper article "Birth of a Nation's Electronic Campus," by Fred M. Hechinger, education editor. New York *Times*. p. C4. Ag. 26, '80. © 1980 by The New York Times Company. Reprinted by permission.

Both plans, to get acceptance from the higher-education establishment, must prove that they will not take any of the regular clientele from colleges, which are already concerned about the prospects of declining enrollments.

The "for adults only" proposal may have a somewhat better chance to allay such fears because there are undoubtedly many adults who will be unable to attend established institutions for further education. The University of Mid-America claims, moreover, that many adults, once their appetite is whetted, will eventually want to complete some of their studies on a real campus.

Even so, many colleges and universities, which are pinning their hopes for survival on a future influx of adult students, will not be enthusiastic about an electronic competitor.

They may be even less enthusiastic about Mr. Annenberg's plan to reach out for the real or imagined residue of left-out college-age youths. In the scramble for bodies to fill vacancies, that group will be a fought-over commodity, especially if the Federal Government can be persuaded to provide more scholarship aid.

Another issue is money. Even so generous an infusion as Mr. Annenberg's would only cover a fraction of the cost for the Open University.

Fortunately, there are many ways of overcoming these obstacles, provided the sponsors of America's Open University are willing to be flexible in making their schemes compatible with existing institutions and their future problems.

One way is suggested by the nonprofit National University Consortium, which plans to enroll next month several thousand students in a nationwide system of television-assisted courses leading to the bachelor's degree. Pilot projects of this program, which will initially involve 11 television stations and 11 colleges, began at the University of Maryland in 1972.

The consortium's key lesson for an Open University compatible with existing higher education is that it requires degree candidates to enroll and pay tuition at participating colleges.

Another opportunity might be offered to colleges and

their faculty through royalties from the production of courses on tape or video disk. . . .

Perhaps the greatest ready-made source of advice and actual materials may be the experience and productive output of Britain's Open University. Its extensive list of textbooks specifically produced for self-instruction, supported by televised or radio-transmitted lessons, has already become an export item.

The British Open University Foundation Inc. (110 East 59th Street, New York, N.Y. 10022) has been set up to spread the gospel and offer advice. It publishes occasional newsletters, of which the current edition contains a listing of course materials especially selected for their adaptability to American college courses.

One aspect of the British Open University worth taking to heart in any American counterpart is its insistence on a combination of long-distance learning and personal contact.

The lessons that are mailed out and the frequent tests returned by students to the central campus are dealt with by a sophisticated, "untouched-by-human-hand" computer system, but that system is backed up by an army of flesh-and-blood tutors. Every student is in constant touch with a tutor and, in addition, may meet frequently with advisors at one of several centers. Advice can be obtained by a "hot-line" telephone when it is needed. Many students spend at least a few weeks on real compuses, and they often complain that the time is too short.

All of this suggests opportunities to merge a future American Open University with existing campus resources. The tradition of American higher education and the size of the United States argue against central control through one Open University center, except for administration. Both academia and television are decentralized in this country, and a new Open University might tread on dangerous ground by ignoring that pattern.

At first glance that pattern may appear as an obstacle to the creation of the type of university envisioned by Mr. Annenberg. But, in fact, the availability of over 3,000 campuses could make possible a successful combination of long-distance learning with personal instruction, guidance and evaluation.

A recent study by the University of Mid-America stresses the role of an Open University as a nationwide investment of educational guidance that would serve students of all ages, as well as traditional and nontraditional institutions. Such a service may suggest a merging of present plans and might make possible a more realistic sharing of the financial burden among various sources.

The ultimate test of these plans may well be whether America's Open University can become a supportive new link in the nation's shaky and frightened system of higher education, instead of a victim of that system's panicky determination to stonewall any attempts by a competitor to gain a foothold.

V. THE PRESENT

EDITOR'S INTRODUCTION

There is turmoil in television land. The networks, which until now have had the most control over the shows that reach our TV screens, now find this control threatened by cable companies, video tape recorders, video discs, and satellite technology. The most powerful weapon that the networks have in the battle to retain their power is the size of audience they can offer to advertisers. The traditional structure of broadcast TV, in which the three networks—ABC, NBC, and CBS—develop a broadcast programming schedule beamed across America via affiliate television stations, has guaranteed these three companies a phenomenally lucrative yearly income. Competitors trying to reach this same market have been virtually shut out.

The new technologies have finally produced a way to siphon off the networks' audience. Cable TV companies, which every year wire more and more homes, offer alternative shows, usually for a fee, which compete with broadcast TV. Video discs and videotapes, both of which can be played back through television sets with the proper equipment, represent another depletion in the audience for broadcast TV. Instead of being at the mercy of network television schedules, viewers can opt out of the schedule altogether and watch material from their own video disc or videotape library. New satellite technology offers the potential of direct satellite-to-viewer broadcast, bypassing the traditional local television station.

L. H. Goldenson, chief executive officer of ABC, feels that in the competition between the cable companies and the networks, the federal government has unfairly discriminated against the networks. One of his key complaints is the low fee that cable TV companies are required, by government regulation, to pay broadcasters for use of their shows. In a speech delivered to the National Press Club, he says, ". . . it is vital to the health of our industry and the service we provide the public that they not prosper by stealing from the system that already exists."

A byproduct of the advances in video technology has been the increasing sophistication of television commercials. "These bright, seemingly carefree commercials . . . are actually the culmination of months of intensive effort by creative directors, musicians, singers, animators, and other technicians. . . . Combining broadcast technology with musical talent, they have updated Ivan Petrovich Pavlov's classic experiment, replacing the psychologist's hungry dogs with legions of viewers," writes Mark Voorhees, reporter for the Hunterdon County *Democrat,* in the *Progressive.*

Jeff Greenfield, the author of *Playing to Win,* examines the current state of cable TV in an article from *Saturday Review.* While L. H. Goldenson claims that cable TV threatens the public affairs programming of local TV stations by reducing those stations' viability, Greenfield finds the cable companies producing more innovative local programming than the broadcasters. The local cable companies "can reach down into localities and neighborhoods in a way the more broadly based local stations cannot."

The last pieces in this section take a look at current television programming trends. The kinds of role models that television praises is the subject of an article by M. C. Miller and Karen Runyon, contributing editors of the *Nation.* They examine several TV shows and find that ". . . by turning us into a uniform mass, cutting us off at the roots and using us to make a lot of bread . . . television actually diverts us from diversity." The shows they criticize display characters who triumph by giving up individuality in favor of conformity.

"Thrill shows [that] appeal and cater to the viewers' infantile instincts" is the subject of a piece by Martha Smilgis, contributing editor to *Time.* Smilgis dissects TV sensationalism and finds that "gore springs eternal at the networks."

COMPETITION IN THE TELEVISION INDUSTRY[1]

I'd like to offer some concrete thoughts about what the future of broadcasting should be like. But before that, let me briefly review some of the past with you. It strikes me that broadcasting has passed through two phases since the Communications Act of 1934 charted our national system of radio and later television. One key provision of that act stressed that the broadcast media should be available to everyone, rich and poor alike. A second provision called for a fair, efficient and equitable ditribution of broadcast facilities among states and communities.

Thus, we built the original twin pillars of broadcasting: a commitment to nationwide, free communication and an equally important commitment to local service. Upon one pillar we erected today's networks; upon the other grew the local radio and television stations that have become community institutions.

Our government leaders had a firm belief in the principles enunciated in that 1934 Act. Toward that end they worked hard to foster a climate in which nationwide radio and then television could grow and flourish. The creation of ABC itself is but one example. It was a decision of the Federal Communications Commission which permitted two smaller companies to merge in 1953 and thereby take a giant stride toward the development of three vigorously competing commercial networks.

In the 1970s, however, our industry entered a second phase. Attitudes toward free television began to change in Washington. Instead of receiving support and encouragement, television broadcasters found themselves confronting an unfriendly government, a government with a different goal: the promotion of new technologies that held out the

[1] Reprint of speech by Leonard H. Goldenson, chairman of the board and chief executive officer, American Broadcasting Companies. *Vital Speeches of the Day*. 47:57–60. N. 1, '80. Used by permission.

promise of greater diversity, but also required the viewer to
pay a fee.

What are these new technologies? Well, first of all,
they're unlike what peceded them, the traditional advertiser-
supported broadcast system we call free, over-the-air television.

The new systems all cost the viewer money. They fall
roughly into three categories:

One is cable television, sometimes called Community An-
tenna Television—CATV. Such a service usually provides
subscribers with local station signals—with some distant ones
thrown in—for a monthly fee. It comes into the home by
wire.

A second is pay cable television, which is added on to regular cable, and costs more money. Pay cable charges extra for
certain channels that carry more current movies and sports.

Third is subscription television—sometimes called over-
the-air pay TV or STV. This is an over-the-air system that
sends out a "scrambled" signal. For a monthly fee the subscriber gets a decoder for current movies and sports.

The change of philosophy in Washington was gradual. In
the late 1960s, when the government first tried to devise
ground rules for the new pay TV development, its underlying
premise was that these new services should add to, not replace or damage, the existing system. Our policymakers recognized that cable and pay cable were media which would
never be available to all citizens. The cost of wiring the entire
nation was prohibitive, and many citizens could not afford to
pay for their television service.

Moreover, without some restrictions, it was feared that
the most popular types of programs would gravitate to pay
television. So, in the late '60s, the FCC said that the new pay
systems could not siphon certain types of programs traditionally offered on free television—such as major sports events—
and then offer them to the public for a charge.

The Commission also recognized the importance of local
stations. It acted to maintain their viability. First, it limited
the number of signals from distant markets which CATV

could import. Second, it protected programs licensed exclusively to local stations. Moreover, the FCC—following the dictates of Congress in the 1962 all channel legislation— made it clear that development of UHF channels took precedence over the growth of cable and pay cable services.

From our point of view at ABC, the government in those days was acting within the tradition and intent of the original Congressional charter for television.

But more recently, in the second phase of television history which began in the early '70s, an FCC majority said, in effect: Let's put all systems in the same ring together. But, to balance competition, let's take free television, blindfold it, tie its hands behind its back, and pin it to the mat before we even start the match. Now that may be a good way to fix a wrestling bout, but it's not the way to regulate an industry.

The record of these past few years is highly revealing, as well as troubling. Conventional cable, for example, has become a flourishing multibillion-dollar business in large part because it does not have to pay market prices for its programs. Before the 1976 Copyright Law, it paid nothing for the use of broadcast signals. Even with that law, as one observer has said, "the vast majority of cable operators pay more for postage stamps than for their programs." This is a government-forced subsidy. Cable is being given a free ride. And the ones pulling the wagon are the program producers and broadcasters. Yet the FCC, which has the power to act, has bucked the problem to Congress. And Congress has not yet faced up to the matter.

Meanwhile, this summer, the FCC dropped two of the last vestiges of protection for the rights that program producers sell to local broadcasters, the so-called "syndicated exclusivity" and "distant signal" rules. With these rules gone, a cablecaster now can help himself to virtually any broadcast program anywhere in the country, regardless of the program owner's intent to limit the area in which the program may be shown.

Also, the Commission and the courts first weakened and then wiped out all the rules for both pay cable and over-the-

air television, rules that had prevented so-called siphoning of
major sports and entertainment attractions from free TV to
pay TV.

Congress has declined to address the subject—even
though pay cable is moving rapidly to a position from which
it can outbid free, over-the-air television for the rights to most
poular sports programs. If there is any doubt about pay TV's
intentions, let me cite you a recent experience of ABC. In
winning the rights to telecast the 1984 Summer Olympic
Games, we were very mindful of the fact that the bid from
pay TV was not far below our own. And the promoter behind
that bid has been quoted as saying, with some contempt:
"The American public thinks it has an inalienable right to
watch everything free."

Which, of course, raises a basic issue: Does the Congress
really want the public to pay for sports and entertainment it
now receives free? Does a Congressman, or a Senator, or a
President really want to run on a platform that calls for the
public to pay for television programming it now receives
free? Will the public support such a candidate?

Satellite-to-home broadcasting represents another potential source of conflict. So far, Washington has looked favor-
ably on it. But satellite broadcasting, as now envisioned,
would completely bypass local stations, which are a vital
source of local news and public affairs programming. Again,
neither Congress nor the FCC has faced up to the economic,
social and political consequences of such a drastic change.

For a moment, compare with me this record of unabashed
promotion of cable and pay television. Compare it with the
regulatory treatment of free television broadcasters.

—A television broadcaster may operate only one channel
in a community; a cablecaster may operate 12, 20, 40 or even
78, as is contemplated in Pittsburgh.

—A television broadcaster may operate in no more than
seven communities around the country; a cablecaster may operate in as many as he wants.

—A television broadcaster may operate only one national
network; a cablecaster may operate as many as he has channels to accommodate.

—A television broadcaster may not own cable where he has a television station. And a television network may not own cable systems at all. A cablecaster may own cable systems and networks wherever he wants. Even a foreign national may now open and operate cable systems and networks in this country, thanks to a recent FCC decision.

—A television broadcaster must present a substantial amount of news and other public service programs; a cablecaster need not present any. On the other hand, we're not permitted to present pornographic material, not that we ever would—but a cable system is free to and sometimes does.

—A television broadcaster—even if he runs a subscription TV station—must produce his own programs or purchase them in the competitive marketplace; a cablecaster, for only a token payment, may help himself to any program a broadcaster has already made or purchased. The money he saves, of course, then can be used to buy the most desirable TV programs for his own pay system.

Clearly, what we have seen is a quiet but profound reversal in government policy. The government is promoting those systems which require the viewer to pay a fee. At the same time, it is placing new and more difficult burdens on free television stations and networks. Washington has tilted the balance—against free television and in favor of pay television.

Some say ABC opposed development of any new means of program distribution just to preserve the status quo. Nothing could be further from the truth.

We do not question that the new technologies can make a positive contribution. They should have an important place in American television. But it is vital to the health of our industry and the service we provide the public that they not prosper by stealing from the system that already exists. Likewise, it is vital that viewers not be discriminated against because of economic status or geographic location and be forced to pay for what they now get free.

Studies show that cable concentrates in the affluent neighborhoods rather than the inner city. This contrasts with free television which has been available to all for many years.

It is the most important source of news, information and entertainment in our society. Also bear in mind that the new technologies—either individually or in combination—are unlikely to be available to all of our citizens even by the end of this century.

We at ABC welcome competition in the television industry, but we believe strongly that in the 1980s the government must move to ensure that the competition be both fair and equitable for all parties.

Let me be blunt: It is time for the government to get off our backs. It was one thing for the government to expect us to operate under tough, restrictive rules when the national communications system was served primarily by free broadcasting. It is quite another, however, for the government to promote pay television and other systems by arbitrarily discriminating against free television.

Today, I propose a six-point program designed to let all parties compete fully and fairly in the television markets of the 1980s:

—First, the government should restore to the producers of television programs and those who buy the rights to those programs the same contractual privileges any other copyright holder enjoys. This can be achieved either by amending the Copyright Act of 1976 or changing the Communications Act. A change in the Copyright Act should provide full compensation when a cablecaster uses a broadcast program. Or the Communications Act should be amended to require the cablecaster to obtain retransmission consent for use of broadcast programs. Otherwise, local stations cannot be expected to continue to support the broad range of services their communities have come to expect.

—Second, the Commission should repeal its multiple ownership restrictions in broadcasting. If cable operators are free to program up to 78 channels in as many markets as they wish, then surely broadcasters should not be limited to one channel in seven markets. If a multi-system operator can own a cable system in every community, then surely there is no justification to restrict broadcasters—or newspaper owners.

To restrict one competitor while leaving others free makes no sense and serves no public purpose.

—Third, the FCC should repeal all rules restricting broadcaster participation in cable ownership. Specifically, it should remove the ban against ownership of both broadcasting and cable facilities in the same market. It also should lift the ban against network ownership of cable.

—Fourth, the Commission should permit any television station the right to offer over-the-air subscription service. Specifically, it should eliminate the present requirement for a minimum number of stations in an area before subscription television is authorized.

—Fifth, the Justice Department should dismiss its antitrust suit against the National Association of Broadcasters. This case boggles the mind. It challenges that part of the NAB Television Code which voluntarily limits the number of commercials on the air. If it succeeds, we'll either have more commercials or more direct government regulation—a classic case of the government stepping in to fix something that's not broken.

—Finally, I propose that the FCC relax its rules that now restrict television networking. Let the networks contribute to further program diversity by offering a second network service—perhaps one of more specialized appeal. In the end, we'll have a more competitive system, and the American people will be the beneficiaries.

The new directions I am proposing would correct the imbalance struck in government policy over the past several years. Such conditions would permit everyone to compete fully and fairly in a free marketplace. Most importantly, all the American public could continue to receive maximum benefits from the traditional free television system, while at the same time the opportunities of the new technologies are becoming more fully developed.

We at ABC believe we have a great deal to bring to the new technologies. With so many new channels becoming available, many have wondered whether the promise of wider choice will turn out to be sterile for lack of quality programs.

Our company has confronted similar challenges for more than a quarter of a century. We know that by working with the finest men and women in this industry, by aggressively pursuing the course I've outlined here today, we can once again meet the challenge and create even greater opportunities to serve the American public. . . .

SALIVATION THROUGH TELEVISION[2]

A strong, handsome runner strides in slow motion through a forested park as light filters down through a canopy of leaves. Woodwinds and strings set a gentle mood.

Marty has an appetite for life, which means he doesn't sit it out.

A close-up of the runner's torso and head fills the screen. His wavy hair, brushed back by the wind, bounces in time to the music.

For people who have an appetite for life, we have a way to satisfy it.

The runner's wife appears, a bar of margarine on the kitchen table beside her. She interrupts her work to hug her husband when he enters the room.

He also has an appetite for food like Fleischmann's, a delicious part of a low-cholesterol, modified-fat diet.

The couple seems almost to dance to the background music. As quickly as the kitchen scene appears, it vanishes, and the runner is again among the trees.

As the tempo and volume of the music rise, the man runs, eats toast with his pig-tailed daughter, and wrestles playfully with his children. More instruments and vocalists join in, and soon the voices, with perfect timing, are extolling the virtues of Fleischmann's margarine.

[2] Reprint of magazine article by Mark Voorhees, reporter for the Hunterdon County *Democrat*, Flemington, N.J. *The Progressive.* 44:28–30. Reprinted by permission from *The Progressive*, 408 West Gorham Street, Madison, Wisconsin 53703. Copyright © 1980, The Progressive, Inc.

The handiwork of Wells, Rich, and Greene, the New York advertising agency of Standard Brands, Inc., makers of Fleischmann's margarine, may be seen and heard on any weekday afternoon, sandwiched between the game shows and soap operas of commercial television. Like most of the rest of the $3-billion-a-year television advertising industry—an enterprise that harnesses enormous talent and technology—it epitomizes an old merchandising maxim: When you can't sell the product, you sell something else.

In her book, *The Show and Tell Machine,* Rose Goldsen sums up the successful promotion technique: "What advertising puts into mind is not the product, but some kind of associative link to it."

Tony Schwartz, a Madison Avenue operative who has created more than 5,000 radio and television spots, carries the point a step further: "Here the key is to connect the products to real lives of human beings," Schwartz writes in his bible of advertising technique, *The Responsive Chord.* "If the advertiser can render a deep commercial on the feelings [of the audience] . . . a real experience is created for the listener or viewer.

"When the consumer sees the product in the store, whether he or she consciously remembers it or not, the product may evoke the experience of the commercial. If that experience was meaningful, and there is a need, the consumer is likely to buy the product.

"The critical task is to design our package of stimuli so that it resonates with information already stored within an individual and thereby induces the desired learning or behavioral effects."

To implement that high-sounding psychological principle, television has developed some formidable tricks of the trade. In the Fleischmann's commercial, music binds together more than fifteen-separate scenes, then highlights the margarine in the midst of it all with a well-timed crescendo. The adroit use of music in the Fleischmann's commercial, as in others, is known in the advertising trade as a "bandaid." Creative directors and executives of ad agencies judge bandaids by their ability to set a mood and shape the pace of the ad.

Jingles are another trick of the trade. These are the attention-getters, the audio billboards. Everyone knows and sings them. "They cut through layers of indifference," wrote Randy Cohen in *More* magazine, "to grasp the viewer in a hammerlock of harmony."

As with the bandaid, the trick of a jingle is to link the product to enticing images. For this reason, jingles are usually paired with lively scenes of sailboats gliding over cresting waves, disco roller skating, a rough-and-tumble game of football, or a setting sun. The most successful jingles are choreographed with such masterful precision that their real impact is largely unnoticed.

When the friendly, freckled McDonald's counter clerk pops up with a welcoming message, the cheery music subsides. As friendly voices chorus, "You deserve a break today," the french fries and milkshakes dance enticing jigs. Some twenty-five scenes occur in sixty seconds.

"The effect is to lure your attention forward like a mechanical rabbit teasing a greyhound," explains Jerry Mander in *Four Arguments for the Elimination of Television*. "Each time you are about to relax your attention, another technical event keeps you attached."

These bright, seemingly carefree commercials, like the "bandaid" spots, are actually the culmination of months of intensive effort by creative directors, musicians, singers, animators, and other technicians. The results are impressive: For many youngsters, jingles have replaced nursery rhymes, and even adults occasionally tap their feet and whistle a jingle.

"Jingles are mantric," says songwriter Charlie Morrow. "They are repeated endlessly and are invariable. The jingle is a hypnotic element. . . . It tries to rivet [products] to your brain."

Advertisers pay eagerly for the riveting: A catchy jingle can bring its composer $10,000. Steve Karmen, the King of the Jingles, is said to earn $1 million a year for writing such tunes as *I Love New York* and *When You've Said Budweiser*. Yet Karmen's fees are small change for advertisers, who dole out $1,000 a second for prime air time.

Such popular music and rock stars as Ray Charles, Aretha Franklin, and the old Jefferson Airplane have cashed in on this profitable endeavor; Barry Manilow, Melissa Manchester, and others have taken time out from their popular music careers to write a jingle or two, as well.

All this fits snugly into the marketing strategies of advertisers. They depend on selling a lifestyle as much as a product, and jingles are a proven link to the appeal of popular music.

"Jingles reflect the current music scene in the country," says Buck Warnick, music director of Young and Rubicam, America's largest ad agency. "With disco being hot, you'll hear that lively beat. *Star Wars* really prompted the spacey, electronic sounds so popular a few years back."

In their book *Rock 'n' Roll Is Here to Pay*, Steve Chapple and Reebe Garofalo explain the link between commercial and popular music: "The endorsement of a hip rock group seemingly transformed the advertised product, no matter how mundane it actually was, into a flashy youth product, in the same way that associating a naked woman with a particular model of camera gives it sexuality."

And then there is the world of "special effects."

A synthesizer, as its name suggests, creates sound. It uses transistorized electronic signals and, if programmed skillfully, can mold sound into melodies, rhythms, and acoustic effects. Says Suzanne Ciani, who has become remarkably adept with synthesizers and other electronic gadgets, "It's an instrument with a brain—it has a system of language like the human brain. I give it words or signals, and it makes sentences of sound."

Ciani's Coca-Cola commercial, showing Coke being poured onto ice, illustrates how electronics can augment the sound of music. That tingly, airy burst of bubbles may sound like "the real thing," but actually it was born in Ciani's synthesizer.

"I tried to create that burst of good feeling that you get from drinking a Coke," Ciani says. She clearly succeeded; in just five seconds, her synthesizer puts a warm, provocative sound in the viewer's mind. Once again, the musical sleight-of-hand forges a link between a mundane product and a vivid, appealing image.

Ciani, with several degrees in computer science and classical music, has the special-effects market cornered. She is often called into the studio to create new sounds evoking familiar images. She has fashioned the ugly feeling of a sore throat, the "tingly feeling of relief" of a Vicks cough drop, the pounding of dogs' feet for a Greyhound bus commercial, and the "submarine disappointment" of a wallet drifting to the bottom of the ocean as its vacationing owner watches.

Ciani can make sounds to go with post-nasal drip, arthritis, and headaches. She can manufacture bodily ailments faster than drug companies can make products to cure them. "The motivation in this kind of music is to produce the discomfort and the tensions, however subconsciously, in the viewer," she says.

Giving people subconscious headaches does not bother Ciani. For her, music is the supreme consideration: "I use whatever will help me communicate. I just take advantage of technology."

With Americans tuning in for an average of fifty hours of television or radio each week, technology is clearly not the only thing advertisers are exploiting.

Combining broadcast technology with musical talent, they have updated Ivan Petrovich Pavlov's classic experiment, replacing the psychologist's hungry dogs with legions of viewers.

The goal this time is not an understanding of animal behavior—it's profit. And the bait is not a meal, but fleeting strains of music, or promises of a better life through a "better" brand of peanut butter, a "new, improved" shampoo.

For people who have an appetite for life, we have a way to satisfy it.

At least Pavlov gave his subjects meat.

HIDDEN TREASURES ON CABLE TV[3]

Will the television set of the future have 30 or 60 channels, two-way hookups, special channels for foreign-language programs, advice to consumers, and sexually explicit programs? Will television be able to break free of its reliance on mass tastes and passive audiences, and an advertiser supported economy that makes controversy a risk for producers?

For more than one in every five television households, such questions have already begun to be answered. In at least 15 million homes, the "television technology of the future" is the television technology of the here-and-now. These are the homes wired for cable, a system that transmits signals through a series of microwave relays and closed-circuit lines directly from a transmitter into home receivers.

Cable TV is not, strictly speaking, "broadcasting" at all, since the signals aren't sent through the air; this fact is what enables cable television to provide ghost-free signals and liberates television from its most fundamental failure—scarcity. Because the signals don't have to compete for room in the broadcast band, there is vitually no limit to how many cable channels a television set can receive. In Manhattan, cable TV subscribers receive 26 channels; in Columbus, Ohio, Warner's Qube system provides 30 channels; proposals for the franchise in New York's Queens County have promised up to 125 channels.

For viewers, however, the real question is not how many signals they can receive for their $10 a month, but what's on these channels. Is the technology simply providing clear reception of broadcast channels, plus movies and sports on an extra "pay cable" channel such as Home Box Office or Showtime? Or is cable television delivering on the possibilities offered by abundance?

[3] Reprint of magazine article by Jeff Greenfield, who recently served as a judge for the National Cable Television Association's award competition. *Saturday Review.* 7:22–24. Jl. '80. Copyright © 1980 by *Saturday Review.* All rights reserved. Reprinted by permission.

Recently, I had a chance to see the kinds of programming available on cable systems all across the country. While the programming I saw was selective, it did demonstrate that cable has the potential of producing something close to a revolution in television, making cable in fact what its developers saw only as potential.

Consider first the question of community service. Most commercial television stations talk about helping their communities, but it is in the main just that—talk. Yes, there are public-affairs programs, usually plugged into Sunday morning slots when most of the audience is asleep or at church or play, but the vast majority of local stations either run network offerings or else choose from the wide array of syndicated offerings: game shows, talk shows, reruns of network programs, movies.

The cable systems, by contrast, could not duplicate this kind of "service" even if they wanted to. They cannot afford the highly rated syndicated shows such as *Donahue* or *Family Feud;* they cannot expect viewers to pay a monthly charge for programming already available; and they cannot win lucrative cable franchises from communities without delivering something different. Moreover, these are community systems with a "targeted" local audience. For both pragmatic and "noble" reasons, therefore, they can reach down into localities and neighborhoods in a way the more broadly based local stations cannot.

Thus, the Fresno-Madeira system serving Fresno, California, uses three of its 30-channel capacity for locally originated programs of special interest to its community. This includes consumer information such as comparative prices in local grocery stores, extensive coverage of a federal Agriculture Department hearing on controversies in the farm-rich region, and special Spanish-language programming. It also can swing into action almost immediately when a local crisis erupts. When a plant accidentally released pesticide into the air, the cable system provided on-the-spot coverage, with tough-minded interviews and with an "open mike" program advising residents of potential health hazards and protective actions that could be taken.

An even more extensive example of community service, and community involvement, is provided by the Berks Cable Company in Reading, Pennsylvania, one of the oldest cable systems in the United States. This company has 14 studios, each of which can originate cable programming, and 64 sites at which pictures can be originated. What this means is, in effect, a genuinely "wired" community. Berks Cable provides bases for local political debates and headquarters for the counting of local election returns—races of intense community interest that may be shuffled aside by other stations on election night when bigger races are being held; it has set up conversations with local officials from 10 different areas (in one case, students from different schools simultaneously questioned the Pennsylvania secretary of education); it links senior citizens and children in a discussion about the generation gap; and it brings in doctors and lawyers who can answer questions from subscribers by telephone about neighborhood health and legal controversies.

Why is this so significant? Mass television is largely unresponsive; the lives of "ordinary" citizens almost never make the evening news or entertainment programs, and people may begin to feel their own lives and accomplishments are somehow unimportant because they are never seen on the powerful medium. The cable systems now in operation are helping to change that perception. When a local symphony or a high school football team is seen on cable television, its effort is somehow validated; participation in an event is encouraged.

Similarly, cable systems are also capable of encouraging a sense of community heritage, the fast-disappearing traditions that are so often erased by the constant bombardment of flashy programs and commercials. A cable system in California's Marin County, for example, produced a superior documentary on the last manned lighthouse in the region, at Point Bonita. Interviews with retired lighthouse operators and their families brought to life this soon-to-be extinct occupation, and photos of long-ago disasters at sea emphasized the dangerous nature of these jobs. The dedication and isolation of these men and women, almost unimaginable in our age, were captured in the faces and words of people who seemed to have stepped out of a Grant Wood painting.

A comparable experience was captured by the Sioux Falls Cable Company in South Dakota, in a long, leisurely interview with a one-time homesteader, an immigrant from Bohemia who settled in Nebraska and survived winter storms and deadly diseases to preserve his land. Such efforts are precisely the kinds of oral and visual histories that link the present to the past, and that could make television more than the ephemeral medium it is today.

If all this sounds too high-minded, too serious for what is essentially an entertainment medium, there are encouraging signs that cable television can fill a badly needed void here, too. Interesting, the most encouraging evidence is not provided by the pay-cable systems, such as Home Box Office and Showtime, for which cable subscribers pay $10 or so a month.

Because these companies are aiming for a mass market— HBO now has more than four million subscribers and Showtime recently passed the million mark—they seem determined to provide popular movies within a few months of their theatrical release, and specials featuring big-name stars such as Diana Ross, Bette Midler, and Donnie and Marie Osmond. While the lack of commercials and censorship is refreshing, the shows so far do not suggest a great reach of imagination.

Local cable companies, by contrast, are occasionally trying for something different. In part, they may simply be providing a showcase for local talent; Marin County's *Showcase II* clears out a studio and brings in local rock, folk, and jazz talent for an hour of strikingly original entertainment. Other efforts are bolder. Durham Cablevision in North Carolina put on a 30-minute local news parody, *Channel 86 News Fest,* which was a merciless send-up of the inanity of local news, complete with an illiterate sportscaster, a prop-happy weatherman, and an urgent report of an impending "meltdown" that turned out to be a Good Humor truck with a refrigeration breakdown. It was funnier and more incisive than most of the "Weekend Update" segments on *Saturday Night Live.*

And Santa Barbara Cable TV enraged local residents by parodying the community's Fiesta Week with a happily malicious account of the *real* story of the town's traditions and rapacious real estate development.

For entertainment that still manages to teach history, Telefrance's documentary on Josephine Baker (cablecast by Manhattan Cable) would be hard for any broadcast outlet to match. This one-hour blend of interviews and rare 55-year-old footage took us back to the Paris of the late 1920s, where the beautiful black dancer-singer created an instant sensation on the Champs Élysées, and followed the career of the exceptional performer. Apart from demonstrating that the Baker legend was well earned, the program gave us a rare glimpse into a time that is impossible to appreciate from written history and journalistic accounts. This is the kind of television that could be used in any classroom study of postwar Europe. And it is exactly the kind of television that no network would dare telecast, for fear that it might end up alienating segments of the economically crucial "mass audience."

All this is certainly *not* evidence that the millennium is here. Far too much cable television is made up of stultifying studio interviews, or a melange of sports and movies, with an occasional descent into titillating soft-core pornography. But neither should the potential of cable—indeed, the reality of cable—be minimized. By freeing the medium from the crushing burden of having to satisfy most of the audience all of the time, cable is clearly going to give American viewers the kind of choice we have had for decades on our newsstands. Right now, a special sports service is providing extended coverage of college and professional events that networks cover only on weekends; another system is broadcasting live proceedings from the floor of the House of Representatives to cable subscribers across the country. Last month, the first 24-hour-a-day all-news TV service began cablecasting from Atlanta to systems all over the country.

Throughout its history, television has been assailed more ferociously than any other mass medium. In fact, it has never been worse, if not better either, than any other popular medium. Its fundamental curse has been *scarcity*—the lack of alternatives. There has been no room on the broadcast band for minority tastes, off-beat satire, high academic pursuits, newly emerging talent, or the concerns of special neighborhoods, ethnic groups, age groups. Cable has now made scarcity a thing of the past in 20 percent of American TV households. And the evidence suggests that with abundance, the choice we have been denied for more than 30 years will finally be ours. Whether this is good—whether the culture would be better served not by better television, but by less—is another question. But to the extent that choice is good, cable is unquestioningly beginning to provide it.

ROLE MODELS ON TV[4]

In its pursuit of one thing (profit), television constantly assures us that we live in a land of innumerable things. It proclaims America's *diversity*—the varied wilderness, the motley populace, the many freedoms. First of all, there is that spectacle of topographic *abbondanza.* The actual countryside may be turning into one transcontinental shopping mall, but television still presents us with a national landscape of staggering variety. A commercial for Visa shows dozens of monuments and natural wonders as we hear a chorus of eager eunuchs sing the names of the fifty states; the evening news "profiles" this or that state on the eve of its primary, showing scenes of city night life, then dawn on some farm, a traffic jam, then a waterfall, and so on; and the endles succession of ads and shows further implies an endless variety of neighborhoods, landmarks, regions, terrains. . . .

And then there are the people, equally diverse: white and black, white and brown, white and yellow, white and red, straight and hip, rich and less rich. Television shows us a gratifying reflection of ourselves as various and tolerant, quick to

[4] Reprint of article "Television," by Mark Crispin Miller and Karen Runyon, contributors to *The Nation.* 230:506–8. Ap. 26, '80. Copyright 1980 The Nation Associates.

accept, a horde with a heart of gold. But what does this pleasant image really mean? And what is television really selling when it praises our "diversity"?

Our favorite medium flatters us with subtle formulations of a long-standing American myth. Although it seems celebratory, this myth has always suggested a deep uneasiness. The notion of "the family of man" has enjoyed its widest currency in America, "the melting pot," whose people are (as Carl Sandburg put it) "a vast huddle with many units." This fond conception at first seems incongruous with, say, Father Coughlin's tirades, Earl Butz's jokes, or most of our history. Haven't many Americans, in fact, seen this grand "diversity" as mere mongrelization? But the question is irrelevant, because what the concept of "the melting pot" actually celebrates is not diversity but its containment. The whole— whether "pot" or "huddle" or extended "family"— is greater than its untrustworthy parts. The famous roll call in American war movies clarifies this assumption—"Goldberg!— O'Houlihan!—Finelli!—Raskolnikov!" It is not this ethnic multiplicity that we are meant to admire but the controlling unit which can keep that "diversity" in manageable order.

Television continues to reflect this fear of diversity. That ethnically various platoon from films like *Battleground* ("Jarvess! Rodriguez! Stazak! Wolowicz!") and *Air Force* ("Quincannon! Munchauser! Weinberg! Winocki!") has been reincarnated on programs set in urban high schools. That gritty squadron has become the likable gang, kept in line by a teacher who is sympathetic, white and bigger than they are. The farcical *Welcome Back, Kotter* presented us with the Sweat Hogs, a high-spirited quartet of imbeciles named Washington, Horshak, Barbarino and Epstein ("Juan Epstein," which ethnic conjunction made it unnecessary to hire another actor). The four only clowned around ... never seriously opposing the mellow Mr. Kotter. *The White Shadow* relies on the same formula: Coach Reeves, a no-nonsense ex-athlete and veteran, teaches sportsmanship and discipline to his basketball team (Coolidge, Gomez, Goldstein, Salami), who would, but for his guidance, be out on the street, inflicting their diversity on decent citizens.

The players' variety is not only contained by the context of "the team" but is actually subverted by a fundamental sameness. Preserving no real differences, their diversity dwindles into a range of purely visual contrasts. This trivialization of diversity has become familiar over the past decade. On "liberal" shows like *All in the Family* and *The Jeffersons*, blacks and whites differed only in hue. These shows implicitly denied the cultural and economic differences between the races, dismissing as "bigoted" any awareness of actual diversity. The only alternative to the racist reactions of Archie Bunker and George Jefferson is the "liberal" reaction, which is to tolerate differences into extinction. Those calls for "brotherhood" actually have expressed a longing for homogeneity.

Times have changed. Those commercials for brotherhood seem dated now, as television begins to respond to the rising nostalgia for "American values": free enterprise (*Dallas*), clannishness (*Family, Eight Is Enough*), frontier mettle (*The Chisholms*) and jingoism (*When the Whistle Blows*, ABC's nightly update on Iran). This rightward shift has qualified the ostensible celebration of diversity, which is too suggestive of tolerance to suit the country's reactionary mood. Of course, the myth of diversity cannot be discredited altogether, since it is an essential feature of our ideology. Television therefore continues to invoke diversity, but only to subvert it with subtle endorsements of the power structure. In program after program, television presents us with a seeming variety which is really nothing more than an exhausted opposition. We see the same old symbols of authority surrounded by their failed alternatives.

This is the case not only in those above-mentioned tributes to the American Way, but in many of the current sitcoms. Co-optation has become television's most serviceable comic premise: yesterday's rebels have come home to Papa; yesterday's ethnic gets to use the country club. This is what happens in *Angie, The Associates, One in a Million, WKRP in Cincinnati.*

On television, blacks have moved out of the ghetto and

into massa's house. On *Diff'rent Strokes*, Arnold and Willis, two young black boys, have been adopted by a wealthy bore (i.e., white man) named Drummond. The kids are irrepressible, livening up Drummond's stuffy household with lots of sass and soul. And on *Benson*, the governor's black butler keeps his cool while all about him are losing theirs. Surrounded by do-gooders and martinets (i.e., white people), Benson keeps everything in working order, with the kind of resourcefulness and common sense that would even reflect well on a free man. But Benson seems content to stay in the mansion, making sandwiches and streetwise comments.

These shows pretend to "bring us together," ostensibly demonstrating that diversity has great rewards for those who will take part in it. The blacks and whites seem to exchange the gifts of their respective cultures like ambassadors from two sovereign nations. But in fact the white man has all the power, which is what makes television's treatment of racial "diversity" so repulsively sentimental. Real hatreds and resentments are suppressed in a maudlin fantasy of transcendent companionship: Benson and the governor sit in their bathrobes, exhanging views over a midnight snack; little black Arnold may tease big white Drummond, but he really loves the guy, and in recent TV movies like *White Mama* and *Jimmy B. and Andre*, a black child and a white grownup come to cherish each other, against all odds.

It is all terribly heartwarming, precisely because it can never stop reminding us of the frightening alternative that surrounds us. We see these characters fraternize like equals, or hug and kiss like loving relatives, but we know very well that Arnold and Benson are powerless, and this makes them latently menacing. What these shows inspire is not tolerance of diversity but gratitude for capitulation and restraint. We want to thank Benson for his folksy docility, because so accomplished a slave could, like Babo in "Benito Cereno," suddenly take a knife to his master's throat. And we are grateful to the governor for his magnanimity, because so exalted an overlord could, if he felt like it, squash his able servant like a bug.

While these "liberal" shows deny diversity by pretending to embrace it, more patently conservative shows deny it by pretending to tolerate it. In a recent episode of *The Chisholms,* a dramatic series about the frontier days, young Bo Chisholm is drawn to a Franciscan padre who has hired him to help build a chapel. The fatherless Bo admires the padre, who reminds him of the late Mr. Chisholm. Everybody in this Baptist community, including Mrs. Chisholm, is upset about this "Romish" influence. But Mrs. Chisholm, it turns out, is only worried that Bo might forget his father: the padre's religion is basically beside the point, as social differences are, once again, subsumed by individual relationships.

The last scene has the Chisholms and the padre singing a hymn together in the padre's chapel. We have learned that there is no difference between Catholics and Baptists: they are all Christians, all working hard to tame the land, to build churches (and maybe a shopping mall). Moreover, the padre *is* just like Bo's Dad: he is plain-speaking, strong, knows how to lob a knife, etc. In fact, they're all so similar that it becomes hard to imagine what all the fuss was about.

But all this climatic sameness cannot overcome our sense that there was, in fact, some difference between the papist and the true Americans. Although Mrs. Chisholm throws a bigoted neighbor out of the house, showing us that the padre's (slight) aberrancy ought to be tolerated, the show implies strongly that, while the Chisholms have just what it takes to make America great, the padre's Romish self-indulgence could never have settled this great land: the papist has introduced Bo to wine, women (i.e., a picture of a courtesan) and high wages (which pleasures have presumably made the nation's Catholic boys too feeble to make it out West so that *they* might have helped build a chapel). While the threat of difference is finally mitigated by the superiority of the American Way, we also infer that "the American Way" is not "the Catholic Way."

A recent ABC TV movie called *Amber Waves* was advertised in *TV Guide* as "A Story That Could Happen Only in America . . . Two Men. Different as they can be. One, losing hope. The other, helping him find it again. Fighting together to reap the next harvest. Drawing raw courage—new strength—from the rich and shining land they both love." In fact, this is a story that could just as easily take place in another country, and, in this case, did: the tale is "framed by footage of luxuriant wheat fields shot in Alberta, Canada," according to the *TV Guide* "Close-Up." The movie is as misleading as its advertising, and a rich and shining example of what the new mood, as reflected on television, does to the myth of diversity.

Bud Burkhardt is an independent grain harvester. Craggy-faced, hard-driving with men, tender with women and dogs, Bud is an embattled figure: he can't get reliable help, and is always one step away from foreclosure. Moreover, he learns that he has lung cancer, but puts off an operation because he has to see the harvest through. Nobody will help him: an old friend refuses, and Bud's son, who stays on in Canada after having dodged the draft, also turns him down. (Bud is too manly to tell anyone that he is dying.)

Fortunately, circumstances throw Larry Koenig, a cocky, city-slick New Yorker (Jew?) and fashion model, into Bud's employ. The kid saves the day by learning and applying Bud's values, and so Bud concludes that "yeah, there'll be crops next year."

In other words, the son with the wrong attitude is replaced by one who is more adaptable. Burkhardt purports to understand his own son's self-exile and even justifies it, more or less: like the Carter Administration, he has pardoned his son for draft dodging, while not exacty blaming the country or his own generation for the Vietnam War. But the viewer is less forgiving. He sees a desperate man trying to reach an absent son by telephone, coughing pathetically and popping his pills. Fatherly forgiveness notwithstanding, the viewer infers that a kid who turns his back on his own dad must have found it easy to betray his country.

Before he can replace the rebellious son, Larry must give up his city ways along with his expensive clothes, so that he can slip into something less comfortable. It is hard to say which is the more effective way of denying regional diversity: disparaging one region in favor of another, or insisting that we all have the same basic values. At the end of *Amber Waves,* Bud realizes that Larry had "it" in him all along; "it" just had to be nurtured, like the waving wheat.

And that reference to those "amber waves" suggests how television tries to "bring us together": by turning us into a uniform mass, cutting us off at the roots and using us to make a lot of bread. For all its apparent celebration of "diff'rent strokes," television actually diverts us from diversity. It would have us consume together in peace, and to that end works ceaselessly to turn us against two entities: the true individual and the autonomous group. Wherever these two entities are threatened with extinction, there is no real diversity at all.

REALITY SHOWS[5]

The sign outside one of the more celebrated spas on the strip proudly trumpets TODAY! GARY WELLS JUMPS CAESARS PALACE FOUNTAINS. So he does, and the result fully lives up to the name of the stunt's sponsor, ABC's thrill-pandering series *That's Incredible!* While gawkers gawked and cameras whirred, Wells, a professional stunt man, gunned a motorcycle up a ramp, sailed over the water fountains outside the showplace, but crashed on his descent. Result: a ruptured aorta and fractures of the pelvis, thigh and lower leg.

For *That's Incredible!,* which is considering if and when it should air its footage of Wells' jump, the stunt was just one of many heart stoppers that have helped the show pull almost a third of the viewing audience in its Monday night prime-time slot. It was also the third injury to have occurred in filming for

[5] Reprint of magazine article "Incredible? Or Abominable?" by Martha Smilgis, contributing editor. *Time.* 116:90+. O. 13, '80. Reprinted by permission from TIME, The Weekly Newsmagazine; Copyright Time Inc. 1980.

the show. Another stunt man, attempting to jump in the air while two cars sped under him, nearly ripped off his foot when it caught in a windshield; he had to have reconstructive surgery and is still in serious condition. Still another daredevil suffered severe burns and lost his hands in the course of running through a 50-yd. tunnel of fire. For this, he was paid $8,-000, from which he cleared only $2,000 after expenses.

That's Incredible! is only the most sensation-mongering of half a dozen shows in a new TV genre known as reality programming. These shows offer viewers, by means of minicams, glimpses of real events and people. The cameras of *That's Incredible!* have dwelt on a man tied by his heels and hanging over a pool of sharks, a woman covered with bees, a miracle-working priest, a one-legged football star and a professor who pours acid over his hands. An NBC version of *That's Incredible!*, called *Games People Play*, has sent crews around the country to film folks engaged in such competitions as women's arm wrestling and belly bucking, in which a pair of beefy brawlers try to butt each other out of a ring. Like *That's Incredible!*, *Games* invariably winds up with a harrowing stunt designed to stir even the most hardened disaster freaks.

On one *Games* show, a stunt driver named Spunky piloted a car off a 45-ft.-high ramp into a lake. The camera focused on the clenched face of his wife as rescue divers made their way to the sunken auto. Would Spunky survive his dive? (Answer: yes.) In another segment, motorcyclist Rex Blackwell roared off a ramp and over two parked helicopters as their blades whirled at 350 r.p.m. "He barely cleared the last blade!" exulted the commentator as a slow-motion replay showed just how close Blackwell had come to being converted to steak tartare.

Another variation on the reality theme is ABC's *The Amazing Animals*, a sort of *Games People Play* for wildlife. Host Burgess Meredith runs footage of such wonders as two-headed snakes, spiders that square dance and cannibalism among rats in overcrowded cages. While some of the reality shows are going strong, others are suffering from TV's penchant for overexploiting a popular idea. After four weeks,

CBS last month dropped *No Holds Barred,* billed as a comedy series highlighting the "crackpot side of modern life" through the "oddball characters that make America unique." *That's My Line,* a remake of the game-show classic *What's My Line?,* also fizzled.

Broadcasters trace the development of such shows back to the appearance of NBC's persistently popular *Real People,* an hour of sometimes amusing interviews in the heartland. A recent show followed A. J. Weberman, a "celebrity garbageologist" who among other feats has retrieved memos from Richard Nixon's trash can and empty Valium bottles from Gloria Vanderbilt's. ("The best thing I ever found," he says, "was Jackie Kennedy's pantyhose.") While *Real People,* which gets more than a third of the audience in its Wednesday prime-time slot, spawned a series of other "entertainment news" shows like NBC's *Speak Up America,* it also turned TV executives on to the fact that low-budget programs produced without costly sets and high-priced talent could be hugely successful. While the tab for producing a half-hour sitcom might come to $300,000, the bill for an hour of reality programming may be $250,000 or less. Another spur to such shows has been the 2½-month actors' strike, which made the filming of dramas and sitcoms for the new season impossible at any price.

Reality-show producers admit that their aim is to be sensational. "The goal is a spectacular piece of film," says *That's Incredible!* Creator Alan Landsburg, 47, a veteran TV producer whose credits include the series *In Search of . . .* and the Jacques Cousteau specials. Landsburg will schedule any story "as long as we decide that the audience reaction will be 'Wow! That's incredible!' We opt for subject matter that is startling."

Or downright appalling, many critics would say. The thrill shows appeal and cater to the viewers' infantile instincts. Film Professor Richard Sklar of New York University compares these programs to a circus sideshow. "The grotesque aspects of popular culture—burlesque, vaudeville variety and pulp magazines—are finding expression on TV today. Television does not go out on a limb; it trails what is happening in society." Some of the toughest condemnations of the shows come from broadcasters. Morely Safer of *60 Minutes* blasts such programming as "the worst brew of bad taste yet concocted by the network witches."

Fortunately, the staying power of the programs is doubtful, as the recent casualties show. Still, gore springs eternal at the networks. This month, ABC plans to air the second installment of *Catastrophe! No Safe Place*, a three-part disaster roundup in which Charles Bronson narrates horrors like the *Hindenburg* explosion; and *The World's Most Spectacular Stunt Man*, a special featuring four feats by a Hollywood pro. It could be, cracks PBS Producer Tony Geiss, that public TV may be forced to counter with its own entry in the reality competition: *That's Intelligent.*

VI. THE FUTURE

EDITOR'S INTRODUCTION

The one inevitability for the future of television is *more*. All of the developing television structures and technologies are promising the TV consumer a geometric increase in choices of programming. The articles in this section mainly explore how our lives will be changed by this dizzying revolution in communications. Will our lives be better after we begin being bombarded with more TV shows, TV stations, videoized information, and video services than we could ever hope to watch or digest?

"What is at stake is how we talk to each other as a nation, how ideas and information are transmitted, who gains access to the system, at what cost and under what conditions," advises Sol Hurwitz, vice president of the Committee for Economic Development in a speech at Harvard University. Hurwitz thinks America's corporations are woefully underprepared to deal with the video communications revolution. In his view, those who are prepared to deal with it will assume great power in the future.

The "small rich audience" has traditionally been the primary consumer of public TV, which specializes mainly in cultural and educational fare. Many observers have identified the rise of pay TV as the death knell for public broadcast stations, noting that it would be more efficient to "narrowcast" public-TV type programming directly to those willing to pay for it rather than retain the "free" broadcast format that mandates a constant search for supporting funds. Paul Warren, a writer specializing in television, says in an article from *TV Guide* that "an educational channel might become a subscription-TV station, sending out scrambled signals of cultural programming to subscribers who have paid monthly fees and have decoders installed in their homes."

R. M. Baruch, chairman of Viacom International, believes that the content of future video will surpass the programming of today. Speaking to an audience at the Town Hall of California, Los Angeles, he emphasizes that the new wave of TV development will create a very choosy audience. "A responsive, participating audience is certain to emerge. It will be a demanding audience, more sophisticated in taste and preference than any audience before."

On the other hand, Chris Welles, a contributing editor to *Esquire* can't help but be pessimistic about the future of TV programming. "I would love to believe that armed with the new video, viewers will soon shout they're mad as hell and will resolve not to take it anymore. But if one searches for even a few traces of yearnings for better programs and inclinations toward revolution, next to nothing is found." He sees a vast new wasteland growing up to replace the old one.

Andy Miesler, senior editor of *New West*, takes a humorous look at a future world where TV technology takes care of all aspects of life. "Television will cook your meals, handle small-claims court lawsuits, [and] attend high school reunions." His humor, however, is based on a disquieting possibility—a future country of citizens who have given up communicating with each other except through the mediation of video.

THE CORPORATION IN A WORLD
OF MEDIA DIVERSITY[1]

The corporation and the media, two distinctly American institutions, fundamental to our way of life, are in the throes of change: dramatic, revolutionary, explosive change. The corporation, the very foundation of the private enterprise system, has gone public, in more ways than one. It is subjected to public rules and regulations, to public disclosure and

[1] Reprint of speech by Sol Hurwitz, vice president, committee for economic development. *Vital Speeches of the Day.* 45:412–416. Ap. 15, '80. Used by permission.

public scrutiny in ways never before imagined. The media, once viewed as separate and distinct channels of communication, are now so tied up with one another technologically, even economically, that it is virtually impossible to isolate the individual parts of the system. Scarcity of channels, the controlling factor in government regulation of telecommunications, is an obsolescent concept. Advancing technologies now promise a media world of unparalleled abundance, diversity, and choice.

For the American corporation the earth-shaking advances in communications are today what the revolution in transportation was more than a century ago. Transportation brought an unprecedented acceleration in the movement and distribution of people and goods in this country. It changed the face of America. In a similar way, modern communications is speeding the delivery of images, ideas, and information. If anything, the implications of the communications revolution—for the corporation, for society, for all of us—are more profound. For we live in an era in which it is possible—technologically—for every thought, experience, and event to be transmitted, stored, and retrieved. It is possible—technologically—for everyone to talk to everyone else, to obtain instant information and total knowlege about all things, everywhere on earth.

In 1854 Henry David Thoreau commented on the communications revolution of *his* time. "We are in great haste to construct a magnetic telegraph from Maine to Texas," he said, "but Maine and Texas, it may be, have nothing to communicate." At a time when everyone can talk to everyone else, the biggest challenge may be deciding what to say, deciding how and what to communicate.

My contention is that the large corporation, among many other institutions in our pluralistic system, ought to play a role in deciding how and what we communciate, for two reasons: because it is in its own interest to do so (business would not have thought of staying out of decisions regarding transportation a century ago) and because it is almost unique in its ability to mobilize the resources necesary to advance the larger public good. Still, for reasons that elude me, the large business enterprise has—with very few exceptions—failed to immerse itself in the public debate over the future of our national communications system. It has failed to grasp the reality of media diversity and its serious implications for the corporation and for society.

These failures are all the more serious in light of the severe public pressures that are being brought to bear today on the highly visible large corporation. The most intractable problems facing large corporations are external to the company. They involve powerful political, economic, and social forces that can determine whether a company will make a profit or loss, or even survive as a self-governing private institution.

True, some positive steps have been taken. Mobil Oil is one of a handful of giant corporations that have integrated the media into their corporate strategies—and it has produced some unexpected dividends for the public. In an effort to upgrade its public image, Mobil appears to have cornered the market on television programs dealing with Victorian and Edwardian England. They are outstanding. Not to be outdone, the Exxon Corporation has captured the Elizabethan market with a Shakespeare orgy, all 37 plays in living color. The television audience for Shakespeare's plays will far exceed the combined live audience for Shakespeare from the time his plays were first produced to the present.

One mustn't read insidious motives into these actions. They are superb achievements by any standard. But, they are not enough. The corporation's public is extremely diverse. To tell its story to an audience that includes millions of shareholders and employees will require sophistication, versatility, and a multitude of media. Take AT&T: three million shareholders, nearly a million employees. And there are millions more in its huge constituency: suppliers, customers, and consumers, people from all sections of the country, all classes of society. They are the nation in microcosm.

There are special interests and institutions, too, that must be dealt with: *competitors*, vigorously striving to invade a corporation's market and capture its customers; *labor unions*, competing for the allegiance, welfare, and wages of employees; *public interest groups*, monitoring the corporation's actions, measuring its social performance, agitating for changes in corporate behavior; *government*, federal, state, and local, commanding, controlling, regulating, taxing, enticing the corporation toward various forms of conduct.

And there are the *news media*, waiting to exploit every David-and-Goliath confrontation on the front page or the Six O'clock News, waiting to publicize every corporate shortcoming. What's the first law of television news? "If it doesn't light up or blow up, don't show it."

Well, relief is in sight. Corporate management will soon find no shortage of outlets on which to tell its story. With the explosion of technology, corporations are entering a new world of media under a great mushroom cloud of abundance and diversity. The terrain is unfamiliar so they had better learn how to navigate. There are new landmarks in this strange country. Let's look at them.

Cable television. It's no longer merely the means of importing distant signals to remote areas or upgrading the existing service. It's the beginning of Wired City, U.S.A. Twenty, forty, even eighty channels with a multiplicity of uses for every corporation, school, and home in the United States. It's coming. Not just commercial, public and community television, but banking and shopping, electronic newspapers and facsimile reproduction, monitoring, testing, the transmission, storage, and retrieval of information of every description. And over the horizon are *fiber optics* carrying maybe a hundred television channels in small glass tubules as thin as a strand of hair.

An experiment in Columbus, Ohio, has 13,000 homes wired to *two-way cable.* In effect, people can talk back to their television sets. You have a touch-button keypad console about the size of a little calculator. You have a choice of 30 channels, and you can command your TV set to bring you what you want. Ten channels feed you the commercial and public television stations, a public access channel and a program guide channel. Another ten offer so-called "premium" selections—mostly movies, such as *Julia* or *Equus,* that have yet to appear on commercial TV. Premium Channel 10 pipes in soft-porno flicks, but only if you order them at $3.50 a throw. The premium channel can be locked, by the way, presumably so an unsuspecting kid who wants to watch *Little House on the Prairie* doesn't turn on *Dr. Feelgood* by mistake. Now, a third set of channels are called community channels and they give you, among other things, the power to instantly say "yes" or "no" to a politician on any issue he puts before you. It's a kind of political *Gong Show.* Even as candidates or public officials are speaking, the public is gauging them. Can you imagine the paranoia that will set in among politicians if two-way cable gets going and the people gain the power to effectively vote the rascals out of office even before the election—with the touch of a button?

There are new landmarks . . . Let's look at them. *Video cassette machines* can record programs off the air. Recordings can be taken from one channel while the viewer is watching another, or they can even be made, with the help of a pre-set timer, when the viewer isn't home. Out for the evening on Saturday? Just set the timer before you leave and—presto!— *Saturday Night Live,* recorded when you get home. Play it back Sunday night, Monday night, any night you like, as many times as you like. Videocassettes can transform America's television viewing habits. They can emancipate the viewer from enslavement to the broadcast schedule.

There are new landmarks . . . Let's look at them. *Satellites,* orbiting the earth above the equator 23,000 miles into the atmosphere. They cast a giant transmission net over the United States. Satellite networks let you deliver a program to hundreds of localities at a fraction of the cost of conventional transmission. Satellites, therefore, may provide an answer to the question of how cable systems can fill those dozens of channels. Satellite interconnections can form mini-networks of cable systems or over-the-air stations to meet common programming or geographic needs. Public televison and radio have already converted to satellite, improving their receiving capacity and boosting their audio quality immeasurably.

And let's not forget the *computer.* Our host, the Harvard

Program on Information Resources Policy, has coined the term *compunications* to describe the emerging common technology between computation and communications. Data processing and communications are all but indistinguishable today. The computer's influence is felt in every area of modern communications.

Slowly, the future begins to take shape. Tomorrow's integrated communications center will include a desk computer, a videocassette recorder, and a standard television receiver connected to a cable television system. The TV picture tube becomes a display device for information, education, and entertainment in endless quantities and varieties, available on command by flicking a switch or pressing a button . . . in the home, in the school, in the office of tomorrow.

It's another country, this land of media diversity. There are new opportunities for access and new choices to be made. Corporate decision-makers will have to learn to recognize the landmarks, to read the signs.

There are new advertising options. The Madison Avenue crowd will have to explore them, or they may be locked out of the homes of the future. Cable television now penetrates 20 percent of the nation's television households, 14 million homes. Bill Donnelly, the media guru at Young & Rubicam, says a 30 percent penetration of television homes is the magic number, the critical mass, and he predicts we will reach that critical mass in 1981. That's when advertisers will start betting big bucks on cable. The leap in cable advertising, according to Bill Donnelly, will be followed by more attractive programming. And, close on the heels of the program improvements will come a spurt in the number of cable subscribers—say, to 50 percent—and we're on our way to Wired City, U.S.A. Even today, local advertising on cable is expanding. It's a good way to reach a highly selective market segment at a reasonable cost. The bargain rates have attracted the notice of local branches of some of the nation's largest corporations: Ford, General Motors, Exxon, Sears, McDonald's and Holiday Inn. A cable network linked by satellite could become a national advertising medium to be reckoned with. It's a development worth watching.

No wonder the television networks are getting nervous. A few short years ago there was a line at the doors of ABC, CBS, and NBC for prime time advertising spots. Not any more. Advertisers are finding alternatives. Look at Mobil Oil. For *Edward the King*—a series that CBS refused to broadcast— Mobil put together an ad hoc "fourth network" of 49 stations in major broadcast markets. In cities like Los Angeles, Washington, and New York, *Edward* is beating out the networks in the same Wednesday 8 p.m. time slot. There are independent television stations in enough markets in this country to form a "fourth network" capable of reaching somewhere between 55 and 60 percent of U.S. television homes. With the right programming it could provide a formidable challenge to ABC, CBS, and NBC. Bill Paley, the chairman of CBS, is desperate. He's suggesting the three networks agree to set aside a segment of prime time for high-quality programming—in contrast, I presume, to what they are now offering. He sees the handwriting on the wall. It spells "cable television," a "fourth network" and "public television"—alternatives that network officials cannot afford to ignore. When you bury your head in the sand, the saying goes, you leave the rest of your body exposed.

There are so many new opportunities for corporate access to the media, so many new choices to be made. I mentioned public broadcasting: 280 public television stations, about 200 public radio stations. The system covers 87 percent of the nation's population. . . . A new Carnegie Commission report on the future of the system [is] titled *A Public Trust* and it's available in paperback. Get a copy. It offers a blueprint for tomorrow's public broadcasting system. The report recommends an increase in the level of support for public broadcasting from the present sum of $482 million to $1.2 billion by 1985. Among the diverse sources of money that the system will require, it recommends a boost in corporate support from the present $40 million to $70 million annually, including relatively more business support for public radio and for individual public radio and television stations, as opposed to the present huge grants for national programs.

But more significant than the Carnegie Commission's plea

for more funds, or its warning of the risks of government intrusion, or its lengthy debates over centralism vs. localism, elitism vs. populism, is the recognition that public broadcasting is operating in a new telecommunications environment. The report's vision extends beyond public broadcasting into the realm of the emerging technologies, and it asks some fundamental questions: "What is or should be public broadcasting's posture in this new environment? How should it make use of the new communications techonologies? Will public broadcasting become superfluous or does it have an integral role in a copious information environment?" It seems to me that the corporation, among other institutions, has a constructive role to play in finding answers to those questions and to others that will determine the future of what the Carnegie Commission aptly calls "the national treasure" of public broadcasting.

But much more than public broadcasting is at stake here. What is at stake is how we talk to each other as a nation, how ideas and information are transmitted, who gains access to the system, at what cost and under what conditions. Clearly we must explore the frontiers of technology, but we must also understand its practical limits. If the move from scarcity to abundance in communications does not guarantee more complete or better managed information, if it only guarantees *more*, then it raises large questions about its ultimate value, including the very complicated questions of individual freedom and privacy.

Most corporations are not prepared to *ask* such questions much less answer them. They are accustomed to grappling only with isolated communications issues, not to looking at communications as a unified system of interdependent parts. Very few large corporations are prepared to deal coherently with the revolutionary changes that are occurring and to relate them to the very real public problems and challenges that the corporation is facing from so many different sources.

What can be done? If corporate management wants a voice in the decisions that are shaping the new world of media diversity, it will have to take decisive action. I believe there are three important steps it can take to gain a voice in those decisions.

First, it must *organize,* or *reorganize.* It must create a capability within the corporation, an office responsible to the chief executive officer and the board of directors, that can monitor national policy developments, recommend policy options, and guide corporate decisions with respect to communciations policy. Its purview would include matters ranging from the corporation's use of communications satellites to support for public television. A resource of this kind could also help the corporation examine its internal system of communications, as well as explore the use of new technologies in developing a better informed and more productive work force. I know of no corporation, outside of those whose business is communications, that is presently structured to provide such a capability.

Second, it must *spend money* and apply other corporate resources to identifying the critical policy questions—economic, social, technological—and the talented people and institutions that can answer them. It must nourish and support *with money* centers of high quality research, those that have the capability for examining new technologies in an integrated fashion—objectively, coherently—and projecting the implications of alternative public policies. It must *spend money* to stimulate and sustain the creative process that leads to program quality and diversity.

Finally, it must *get involved* in the policy debate. At this very moment Congress is rewriting the Communications Act of 1934. For the first time, there is an awareness that new technologies and the promise of greater media abundance, diversity, and competition may lessen the need for federal controls. Undergoing intensive review are long standing policies dealing with fairness and equal time concepts, with media concentration, and with the licensing of commercial broadcasters and the economic and social responsibilities that go with it. As institutions with a vital stake in the future of electronic communications, corporations ought to have a voice in the policy debate that will help determine that fu-

ture—not as special pleaders, not as rear-guard defenders of
the status quo, but as enlightened business leaders who have
large public constituencies with a diversity of interests and
needs to satisfy.

This last point is important. No one is expecting business
to neglect its responsibility for the bottom line or to ignore its
other private interests. The challenge for business in the debate over the future of the media is to learn how to tell the
story in both public and private terms, to learn how to mobilize its private interests for the public good. The revolution in
communications is upon us. It is ineluctable, inescapable, ir-
reversible. Sooner or later business will have to get involved. I
say better sooner than later.

BYE-BYE, PLEDGE WEEK[2]

Tincupping, they call it in the world of public television.
Viewers have come to loathe it almost as much as the commercials they've turned to public TV to avoid—a seemingly
endless round of pledge weeks, pledge festivals and auctions
that have helped fund the medium for years.

Perhaps the only people who hate tincupping more than
viewers are the PTV station managers and fund raisers themselves. Fund raising is often seen as demeaning and boring,
but there has never been any other choice for 288 public-TV
stations—usually long on programming ideas but short of the
dollars to pay for them.

"We have to find other means of raising funds," said Neil
Mahrer, senior vice president for marketing and administration for the Public Broadcasting Service (PBS). "Stations have
to look at all possibilities, especially when we see that the
traditional means of funding are falling far short of what is
needed to fund TV."

[2] Reprint of magazine article by Paul Warren, senior editor, *Television Digest*. *TV
Guide*. 28:11–15. O. 11, '80. Reprinted with permission from TV GUIDE ® Magazine.
Copyright © 1980 by Triangle Publications, Inc. Radnor, Pennsylvania.

Since the 1960s, public TV has relied on money from four general sources: fund raising, Federal and state governments, foundations, and corporate underwriters. In the past, public TV has been able to survive, if not exactly prosper, with these benefactors, but those days are rapidly coming to an end. Federal money, the backbone of the system in the past, is likely to comprise an ever-shrinking pot of revenue in the future.

This all adds up to one thing in the halls of public-TV stations across the country: fear. Where public broadcasters used to gather to discuss programming or the latest battle in the never-ending civil war that is public TV, money and how to get it now dominate conversation. As one station manager put it: "People are scared. Big stations and little stations alike see that the money is running out. We're all being put in a vise. There is a lot of fear in the system."

But while a lot of fingernails are being chewed at some stations, others are making entrepreneurial moves that would impress a Freddie Silverman. The moves revolve around the most-heard words in broadcasting today—"the new technology." Satellites, pay- and subscription TV, videodiscs and videocassettes are all being looked at by major program-producing stations with an intensity usually reserved for moaning about the Corporation for Public Broadcasting, which funnels the scarce Federal dollars to public TV.

Most of the action centers around pay-cable TV, which is making a lot of people rich in the commercial-TV world. Major producing stations—including WNET, New York; KCET, Los Angeles; WTTW, Chicago; and WGBH-TV Boston—all have or are considering deals with Home Box Office and Showtime, the major pay-cable outfits. The agreements call for coproductions, allowing both a station and the pay-cable company to finance an expensive production. The deal generally is that the pay-cable company gets first crack, allowing public-TV viewers to see a show only after it's been on pay cable.

While a number of stations are examining the possibilities of becoming suppliers to pay-TV—and videodiscs and videocassettes—an even more radical idea has emerged from the Corporation for Public Broadcasting (CPB), which is probably more aware than anybody that money is drying up. A consultant to CPB has proposed that public TV itself experiment with a pay-TV operation. The consultant proposed that an educational channel might become a subscription-TV station, sending out scrambled signals of cultural programming to subscribers who have paid monthly fees and have decoders installed in their homes. And about the same time as the consultant submitted his report, KQED in San Francisco applied to the FCC for permission to turn its sister station, KQEC, into an STV operation.

A much more ambitious proposal has come from the Carnegie Corp., whose study on public TV in 1967 resulted in Congressional establishment of the public-TV system. Carnegie, also worried about the problems of Federal funding, recently proposed that public broadcasters establish their own satellite-delivered pay-cable system called PACE (which stands for performing arts, culture and entertainment). The plan calls for PACE to be launched in 1982 with a $30-million pot—half from corporate and foundation grants and the rest being borrowed. Under Carnegie's proposal, PACE would feature high-culture programming that would be sold to consumers as a pay-TV product and then sold for public-TV-station use at a lower rate. While many in public TV like the idea, there is grave concern that the project is just too big to get off the ground before a commercial pay-TV operator jumps in and makes a bundle, pre-empting the folks from PTV. PBS, meanwhile, is planning a $50,000 study to see if a pay-TV service would make it, and public stations in New York, Los Angeles and Boston are working on a joint project aimed in the same direction.

The whole concept of selling previously free cultural programming and using public stations and resources for pay-TV is expected to attract considerable attention. To make a public-TV station a subscription-TV station requires FCC approval, viewed as impossible to get until recently. Federal Communications Commission Chairman Charles Ferris [Oct. 1977–Apr. 1981—ed.] has made it clear to public broadcasters he's all in favor of their using such traditionally commercial means of raising funds as subscription TV. But viewers, used to getting public TV free, or after giving voluntary contributions, can be expected to scream bloody murder if pay-TV disrupts their habits. And when viewers scream, Congress listens. And since Congress has a hefty hold on public TV's purse strings, there could be trouble.

Another of the new technologies public TV has cast its lustful eye upon is direct-broadcast satellites (DBS), which allow viewers to receive programming direct from a satellite, bypassing a local station or cable-TV company. Washington, D.C.'s Communications Satellite Corporation (Comsat) proposes to launch a DBS system in several years, and public broadcasters hope to get a piece of that action. Officials at the Corporation for Public Broadcasting have proposed joining forces with Comsat in filing for DBS approval before the FCC. The theory is that the FCC will be much more inclined to approve DBS with public broadcasters supporting it. In exchange for support, CPB has proposed getting a cut of Comsat's profits, plus a chance to program one of the DBS channels. Although the entire fate of Comsat's plan was thrown into doubt when Sears, Roebuck and Co. announced it was withdrawing as a Comsat backer, CPB nonetheless is hoping it can cash in on DBS.

Seen by many in public broadcasting as a leading entrepreneur in public TV is New York's WNET, also the public-TV system's major producing station. WNET currently is holding talks with videodisc manufacturer RCA for the possible sale on discs of such productions as WNET's multipart *Civilization and the Jews* project. And the station sees its library of *Dance in America* programs as another prime disc property. WNET and other stations are also considering marketing home-video programs through a monthly public-TV program guide, The Dial, which was launched as a joint venture by four major producing PBS stations this fall. The publication itself, which accepts advertising, has caused considerable controversy and is viewed as a bellwether for Congressional reaction to public-TV-station plans for getting into new areas.

Despite its image as a classroom-oriented medium bogged down in traditional broadcasting, public TV has long been an innovator. It is to no one's surprise that public-TV stations are moving in quickly to explore deals with pay-cable and disc manufacturers. For it was public TV that pioneered the use of satellites to deliver programming to its stations, and it is public TV that is now leading experimentation in this country with the consumer testing of teletext, a form of electronic newspaper that turns a home TV set into an information system.

Public TV also has long experience in programming to small groups, which TV analysts see as the wave of the future. Audiences, because of the new technologies that offer a variety of TV choices—be it disc, pay-cable, specialized programming—will be segmented.

While public TV moves more and more into the traditionally commercial areas of subscription TV and videodiscs, commercial broadcasters are expected to howl louder than ever. Nothing rankles commercial broadcasters more than having a Federally subsidized medium like public TV start to compete with them. Over the years there has been a love-hate relationship between commercial and public broadcasters, the commercial folks happy that public TV takes much of the heat off them to provide top-quality children's and cultural programming, but unhappy when they siphon too many viewers. But if commercial broadcasters are complaining now, just wait for the reaction if a Buffalo PBS station gets approval for its proposed means of raising funds: it wants to carry ads.

LIFESTYLE REVOLUTIONS IN THE TELEVISION AGE[3]

Not too long ago, Walter Cronkite, the dean of American television newscasters, gave us the following quotation:

[3] Reprint of speech by R. M. Baruch, Chairman of the Board and Chief Executive Officer, Viacom Intl. *Vital Speeches of the Day.* 46:209–13. Ja. 15, '80. Used by permission.

"It is a gloomy moment in the history of our country. Not in the lifetime of most men has there been so much grave and deep apprehension. Never has the future seemed so incalculable as at this time. The domestic situation is in chaos. Our dollar is weak through the world. Prices are so high as to be utterly impossible. The political cauldron seethes and bubbles with uncertainty. Russia hangs, as usual, like a cloud, dark and silent, upon the horizon; it is a solemn moment . . . Of our troubles no man can see the end."

That quote was from an editorial that appeared in Harper's Weekly Magazine in October of 1857 . . . over 120 years ago.

There is a school of thought that believes "the more things change, the more they stay the same." There is another school across the street that regards the dynamism of cultural and technological change as a very real force in shaping human destiny.

I got my diploma from that second school. I admit that I am addicted to the future. I see change not only as inevitable, but desirable.

Not that I am without qualms. Modern technology is a gigantic force that must be directed to the service of life. Our growing knowledge of this planet and the stars has unleashed power beyond our wildest imaginings. Our children take for granted miracles that would have boggled the mind of any resident visionary 100 years ago . . . 50 years ago . . . 25 years ago . . . *yesterday.*

More and more, it becomes evident that the key to the survival and prosperity of those curious creatures who inhabit Planet Earth . . . who dream of far-away galaxies . . . comes down to a single word . . . *communication.*

Before we can move forward together we must learn to talk together, and laugh together. Barriers to human communications must be overcome, be they mountains or oceans or suspicions engendered over centuries.

There have been many "revolutions" in the 20th Century. Political upheavals . . . revolutions in science, in transportation, even revolutions in our homes, in the way men and women relate. But there has been no more significant revolution than in the area of communications.

I sometimes think of the communications revolution in

terms of our population explosion. Consider that it took millions of years for Earth's population to reach 250 million . . . the population of the world at the time Jesus of Nazareth was born. It took a little over 1500 years to double that count to 500 million. By 1960, the world population reached three billion and by the year 2000 it is estimated that this little planet will host six billion souls.

This enormous population must, by necessity, communicate better and faster. An acceleration in the state-of-the-communications-art has been clearly demonstrated over the last few decades.

Allow me to reminisce a moment. I remember, back in the 30's, sitting somewhere in Europe, connected by earphones to a crystal set, listening with utter amazement to an early morning shortwave broadcast tell me, to my delight, that Joe Louis knocked out Max Schmeling.

That was in the 30's . . . not so very long ago.

Radio was the miracle of the 30's and 40's. Some 660 AM stations and just a handful of FM stations served the American people. The 50's brought us a new technological miracle . . . television. The impact on radio was severe . . . so severe that some predicted radio's demise . . . they told us radio would become The Shadow's shadow.

But what happened? Today we find 4500 AM stations and 3500 FM stations serving the nation. Radio had to change and adapt but it proved amazingly resilient. Before television: under 700 radio stations. Today, some 8000 stations. Did the frightening technology of television squeeze radio into obsolescence? Not at all! The prophets of doom and gloom were replaced by another kind of profits . . . the kind on the balance sheet.

Today, radio accounts for some seven percent of national advertising revenues. In years to come, as these expenditures grow, so will radio's size of the pie increase.

In the very near future, we shall see the advent of AM stereo radio. The AM stations will achieve technological parity with their FM brethren. In time, FM will have to develop new strategies to excel . . . and outsell their AM rivals. And so it goes. Each laboratory miracle begats another. Each new breakthrough produces new opportunity. If challenge is approached with creativity, not fear, what seems at first to be a threat can be turned into a virtue.

Radio is, and will be very much with us. But let us click off the radio now and turn to television.

In the 1950's, just about 100 television stations sent their signals in black-and-white.

It was early in television's history that our government regulators set limits to television's expansion. Some said they acted with fatal judgment. Others were simply delighted at the manner in which our government goofed ... the ones with licenses already in their pockets.

The early generation of television sets were able to receive channels 2 to 13, which we know as the VHF band. The UHF band, channels 14 to 84, could not be tuned in by most receivers then on the market. Government regulations added to the problem, by keeping UHF an inferior signal. It wasn't until many years later that the FCC rectified some of the horrendous mistakes.

When, in the early 50's, the government ban on new stations was imposed, many communities were denied adequate television service.

When our people are within reach of something good, but can't quite grasp it, they always manifest that unique American free spirit of ingenuity. They reach out.

It was then that strange looking towers began appearing on mountain tops ... towers capable of receiving more and better television signals. Those signals were carried by wire to the nearby towns and *presto* ... cable television was born! The seeds of an exciting new communications miracle had been planted. And the flowers are just beginning to bloom.

But let's not move too quickly. Before we focus on the future, let's take pause to get a picture of what happened to this maverick called television. Just three decades ago this country had as many television sets as it produced triplets. Then, from a few households television burgeoned to its present 75 million American homes. Nearly half of these homes have two or more sets and 13 percent have three sets or more.

Are the sets being watched? You bet they are! Nielsen

tells us that in 1959 the average television viewing, per home, per day, totaled four hours and 58 minutes. Ten years later, the figure was five hours and 45 minutes. This year, according to the president of ABC Television, the average American television home watches six hours and 45 minutes of television every day. Incredible as it sounds, many of us spend more time watching television than we spend on the job, or asleep.

That so many people turn to television for information and entertainment is obviously an overwhelming vote of confidence in an election that takes place every day and every night, all year long. It is ironic that the medium comes in for so much negative criticism when it performs such a positive service for its audience.

Everyone and his brother wants television to get "better", even if you could define what "better" really means. What the critics forget is that nobody wants "better" television than the industry itself. We are not in the business to make bad programs, though some might question that statement. And television has gotten better. The so-called "Golden Age" of television was made of brass compared with today's programs. Sure, television had great moments in the past. But today the programming is more diverse, consistently of much higher quality, more courageous and more innovative than ever before. News is better, sports are better done, entertainment is more varied. One problem is that there is so much good television in any given week it is harder for a single program to stand out for praise.

I have some advice for the chronic complainers: If you don't like a program, there is that little dial on the TV set that allows it to be turned off—use it! Broadcasters smile when the dial is turned on to their programs. When it is turned off, they go into instant depression. Television is a very democratic medium. It responds to its audience ... to the *ratings*. When the audience takes a holiday, the programs change and fast.

We hear constant calls for programs that are more educational and more cultural. It is a lot easier to embrace the cause of education and culture than it is to define. Someone once said, "Those who criticize television the most would like to bring others to the levels which they themselves have not achieved." There are a host of champions for so called "better" programs for the *other fellow* to watch.

Broadcasters do their damndest to serve the most diverse and demanding audience in history with more and better programs. What they often fail to do is speak out in favor of television's achievements. I think broadcasters underestimate the vitality of the medium and its positive impact on the American scene. There is always room for improvement, but there is also room for pride.

Unfortunately, this defensive attitude among some broadcasters carries over into other areas. Those of us who spend a lot of time in Washington have seen spokesmen for the industry decry every new technology as a demon. Some leaders of the television industry oppose new technologies like prudes oppose tight jeans. Limited vision forces them to regard the emerging technologies, such as cable or subscription cable as anathema. Instead of seeing opportunity, they see devils.

The television establishment has done very well indeed over the years, and it will do better in the years ahead. We get a clear sense of this growing prosperity if we look at the competitive media:

In 1978, according to McCann Erickson, the newspaper industry attracted some thirty percent of all national advertising expenditures in this country. Television got some twenty percent.

If the television industry can prosper . . . which it does . . . on a twenty percent market share . . . if the television industry could survive and triumph over the loss of ten percent of its total revenues when cigarette advertising was snuffed out . . . which it did . . . imagine the leverage the industry will obtain when it gains just one or two percentage points from the competition.

If present trends continue, it has been estimated by a research scientist, that by the year 2000, television broadcast revenues (in terms of dollars of the late 70's) will rise from the present estimated four billion to a staggering twenty-two billion dollars.

By the year 2000, the American population should grow to 260 million. The largest demographic growth curve is predicted for the population segment in the 25 to 34 year age group. Those are the most desirable viewers from a television advertiser's viewpoint. It's only logical that increased advertising dollars will flow to television and that the future is very bright. You would think these kind of statistics would allow industry leaders to be a bit more receptive to the new technologies.

Just five years from now we will have 85 million television homes. That's a lush target for advertisers. Is it any wonder ABC paid $225 million for the 1984 Olympic Games? Do you recall when it was thought imprudent for NBC to spend over $130 million for the 1980 games? The dollars needed to support the television industry are out there . . .

In the meantime, cable television has made enormous strides everywhere it is operative. Just as it took color television time to gain acceptance, it will take time for cable to flourish even further. I believe the early 1980's will be the years when cable television gives us a new communications explosion.

Today, there are more than 15 million cable television homes. More important, nearly half of all the homes in America can now avail themselves of cable service.

As the cable industry delivers alternative programming that captures more of the interest of this vast group of potential subscribers, the number of cable homes will grow even more rapidly. In a recent article, I noticed a forecast of 100 million cable homes by the year 2000.

At present growth rates, by 1985 we should have 30 to 35 million cable television subscriber homes. Among the cities now being cabled, or soon to be, are Houston, Nashville, Pittsburgh, Dallas, Minneapolis, St. Paul, Omaha and Boston.

Will the dramatic growth of cable hurt the local broadcaster? Quite the contrary. It is well known that cable-equipped homes watch more television. The cable systems help disseminate broadcast signals over a larger area. Cable viewers will watch network programs and local programs. But they will have an ever widening program choice.

Programming, in our business, is sometimes called *software.* That's a descriptive term, not a criticism. It's the software that attracts the viewer to the TV set. He, or she, couldn't care less how it gets there. Last year, *Newsweek* Magazine stated: "In the long run . . . the only consideration that truly counts is what sort of programming will come inside the new electronic packages." Yet something is happening with the delivery systems that is contributing enormously to the communications revolution.

Years ago, a science fiction writer named Arthur Clarke proposed the idea for communications satellites. As usual, reality followed imagination. By the early 1960's, what began with Sputnik beeping in Russian had given us space communications satellites with names like Echo, Telstar, Relay, Syncom, and Early Bird.

Telstar could only relay a signal for about 12 minutes as it wooshed over the horizon faster than a disco skater dancing to Beethoven. To my knowledge, nobody complained when satellite technology improved and gave us satellites that hang in stationary orbits 23,000 miles over the Earth. This development made continuous satellite communications possible.

The newly emerging cable television industry was quick to capitalize on this amazing technological breakthrough. Signals and programs could be sent, via satellite, to ground stations, and then fed into homes wired for cable service. Satellites gave cable an efficient, relatively inexpensive distribution system.

Regular cable service was supplemented by subscription cable, which provides, via satellite, unedited motion pictures, without commercial interruption. Subscription cable also provides specially produced attractions such as plays, concerts, sports, children's programming and other events to subscribers of this "second tier" of cable services.

Some members of the broadcasting fraternity saw instant doom as cable services grew. The public was told, the Congress was told that the moment pay cable reached four million subscribers it would "syphon" (that was their term, anticipating the gasoline shortage) "syphon" programs and practically all major sports events from conventional over-the-air television.

Today, we are just about at five million pay cable subscribers. Yet, somehow, the television broadcasting industry has managed to endure and muddle through with higher profits than ever. And nobody has stolen our birthright ... the Superbowl. In truth, the public has been the real beneficiary, enjoying services like *Showtime* and others.

Cable television is, at long last, providing exciting specialized services, via satellite, to its subscribers:

Our cable television industry has access to supplementary services offered by *Showtime* and its competitors. Additionally, signals from stations in Atlanta, New York, Los Angeles or San Francisco can be received. Cable subscribers can watch two children's networks, a specialized sports network, a Madison Square Garden network, gavel-to-gavel proceedings of the House of Representatives, an educational network, two religious networks and more. Soon we will offer a 24-hour news network, a black network ... the horizons are as wide as the sky.

Estimates by Drexel Burnham Lambert, Inc. forecast that by 1985, cable revenues will reach $1 to $1.5 billion dollars. Based on the recently developing trend in cable homes to buy more than one subscription cable service, and because of new services now being developed, my own estimate is that by 1985, the figure will be closer to two billion or more in cable revenues.

Half of this two or more billion dollars will be earned by program suppliers like *Showtime* and its competitors. A lot of those dollars will be reinvested to develop a broader program spectrum. Incidentally, these same estimates indicate that increased cable viewing will result in no great erosion of the conventional television audience. The few percentage points lost will be more than compensated by the overall growth in the television home universe.

The wedding of cable and satellite technologies will produce changes far beyond new programs. They will have a deep and lasting effect on our very lifestyles. Let me give you some examples ... or samples ... of the future:

Our company, on one of our cable television systems, is installing a large number of cable-energized burglary, fire and emergency alarm systems. Cable has become a protector of life and property.

Another of our cable systems is completing installation of an interconnected arraignment system which will save taxpayers vast sums of money in New York State by eliminating personal appearances of law enforcement officers and defendants before judges.

Energy conservation has become vital to America's very survival. The cable industry is experimenting with power distribution systems that could also turn appliances on and off using a cable signal from a central computer.

Our own company's cable division recently experimented with a law course fed via satellite from New York University to the McGeorge School of Law in California. At a time when the private college level educational structure is struggling for economic survival, wired instruction can make a major contribution to education.

In this great country, 134 counties are still without physicians. Two-way cable technology can help bring them medical services.

Cable television could well change the shopping habits of the nation. The presentation, and selection, of goods and services is now within our technological grasp. A lot of gasoline will be saved by at-home shoppers. This emerging technology will also have enormous impact on advertising and marketing.

There is a good chance that, by the end of the next decade, meetings like this will be considered old fashioned. Like it or not, depending on what you did last night, cable television, satellite-interconnected video meetings will be an everyday occurrence. The convention business will, in part, go electronic.

Other applications of cable technology are innumerable. We could talk about the future until we reach it, but our time is limited. There are some bases we should touch before sign-off:

By the end of this year, the cable television industry will

have about 2000 receiving Earth stations capable of obtaining a satellite signal. The television broadcast industry will have just two or three dozen Earth stations. I believe that the television industry will finally see the light and utilize satellite technology. How far is the day when the present national networks offer their affiliates not one program at a time, but via satellite, a generous "Chinese" menu of programs from which the local stations can pick up and choose depending on audience preference?

At some point in the 1980's, the relationship between networks and affiliated stations might well be the subject of a new structure in the making.

I should also mention that there are constraints implicit in current satellite technology. The maximum number of satellites assigned to use allowable broadcast frequencies will probably be limited to twenty-five. Eleven satellites are now operational. A twelfth is scheduled to be launched two days from now. There is a limit to the number of signals which can be propagated.

That's the bad news. The good news is that the cost of receiving dishes has declined from $100,000 just a few years ago to the present figure of $10,000–$25,000. In fact, the latest Nieman Marcus Christmas Catalog features your very own Earth station for only $36,000 plus tax.

Does this mean that direct satellite-to-home television is just around the corner, or cloud? I don't think so. The power required both in the sky or on the ground to make such a system practical puts direct satellite broadcasting years in the future from a cost vantage. There are also serious regulatory and political problems which must be solved.

When direct satellite-to-home communications was first proposed, the Soviet Union quickly suggested jamming incoming broadcasts by jamming frequencies, or, in a more neighborly mood, of sending up killer rockets or laser beams to knock out transmitting satellites.

A delicious sample of diplomatese can be found in the latest *United Nations General Assembly Report of the Legal Subcommittee,* which if implemented would leave us very little, if anything to put on satellites especially not news or information which could be prohibited by any of these ambiguous clauses:

I quote:

"States undertaking activities in direct television broadcasting by satellites should in all cases exclude from the television programs any material which is detrimental to the maintenance of international peace and security, which publicizes ideas of war, militarism, national and racial hatred and enmity between peoples, which is aimed at interfering in the domestic affairs of other States or which undermines the foundations of the local civilization, culture, way of life, traditions or language."

Again, the whole concept of satellite-to-home broadcasting brings with it enormous political and regulatory baggage.

We are in a period of great technological advance. We see evidence in the enormous growth of the video tape cassette market, and we will see the video disc catch on quickly. Estimates tell us that by year-end, a million video cassette players will have been sold, using different standards and vastly different formats.

The video disc is about to enter the marketplace. The only thing the video disc industry has to fear is confusion in the buyer's mind. The record industry opted for incompatible standards requiring different players for different records. The video cassette industry did the same. And now potential buyers must not only be sold on the video disc, but on which kind of video disc . . . stylus or laser or what have you.

A software supplier, such as ourselves, will not worry which standard is used to reproduce the software. But we do worry about consumer confusion possibly slowing up a great technology of enormous potential in the fields of entertainment, education and information. We hope the industry finds a way to make its products compatible for their sake, for our sake and for the sake of the buyer.

As these new technologies come to maturity, more and more software will be required. This will be a boon to creative communities such as the one here in Hollywood. One of the most plaguing problems has been underemployment of actors, writers and other creative people. The new demand for product will alleviate much of that stress.

But a word of caution . . . a word to the unions . . . to the guilds representing this valuable creative resource: An urgent word . . . In the past, many of the unions and guilds have recognized the value of supporting new distribution methods and technologies. On the other hand, some unions did not, became greedy to what I believe was the ultimate serious detriment of their membership. Give these new technologies like pay cable the opportunity to take root and grow. My word to the union and the guilds is: Give these innovations the chance to survive their infancy before overwhelming them with demands, clauses, fees and the like. The future is golden. Constraint in the present will result in a bountiful harvest, if the plant is not cut off at the seedling stage.

Conversely, the timetable for the success of the electronic packages depends on the programming offered to the huge potential audience. Give us the creative skills to make the programs and we'll give you a tremendous arena in which to showcase your talents.

A responsive, participating audience is certain to emerge. It will be a demanding audience, more sophisticated in taste and preference than any audience before. It will challenge us to our best, and we will meet that challenge.

We are on the threshold of an exciting decade. Electronic technology is our bridge to the future. We must not inhibit this miracle from finding its place in the world . . . from actually changing our world for the better.

We must match the miracles with miracles of vision . . . miracles of service.

In conclusion, let me leave you with these words spoken by the late Edward R. Murrow:

"In this ever changing world in which many people, in one generation, seek to accomplish the changes of centuries, this country has a great role to fill."

WE HAVE SEEN THE FUTURE OF VIDEO[4]

Nicholas Johnson is smiling, for at last there is hope. As network television's most vociferous critic, he has railed for years against the abominations of the tube, especially the "tyranny of banal mass-audience programming." But the tyranny persisted. Now, however, what is being hailed as the "video revolution" has arrived. "It will be a long time dying," says Johnson, "but the television industry as it's presently known is obsolete." It is only a matter of time, many TV critics predict, before we will witness an electronic unplugging of cataclysmic moment: the demise of the three networks and, even more important, the extinguishment of the "vast wasteland" of images inflicted on our eyeballs for a quarter century.

The instruments of this historic dissolution, as the critics see it, are the three new video technologies that underlie the video revolution:

1. Cable television systems that now transmit over wire to more than fifteen million homes, 20 percent of those with TV sets. For an average of $7 per month, subscribers receive as many as thirty-five channels of programming. About five million homes pay an additional fee for pay-television channels of special programs.

2. Communications satellites that permit low-cost national video transmission to cable systems.

3. Consumer videotape recorders and videodisc players that allow viewers to replace regular network schedules with an extensive variety of home videotape and disc programs.

These technologies, in which such major corporations as IBM, General Electric, Time Inc., American Express, and the New York Times Company have invested millions of dollars, permit viewers and program producers to bypass the heretofore impregnable oligopoly of the airwaves maintained by the

[4] Reprint of magazine article by Chris Welles, contributing editor. *Esquire.* 93:89–95. Je. '80. Used by permission of the author.

three commercial networks. That oligopoly originated mainly from the scarcity of broadcast space on the VHF spectrum, which restricted most communities to no more than three usable channels. Gradually, local stations were linked into three national networks that came to pursue the same business strategy: to maximize profits by attracting the largest possible audiences with what critics term "lowest common denominator" programs. The audiences are then sold, in effect, to advertisers of mass-market consumer products. Network domination of the broadcast airwaves—the only means of electronic visual access to national audiences—always foreclosed serious rivals.

Cable, satellites, and home video devices change all this: They are essentially new distribution systems with virtually unlimited channel capacity. It is as if OPEC were confronted with an inexhaustible new source of petroleum. Numerous video doomsayers predict that the proliferation of new channels will fragment and siphon away the bulk of the networks' audience and their advertising revenues.

As the network oligopoly collapses, we will progress, it is said, toward a glorious new golden age of video programming. It will be a bountiful refoliation of the wasteland, a realization of the promise displayed briefly by television during the golden age of the early 1950s, the era of such widely praised shows as *Playhouse 90*, *Studio One*, and *See It Now*.

The most salient feature of the new video's golden age, according to predictions, will be what futurist Alvin Toffler calls in his new book, *The Third Wave* [Morrow, '80], the "demassification" of television. Says Toffler, "We're going to move from a few images distributed widely to many images distributed narrowly." The new narrowcasting will consist of dozens, perhaps hundreds, of sharply focused channels serving the television audience's vastly diverse affinities and tastes. Instead of docilely submitting to mindless, mass-taste network schedules, the viewer will become his own programmer and create his own schedule from the abundance of much more civilized, intelligent, and imaginative fare delivered by the new technologies. With these technologies as weapons,

Chicago Tribune TV critic Gary Deeb wrote recently, angry viewers "are striking back at the networks that have trampled them and treated them like slobs for so long."

This possesses the irresistible melodramatic appeal of a prime-time miniseries: After years of horrible subjugation, hapless and disgruntled viewers now have the means to dispatch their oppressors into oblivion, seize control of their television sets, and watch what *they* want to watch, not what somebody else wants them to watch.

Close scrutiny of this melodrama, though, reveals some unfortunate plot flaws. The networks, it turns out, are much less vulnerable than they appear. The new weapons being used against them are not very effective and may not be weapons at all. And the viewers don't seem very interested in a revolution.

Michael Fuchs, head of programming for Home Box Office, the largest pay-TV service and a subsidiary of Time Inc., is sitting on a couch in his office in the Time & Life Building. The new videocasters, just like the old broadcasters, are, for the most part, scattered along a short stretch of Manhattan's Sixth Avenue, and from his couch Fuchs has a clear view of the headquarters of CBS, NBC, and ABC.

They also have a clear view of him, which is appropriate, since HBO has emerged as the fourth network. With over four million subscribers, two thirds of the pay-TV market, HBO is by far the most successful new videocaster. With the possible exception of Showtime, its much smaller rival, it is the only one to produce a large volume of original programming, to attract a substantial audience, and to present a serious threat to the three older networks.

HBO's new-video images, however, bear a surprisingly close resemblance to those of its old-video competitors. Its basic fare is popular entertainment: recently released movies, which it can transmit without commercials or cuts (due to its exemption from FCC program regulations); sports events; and original specials, typically nightclub-style shows with stars like Diana Ross and Robin Williams. Among other recent HBO shows was *National Lampoon Presents Disco Bea-*

ver from Outer Space, which included a segment called "The
Breast Game," a bare-breasted parody of TV game shows.

"We're trying to make HBO special," says Fuchs, a
young, fast-talking lawyer who previously packaged TV
properties for the William Morris Agency. "It's not commercial TV. We have tremendous built-in advantages over the
networks—language, nudity. But we're still appealing to a
mass audience. Our people are not freaks. They're the same
people who watch the networks. They're TV watchers." To
build viewer loyalty, HBO is currently developing network-
style series. "We're not looking to reinvent the wheel," Fuchs
says. "Everything in this business is derivative."

HBO arrived at its present programming mix after disappointing experiences with special-interest cultural programs—just the sort of shows, in fact, that critics have been
counting on the video revolution to deliver.

"We learned with a lot of hard knocks," Fuchs says. "We
tried culture. We had *The Pallisers* [a BBC series based on the
Anthony Trollope novels] on the air. I think it would be wonderful if the American public had a cultural channel. But I
don't know anybody in the business who believes the country
is ready for that. We decided the only way we could make
money was entertainment. If tomorrow we said to people: no
movies, all culture ... well, then, good-bye business. In a
way, the process is very democratic. The subscribers vote
every month. You've got to keep your eye on that box office."

Old video is the chief stock-in-trade of most of the other
new videocasters as well. Showtime also features movies and
entertainment specials, including a reunion of *Playboy* Play-
mates and a Miss Nude California contest. Showtime has
taped *The Ed McMahon Show* as a possible pilot for a weekly
series. Most nonpay cable channels are merely signals from
existing broadcast stations. The other channels carry various
satellite-transmitted cable services consisting of such derivative and traditional programming as old movies, network
reruns, and sports events. Beyond automated time and
weather channels, local cable operators do relatively little serious origination of their own. As CBS Broadcast Group presi-

dent Gene F. Jankowski put it in a discussion of cable television, "It is a case of new technology clothing itself in the timeworn hand-me-downs and tattered castoffs of established and accepted broadcasting."

Home video, so far, is no different. Virtually all of the available "software," as videocasters call programming, for videotape recorders and disc players consists of movies. (As much as 60 percent of prerecorded videotape sales are pornographic films.) Most videotape recorder owners use their machines mainly to "time shift," to record regular television broadcasts for later viewing.

Predictions that the video revolution will vanquish established broadcast programming misconstrue what the revolution is all about. The revolution is basically one of technology—the way signals get to your TV set. Cable, satellite, and home video may eventually supplant most over-the-air transmission. But the signals distributed by the new technologies are not a revolutionary new medium that will necessarily make existing television shows obsolete the way the telegraph replaced the pony express. What people call the new video is not a new medium at all. It is television.

As they become more broadly applied, the new technologies will spur wider experimentation with new forms of television. The new video will not be a precise replica of the old video, but it is unlikely to be very different. As television, the new video is subject to the same inescapable economic exigencies that have always dictated the content of the old video. Whether it is dominated by CBS or Time Inc., television is economics first, art and everything else second. Those economics require that television essentially remain a mass medium catering to mass tastes. "The new technology," says Benton & Bowles senior vice-president George Simko, "will be driven by software that appeals to the largest number of people."

Most television programs are extraordinarily expensive to produce: $600,000 or more for a typical prime-time hour. A broadcaster must deliver a very large audience to advertisers just to cover his costs. Moreover, the cost of a program, unlike that of a magazine, is fixed and independent of the size of its audience. This means that a larger audience generates not only greater revenues for the broadcaster but also larger profits and profit margins. The broadcaster has no incentive to aim for a small audience when for the same cost he can aim for a larger audience and make a bigger profit.

Though it obtains its revenues from subscribers, pay television is ruled by the same economic incentives. Most pay-TV subscribers pay a flat monthly fee for the entire service instead of separate per-program assessments. Thus it is in the economic interest of a pay service to spend its program budget on shows that please the largest number of subscribers. "The dynamics of video are that you can't satisfy little disparate tastes," says Fuchs. "We can't do a show on stamp collecting for one percent of the audience."

Some new-video entrepreneurs, nevertheless, are actively pursuing narrowcasting. Narrowcast networks appealing to such special interests as blacks, children, Spanish Americans, and sports buffs are transmitting programs by satellite to thousands of cable systems.

The narrowcasters' financial success has been marginal, though, because they too are ruled by television economics. Since the channels are provided free to cable subscribers, the narrowcasters are dependent on advertising. And as national services, they have had to seek business from the same mass-consumer-goods companies that advertise on the broadcast networks. Those companies buy narrowcast time the way they buy broadcast time—on a cost-per-thousand-viewers basis. As special-interest services, though, the narrowcasts predictably obtain very low ratings—usually a fraction of a percent of the cable audience—and thus very low ad revenues. Total ad income for the cable industry in 1978, according to the FCC, was just $4.9 million, versus $8 billion for commercial TV broadcasting. A channel of USA Network sports events, perhaps the most popular of the narrowcast services, collected $2 million in ad income in 1979. That is about the cost of four minutes of commercials during a Super Bowl broadcast.

Meager ad revenues have forced the narrowcasters to rely

mostly on dated and derivative programming from other media, especially movies. SIN National Spanish Television Network, a Spanish-language station, offers soap operas produced for South American television. Rather than risk developing new forms, most of the handful of narrowcasters producing original programs merely adapt traditional network formats to special audiences. Discussing the time when Black Entertainment Television network, which now airs black movies two hours a week, will have the funds for its own programs, president Robert Johnson remarked that "the black talk shows, sitcoms, and game shows are only a few years away."

Other narrowcasters are trying low-cost production schemes. Cable News Network, an all-news station scheduled to begin operating June 1, intends to produce twenty-four hours of news daily with a staff of 250 and an annual budget of $25 million. By contrast, each of the broadcast network news divisions, which produce far fewer hours of programming, has a staff of over a thousand and an annual budget of $150 million and is expanding the resources and time devoted to news. "Dollars always force compromises," concedes CNN president Reese Schonfeld. "But people who like news would rather watch news, even plain pipe-rack news, then *Charlie's Angels.*" Instead of tightly edited "high gloss" newscasts, he says, CNN will stress more informally produced live, on-the-scene reports.

Most low-budget narrowcast ventures, though, have fared badly. "The public is spoiled," says Fuchs. "They're used to the lushest video." Robert Rosencrans, president of UA-Columbia Cablevision, which produces the USA Network sports service, says he must use the same slow-motion, instant-replay, multiangle camera techniques the commercial networks use. "It's very expensive," he says, "but you can't get away with cutting corners." The less money a narrowcaster spends on programs, the fewer viewers are likely to be lured away from more attractively produced network and pay-TV shows. Fewer viewers, in turn, means an even lower program budget.

"We try to be supportive of these efforts," says Charles

Dolan, founder of HBO and now operator of a cable system in the New York suburbs that is one of the country's largest. "But that doesn't prevent me from being skeptical. I don't think any of them have shown they are viable."

As new-video entrepreneurs continue to look for ways to circumvent television's mass-market economics and develop imaginative alternatives to the old video, some are certain to achieve viability if not prosperity. Though television economics will require most videotape and disc software to have mass appeal, for instance, many experts foresee a respectable market for high-priced, low-budget instructional tapes and discs on such subjects as cooking and golfing.

Rather than develop custom programming or attempt to outbid the networks for programs and talent, as is often predicted, most videocasters will simply continue to plug themselves into existing mass-market video distribution systems. High production costs, the dearth of top-quality talent and product, and the substantial risks of market failure have always required what the trade calls "sequential" distribution. Movies, for instance, are routed from theaters to network television to independent stations. Pay TV, tape, and discs have been forcing themselves into the front end of the movie distribution cycle, ahead of network television. Pay TV will probably sell original shows to the tape and disc market and perhaps even to commercial television.

The major software packagers and suppliers, though, will likely continue to be the three networks. No mere electromagnetic OPEC, the networks have become enormously powerful, wealthy, and efficient. They completely dominate television's production, distribution, and promotion mechanisms. They are creatures less of electronics than of economics, especially economies of scale. They are less dependent on sophisticated technologies than on sophisticated corporate management and strategy.

Compared to cable's $50 million, the networks spend $2.5 billion a year on programming. They produce a rising number of movies, have recently established divisions to create software and hardware for the home video market, and plan to supply programs to pay-TV and even narrowcast services. Not coincidentally, broadcasters own over 30 percent of the nation's cable systems. Says former CBS News president Fred Friendly: "In the end, the networks will dominate [the new video]. They have the money, the know-how, and the savvy."

The new video, in sum, will continue to be more of the same old mass-appeal wasteland software that we have all come to know and to loathe. But do we really loathe it?

At the Sixth Avenue offices of A. C. Nielsen Company, the television industry's scorekeeper, researchers traffic not in dreams, hopes, and fears but in statistical measures of observable behavior.

"If you ask people whether they want to see something like Shakespeare on television, half of them will say they do," says David Harkness, a marketing manager for Nielsen. "They want the interviewer to think well of them. But when you put Shakespeare on TV, nobody watches. You have to be very suspicious when people tell you what their intentions are. That can be a lot different from what they really do.

"I think people are somewhat dissatisfied with TV. But when you offer them something different they don't take it, because they aren't really all that dissatisfied. The American public has a great love affair with the TV set. Consumers today complain about a lot of things. But you don't see mass protests to make TV better."

Some data from Nielsen surveys:

1. Viewing hours per person in 1979 reached an all-time high of 3.9 hours a day, up 11 percent over the past five years.

2. Largely due to cable television expansion, the percentage of TV homes able to receive many channels has been increasing sharply. Between 1970 and 1980, for instance, the percentage receiving eight or more stations rose from 37 to 57.

3. The growth in viewing and viewing options has so far had a negligible impact on the networks' long-standing 90-percent share of the prime-time audience. Of the new video services, only pay TV has displayed any erosion capability. A Nielsen study of a sample month, November 1979, found that

in the seven percent of homes that are pay subscribers, pay channels had an average prime-time share of 15 percent, versus the networks' 79 percent. Nearly all the remaining viewing by the pay families was of other commercial stations. The audience share of all nonpay programs produced specially for cable systems, including the narrowcasts, was about one percent. Only six percent of the pay-TV homes viewed *any* cable programming during the sample month.

4. Instead of replacing network shows, most of the new video seems to be viewed in addition to commercial television. Pay-TV homes, for instance, watch four more hours a week of television than families without pay TV. Says David Harkness, "They're not watching HBO to avoid the trash on the networks. When they're not watching HBO, they're watching *Laverne and Shirley* in heavy quantities. They enjoy TV so much that they're willing to pay for more."

Nielsen does not forecast. But the overwhelming consensus of new and old videocasters is that during the current decade the three networks will suffer an erosion in audience share, mainly due to pay TV, of no more than 10 percent. Even that figure presumes rapid growth in cable and home video penetration. In the past, that growth has lagged behind most estimates.

As someone with a very low opinion of most network television, I would dearly love to believe, as so many critics do, that the industry is grossly underestimating public taste. I would love to believe that armed with the new video, viewers will soon shout they're mad as hell and will resolve not to take it anymore. But if one searches for even a few traces of yearnings for better programs and inclinations toward revolution, next to nothing is found. For years, public television has striven valiantly to present a cultured, civilized alternative to network television. But despite increased emphasis on entertainment programming, no more than two percent of the prime-time audience regularly tunes in. Meanwhile, during any given minute in prime time, close to a hundred million faithful Americans have their sets hooked up to the wasteland. The real enemy, as has often been observed in other contexts, is us.

Those who regard the networks as tyrants fail to appreciate the function most of us assign to television. The millions who watch regularly are not necessarily cultural ignoramuses, intellectual dwarfs, indiscriminate clones of some prototypical Mass Viewer. Many read good books, go to museums, and pursue sophisticated special interests. But when they sit down in front of the TV set, usually at the end of a day of work, they are generally not looking for cultural uplift or particularized information. Says Harlan Kleiman, a former avant-garde Off Broadway producer who now makes programs for various pay-TV services: "People just want to be diverted. TV is chewing gum for the eyes."

Viewers' tastes in televised diversion are sufficiently homogeneous and unsophisticated that most are satisfied, if not excited, by such standard entertainment formats as sitcoms and adventure shows. Studies show that better-educated viewers watch the same programs as less-educated viewers.

The tube may offer more then mere diversion. Regular viewers tend to turn on the set less to watch a specific program than simply to watch *something*. Studies suggest that the swift flow of flickering images can have an anesthetizing, almost stupefying, effect on the brain. Some researchers have termed the set an "electronic fireplace." Television seems effective in obliterating rumination on the often unpleasant outside world, though what, if anything, it instills remains unclear.

While the broadcasters effectively serve the needs of the great mass of the television audience, critics are correct in charging that the broadcasters, for economic reasons, have ignored fringe tastes and interests. If the video revolution is not materially affecting the mass, it is at least presenting more options for those on the fringes. "What we've done is democratize television," says Kleiman, "so that many marginal and peripheral markets can exist. They're only going to get a tiny fragment of the audience, but they're going to have the opportunity to reach that fragment. That's what the revolution is." Pornographic films, local basketball games, bawdy nightclub acts, black sitcoms—the current content of these peripheral markets—may not be much to cheer about. But Michael

Rice, who before becoming head of the Aspen Institute program on communications and society was general manager of Boston's WGBH, perhaps the most adventurous public television station, does not despair. "Critics who have bemoaned commercial television have typically shared the view that what we need is more demanding drama, more controversy, more serious music," he says. "Basically, their complaint is that TV has not been geared to *their* interests and tastes. But there is a lot more to diversity. The Spanish-language network isn't a rival of *Studio One*, but it does serve a special interest. The new video may be more effective in satisfying that kind of diversity than the long-cherished hope that television could raise the level of civilization."

This is not the end of the story. Recall what Michael Fuchs of HBO said about subscribers' voting every month. Network viewers vote every time they turn the dial. Now consider two groups of voters. Though millions loyally tune in *Laverne and Shirley*, there are probably as many who almost never watch TV. Charles Dolan, the cable operator, says that beyond a certain point it becomes almost impossible to increase cable's penetration of a community. Signing up the holdouts, he claims, "is like selling Bibles to people who don't believe in God." These people could start voting.

Then there are the millions who do watch *Laverne and Shirley*. Fred Friendly accuses the networks of a "self-fulfilling prophecy of defeat. They have been degrading American taste, hour after hour." Degrading, perhaps, but not destroying. These people could change their votes.

More options are now available to us as voters. More people are soliciting our votes. More people are watching the ballot box. If enough of us want something different, we have the power to get it.

HOME TV: THE FUTURE LIES AHEAD[5]

In a suburb outside Madison, Wisconsin, ordinary house-wife Marilyn Sprinbok, 32, is watching *Days of Our Lives* on her nineteen-inch Chromocolor portable. The set looks ordinary, too, except for a small, designer-beige junction box perched on top. "Yes, I'm absolutely normal in every respect," says the pert, cheerful Mrs. Sprinbok to a visitor. Suddenly, in the midst of a Knox Gelatin commercial, the little box begins to hum and the TV screen goes blank.

BIG SALE ON HERCULON FLOOR COVERINGS, HONEST BOB'S HOUSE OF VAL-U'S, ARCADIA, INDIANA, reads a bright yellow "crawl" across the bottom of the screen. Mrs. S. utters a squeal of delight, turns to a computer console concealed in a nearby credenza and "calls up" all the information needed to make airline, hotel and railroad flatcar reservations.

"Basically, the problem in your Arab and Islamic countries is that there's nothing in their religion to encourage uniform unit pricing," says Robert Whitefinger, 72. Whitefinger, a resident of Idle Vistas Mobile Rancho, a senior citizens encampment near Bradenton, Florida, is this week's guest host of *Let's Ramble,* a weekly travel program taped and piped, via closed-circuit cable, to all Idle Vista residents not in arrears on their LP gas payments. Whitefinger, a retired manufacturer of industrial aprons, looks right into the camera as he recounts some amusing adventures in the Islamabad bazaar during a recent Good Sam Club package tour. "Cue up those slides, how about it?" he says to an offstage technician.

"We need a coherent and sensible snowmobile import policy—and we need it now," says Congressman Bob Bovril (Democrat, Michigan). Bovril is being interviewed by local Optimist Club officials on a show called *Hello Out There,* produced by OmniVision, a Flint cable TV company owned

---

[5] Reprint of magazine article by Andy Meisler, senior editor, *New West.* 5:8–9. Ag. 11, '80. Copyright © 1980 by the New York Magazine Company, Inc. Reprinted with the permission of *New West* magazine.

by the giant OverCorp conglomerate. But this is no ordinary public affairs program: For one, it is the most popular new show in the cable subscription area. For another, it incorporates a "two-way" factor that may revolutionize the medium.

About midway through the show, which is very dull, a series of high-pitched beeps alerts the viewer, and a close-up of the congressman is freeze-framed.

HOW DO YOU LIKE MY SUIT? reads a computer generated printout across his chest.

All over the Flint area, unseen hands operate small "joysticks" attached to their televisions. Within seconds their votes, tabulated in a special "feedback room," are displayed on the screen.

YES: 31%, NO: 47%, NOT WATCHING—COME AGAIN?: 22%, reads the readout.

Congressman Bovril, who faces a tough reelection fight this fall—his opponent is funded by wealthy creosote manufacturing interests—blanches visibly under his thick Pan-Gloss makeup.

Science fiction? A vision of television's distant future? "Not so," says television visionary Nathan LeNovsky. Dr. LeNovsky, holder of the prestigious Magnavox Chair of Applied Video at the University of Northern California, has just completed an intensive 39-week study of TV's exploding possibilities. "The existing technology exists now," he says excitedly. "In ten or fifteen years, television's 'traditional' function—that of a handy conduit for little tiny dots—will be largely a thing of the past."

By 1990, he says, today's deluxe floor model will be as obsolete as a one-button blender. Right now, at this very second, he admits, "advanced electronic debtor items" like videotape recorders (VTRs), cable TV (CTV) hookups and tiny windowsill radar dishes capable of receiving far-flung satellite transmissions (TWRDCRFSTs) are considered expensive luxuries.

"But marketing breakthroughs will soon transform them into expensive necessities," says LeNovsky. Soon, he predicts, these purchases will be considered no more "optional" than a digital clock radio or electric hedge trimmer.

Even more important: "We're heading toward what I call a 'wired nation' capability," says LeNovsky. Tooth-rattling, impossible-to-bill over-the-air transmissions will be discontinued; bulky cables, inefficient antennae and unsightly foil-wrapped coat hangers will be replaced by fiber-optic wires no thicker than a camel's hair. Literally hundreds of old movies, Reuters newswires and Evinrude safe-boating instructional films will reach your home screen simultaneously. "And when the whole world is wired," adds LeNovsky, "individual television sets, governed by 'smart' on/off switches, will be able to interface ['schmooze' is the technical term] with any television, computer or garage-door opener anywhere."

The myriad possibilities are just beginning to be explored. Marilyn Sprinbok's Zenith, for example, is part of an experimental "credit grid" hooked up to a giant Household Finance computer. Bob Whitefinger's closed-circuit "network" is carried over innocent-looking recreational sewage lines. And the feedback that so vexed Congressman Bovril (and, eventually, convinced him to resign his post and become a highly paid lobbyist for the road salt industry) was made possible by *Backsass*, a $35-a-month feature that will soon become available to subscribers in Syosset, Long Island, and Nutrioso, Arizona.

What else is in store for the unsuspecting viewer?

"A lot," says LeNovsky.

Home television sets, hooked to computerized thermostats and doorbells, will be able to simultaneously adjust room temperature, keep out unwanted visitors, display the latest NYSE stock prices and make major career decisions. Personal finances will be a snap: Citizens will simply type in all income and expenses, garnishees and tax liens, and crack network accountants—keeping a handy videotape record for the IRS—will instantaneously flash back a five-year "discretionary purchase plan" (DPP).

"Television will cook your meals, handle small-claims court lawsuits, attend high school reunions," says LeNovsky.

LeNovsky reaches back to his bookcase. Concealed behind a stack of *Reader's Digest* condensed books is a small, sleek-looking TV set. Inserting a dollar bill into a hidden slot, LeNovsky activates the futuristic-looking computer. There is brief confusion on the screen, a snippet of an old *Watch Mr. Wizard* episode, the theme song from *Big Time Wrestling* and then silence.

PLEASE STAND BY, reads a bright green computer-generated placard.

"I can hardly wait," says the happy Dr. L.

BIBLIOGRAPHY

An asterisk (°) preceding a reference indicates that the article or part of it has been reprinted in this book.

BOOKS AND PAMPHLETS

Arlen, Michael J. The camera age: essays on television. Farrar, Straus & Giroux. '81.
Arlen, Michael J. Thirty seconds. Farrar, Straus & Giroux. '80.
Fang, I. E. Television news. Hastings House. '72.
Johnson, Nicholas. How to talk back to your television set. Atlantic Monthly Press. '70.
Lesser, G. S. Children and television: lessons from Sesame Street. Vintage Books. '74.
Mander, Jerry. Four arguments for the elimination of television. Morrow. '78.
Smith, R. L. and Gallagher, R. B. The emergence of pay cable television. Volumes 1 & 2. Overview and final report prepared for National Telecommunications & Information Administration by Technology & Economics Inc. July '80.
Winn, Marie. The plug-in drug. Viking Press. '77.

PERIODICALS

° American Film. 5:30–5. Mr. '80. God's television. Edwin Diamond.
° American Film. 5:37–40. Jl./Ag. '80. News: television's bargain basement. Laurence Bergreen.
American Film. 6:19–22. S. '80. Thy neighbor's television. Edwin Diamond.
° American Film. 6:74+ O. '80. All the news that isn't news. Edwin Diamond.
American Film. 6:21–8. N. '80. The video scene. Amy Greenfield.
American Film. 6:61–5. N. '80. A question of quality. Robert Sklar.
American Film. 6:13–4. D. '80. About television. Martin Mayer.
American Film. 6:42–4. D. '80. Television's phantom audience. Robert Sklar.
American Film, 6:38–44. Ja./F. '81. What every parent should know about television. D. G. Singer, Jerome Singer, D. M. Zuckerman.

* Atlantic. 245:99–101. Apr. '80. Newspaper days: politics—we are the hostages. W. S. Just.

Attenzione. 2:74–5. S. '80. Media: Uncle Floyd. George Shea.

Bioscience. 30:440. Jl. '80. Chewing gum for the eyes; discussion. J. P. Hailman.

Business Week. p 16–9. S. 1, '80. Convention sponsors ignore the TV ratings.

Business Week. p 62–4+. D. 8, '80. Cable TV: the race to plug in.

Cablevision. 6:72–118. D. 15, '80. Wire wars. Fred Dawson.

Cablevision. 6:128–240+ D. 15, '80. Media concentration. Victoria Gits.

Commentary. 69:75–81. Ap. '80. On the air. Samuel Lipman.

Current. 223:14–8. Je. '80. Media and the news [interview by Marguerite Michaels]. Walter Cronkite.

Editorial Research Reports. v 1, no 17:331–348. My. 9, '80. Television in the eighties. Marc Leepson.

* Esquire. 93:89–90+. Je. '80. We have seen the future of video. Chris Welles.

Esquire. 94:88–9. D. '80. Walter Cronkite: a dossier. Betsy Carter.

Forbes. 126:35–6. S. 1, '80. Video fever. K. K. Wiegner.

Fortune. 102:66–70+. Ag. 25, '80. Boss as pitchman. A. M. Morrison.

GEO. 2:152–3. N. '80. The television factor. Daniel Schorr.

Home Video. 2:34–7. Ja. '81. I have seen the video future and it is sex. Isaac Asimov.

Journal of Broadcasting. 23:393–409. Fall '79. Television networks, competition and program diversity. B. R. Litman.

Journal of Communication. 28:19–29. Winter '78. Children's social behavior in three towns with differing television experience. J. P. Murray and Susan Kippax.

Ms. Magazine. 9:26. S. '80. Reporter herself is news. J. C. Stucker.

* Nation. 230:506–8. Ap. 26, '80. Television. M. C. Miller and Karen Runyon.

* National Review. 32:358. Mr. 21, '80. Dangerous to your health. Michael Novak.

New Republic. 183:6+. S. 6 & 13, '80. White House watch: debate and switch. John Osborne.

New York. 13:25–30. Jl. 28, '80. Superstar agent of TV news. H. D. Shapiro.

New York. 13:38–40+. N. 17, '80. Good-bye, Dallas, hello, videodiscs. Michael Schrage.

New York. 13:12–3. D. 22, '80. Sporting life. Vic Ziegel.

* The New York Review of Books. 27:11–5. Ag. 14, '80. Elections: why the system has failed. Tom Wicker.

New York Times. p D 27. Je. 29, '80. Can television lead children to reading? Grace Hechinger and F. M. Hechinger.

* New York Times. p C 4. Ag. 26, '80. About Education. F. M. Hechinger.

*New York Times. p A19. S. 3, '80. A few words of his own. Russell Baker.

New York Times. p D 43. O. 12, '80. Why network evening newscasts might soon be an hour long. H. J. Gans.

New York Times. p S 2. O. 12, '80. Recalling the joy of watching baseball on the radio. Mark Harris.

New York Times. p D 22, D. 7, '80. Who's behind the Nightline success story? J. J. O'Connor.

New York Times. p A 35. D. 12. '80. Projections and voters. Laurily Epstein and Gerald Strom.

New York Times. p D 1+. D. 18, '80. Video cassettes get a big play. N. R. Kleinfeld.

New York Times. p S 6. D. 21, '80. TV without voice: a neophyte's report. R. F. Shepard.

New York Times. p C 24. Ja. 8, '81. WNYC will aim for small groups. C. G. Fraser.

New York Times. p D 1+. Ja. 9, '81. The computer as retailer.

New York Times Book Review. 85:43–4. S. 14, '80. Paperback talk. Ray Walters.

* New West. 5:8–9. Ag. 11, '80. Home TV: the future lies ahead. Andy Meisler.

* New Yorker. 56:172–4+. O. 27, '80. The air. M. J. Arlen.

Newsweek. 96:24–5. S. 22, '80. And then there were two. D. M. Alpern and others.

Newsweek. 96:101+. O. 27, '80. Magazines to turn the viewer on. Arlie Schardt and others.

Newsweek. 96:65–6. D. 15, '80. Sex and the anchor person. H. F. Waters and G. Hackett.

Next. 2:34–9. Ja. '81. For commercial TV, either a new beginning or the end. Martin Mayer.

Next. 2:62. Ja. '81. In the matter of Benkorama. Lewis Grossberger.

Panorama. 1:60–1. F. '80. Waiting for Uncle Miltie. Scot Haller.

Panorama. 1:40–2. My. '80. Television is a member of the family. D. G. Singer.

Panorama. 1:38+. N. '80. The sexual revolution: is TV keeping pace with our society? Marcia Seligson.

Panorama. 1:52–5+. N. '80. They surely won't throw *this* newspaper on your doorstep. Ron Powers.

Panorama. 1:46–9+. D. '80. Public television in crisis: this could
be the countdown to extinction. Doug Hill.

People. 14:37–8+. Ag. 11, '80. Is television the real power at the
convention? Dan Rather (interview by C. P. Andersen).

People. 14:66+. S. 15, '80. Like most Americans, the McKees are
neck-deep in bills, but they're green ones thanks to Tic tac
dough. A. F. Gonzalez.

° Progressive. 44:28–30. Mr. '80. Salivation through television.
Mark Voorhees.

° Psychology Today. 13:6+. Ja. '80. Reprogramming the media researchers. Howard Gardner.

° Psychology Today. 14:26+. Ag. '80. Television. Berkeley Rice.

Rolling Stone. p 17–9+. F. 5, '81. Walter, we hardly knew you.
Timothy White.

The Runner. 2:45–9. S. '80. Running on TV: boom or bust? J. O.
Dunaway.

Saturday Evening Post. 252:66–71. D. '80. Muppets on the move.
Hank Nuwer.

Saturday Review. 7:26–7. Mr. 29, '80. Television. Peter Andrews.

° Saturday Review. 7:30–2. N. '80. Television news: seeing isn't
believing. Peter Funt.

Saturday Review. 8:36–8. Ja. '81. Can PBS survive cable? Peter
Caranicas.

Science & Mechanics. Summer, '80. 51–4. Satellite-to-home TV.
Robert Perry.

° Sight and Sound. 48:19–22. Winter '78/79. The TV Plexus.
James Monaco.

Sight and Sound. 48:148–50+. Summer '79. Television may never
be the same again. John Howkins.

Sight and Sound. 49:87–90. Spring '80. TV weather. David Thom-
son.

Television and Children. 3:29–31. Fall '80. Television and the
inner drama of young children. Basil Cox.

Television and Children. 3:40–9. Fall '80. Television and children's behavior: past fears, present worries, future hopes. J. P.
Murray.

Time. 116:22–3. Jl. 28, '80. Part ritual, part TV show. J. F. Stacks.

Time. 116:97. S. 15, '80. Degrees for video watchers.

° Time. 116:90+. O. 13, '80. Incredible? or abominable? Martha
Smilgis.

Time. 116:62–6+. D. 1, '80. Battle for the morning. Gerald Clarke
and others.

° Today's Education. 69:48GE–52GE. S.-O. '80. Schools and the
power of television [interview by Maria Robbins]. Terry
Herndon.

Today's Education. 69:55GE–6GE. S.-O. '80. Why we need critical viewing skills. F. B. Withrow.

* Today's Education. 69:66GE–8GE. S.-O. '80. FCC takes a hard look at television. C. D. Ferris.

* TV Guide. 28:11–15. O. 11, '80. Bye-bye, pledge week. Paul Warren.

TV Guide. 29:4–8. Ja. 10, '81. When is TV too scary for children? Katie Leishman.

TV Guide. 29:4–10. Ja. 24, '81. Is CBS news still supreme? Sally Bedell.

* USA Today. 109:61. S. '80. Lively arts. Joe Saltzman.

* USA Today. 109:62–4, S. '80. Mass media. James Roman.

* US News & World Report. 88:70. Mr. 17, '80. Americans are "haunted by a fear of technology." D. J. Boorstin.

US News & World Report. 89:20–1. S. 22, '80. Carter's big gamble.

Videography. 5:65–9. Ag. '80. David Keller: youthful optimist/nihilist. Victor Ancona.

* Vital Speeches of the Day. 46:209–13. Ja. 15, '80. Lifestyle revolutions in the television age. R. M. Baruch.

* Vital Speeches of the Day. 45:412–6. Ap. 15, '80. The corporation in a world of media diversity. Sol Hurwitz.

Vital Speeches of the Day. 46:473–6. My. 15, '80. Press conference. J. J. Duome.

* Vital Speeches of the Day. 46:487–93. Je. 1, '80. Electronic democracy. A. R. Saldich.

Vital Speeches of the Day. 46:670–2. Ag. 15, '80. Press Freedom. W. S. Paley.

Vital Speeches of the Day. 46:753–6. O. 1, '80. American intelligence in the 1980's. Stansfield Turner.

* Vital Speeches of the Day. 47:57–60. N. 1, '80. Competition in the television industry. L. H. Goldenson.

Wall Street Journal. 194:1+. Ja 2, '80. Air war: news departments of the TV networks join ratings battle. J. E. Cooney.